Women of Color and Social Media Multitasking

Women of Color and Social Media Multitasking

Blogs, Timelines, Feeds, and Community

Edited by Keisha Edwards Tassie and
Sonja M. Brown Givens

LEXINGTON BOOKS
Lanham • Boulder • New York • London

Published by Lexington Books
An imprint of The Rowman & Littlefield Publishing Group, Inc.
4501 Forbes Boulevard, Suite 200, Lanham, Maryland 20706
www.rowman.com

Unit A, Whitacre Mews, 26-34 Stannary Street, London SE11 4AB

British Library Cataloguing in Publication Information Available

Library of Congress Cataloging-in-Publication Data

Names: Givens, Sonja M. Brown, editor. | Tassie, Keisha Edwards, 1976- editor.
Title: Women of color and social media multitasking : blogs, timelines, feeds, and community /
edited by Sonja M. Brown Givens and Keisha Edwards Tassie.
Description: Lanham : Lexington Books, 2015. | Includes bibliographical references and index.
Identifiers: LCCN 2015039405| ISBN 9781498528474 (cloth) | ISBN 9781498528481
(electronic) | ISBN 9781498528498 (pbk)
Subjects: LCSH: Minority women. | Feminism. | Women's rights. | Social media.
Classification: LCC HQ1161 .W656 2015 | DDC 305.48/8--dc23 LC record available at http://
lccn.loc.gov/2015039405

We dedicate this book to women of color around the world. To the brave women who create safe spaces and start campaigns to make women of color more active citizens of the world. To women who are inspired in various ways, and for various reasons, to do what they can, do what they must, do what they love to effect positive change within our global community. And we dedicate this book to us, the brilliant team of women who created this work of art and intellect that lifts the voices and shares the experiences of women of color around the world.

#WomanPower

—*Keisha & Sonja*

Contents

Foreword

Robin R. Means Coleman

In 2013, Sharkeisha Thomas, a Houston (TX) teen, became an internet sensation when a video of her inflicting a one-sided attack on her friend, ShaMichael, went viral. The stunningly violent beating—seven punches to the head and a kick to the face—was a set-up. The more solidly built Sharkeisha coaxed the slighter, bespectacled ShaMichael to a housing complex for a beat-down captured on cell phone video by Sharkeisha's buddies.

The video appeared most prominently on *Worldstarhiphop.com*, a commercial blog site that features rap videos, as well as raw videos of brutality and of women in sexually exploitative situations. Sixteen-year-old Sharkeisha went viral, with to-date over 24.8 million views, under the auspices of *WorldStar*, thereby mooring our impression of her identity to that of the site—"ratchet" on both accounts. In fact, one commenter posted, "Sharkeisha was destined to be ratchet." A few commenters interpreted the video as a classic tragedy with ShaMichael as a tragic hero victimized by an evil bully. The attack video, commented on over 30 thousand times, was judged by many as entertaining, with a bounty of "LOLs" and "LMAOs" posted. Notably, the overwhelming majority of commenters derided Sharkeisha's name. One commenter posted: "Sharkeisha sounds like a movie that airs on the SyFy channel about a shark who fucked a ratchet chick named Keisha."

Indeed, Sharkeisha was further propelled into notoriety thanks to the Syfy channel. In 2013, Syfy aired the campy, made-for-TV movie *Sharknado* about sharks, scooped up into waterspouts, who dropped to the ground to snack on people on dry land. The two raptorial depictions—Sharkeisha and *Sharknado*—collided. Sharkeisha was turned into a disturbing memetic image of half shark, half double-minority combatant, thereby rendering her even more animalistic as well as racially and gendered peculiar. As Nakamura (2014, 259) argues, memes love and punish the internet's "bad subjects," often through "overtly racialized and sexist" imagery. In being subjected to memetic transformation (couched in humor), Sharkeisha's crime was not only the assault upon ShaMichael, but also her seeming inability to comport herself as a worthy member of the citizenry. More, the spectacle served as a distraction, similarly denying ShaMichael to be viewed as a legitimately "suffering body" (Ticktin 2011, 11) in need of humanitarian intervention. Sharkeisha's abjection, then, disinvited collectives to mobilize against her escalating cyber exploitation.

I use the case of Sharkeisha, her interpellation with *Sharknado*, her digital visibility, and the public's reaction (or lack thereof) to her, to illustrate the type of issues that the authors in *Women of Color and Social Media Multitasking: Blogs, Timelines, Feeds, and Community* are interrogating. Specifically, the authors here assert that it is necessary to (re)claim digital spaces for women of color.

Through sophisticated, trenchant analyses into a number of timely and provocative case studies, the authors contend that digital interventions such as social media or hashtag activism are uniquely powerful, and need not mirror the strategies of their more analog cousins. In short, past change efforts were confined by limited interactivity—little opportunity for prolonged dialogue, elaboration, or updates over time or across varied communicative spaces. Hence, in the absence of elaborated deliberation, political action often necessarily centered on those easily discerned as worthy; that is, the magnanimous Rosa Parks-esq, rarely the ignominious Sharkeishas. The authors featured here prompt us to consider who or what we find defensible, and ask that we carefully consider that which we are not prepared to advocate for.

The authors in *Women of Color and Social Media Multitasking* explore uses of social media (e.g., Tumbler, Twitter, Instagram) by women of color, laying bare the professional, social, psychological, and political contexts for social media "multitasking"—for example, creating extended communities, locating support for self and others, and working to affect change. What is highlighted here most profoundly is women of color's "technical capital" in which technical expertise is used to mobilize groups to secure power and resources (Brock et al. 2015).

The authors ask, "what does it mean for women of color to enter into or extract themselves from spaces that have only privileged women of a certain hue, value system and gender role performance?" They contend that social media afford women of color the de-temporally and anti-linearly robust means to identify, interrogate, and (re)frame the issues and narratives impacting them and their communities.

By shining a spotlight on the ways in which women of color have critically engaged ideas of citizenship and (resistance to) hegemonic subjectivity, the authors presented in this collection draw our attention to offensives and exclusions from *outside* of women of colors' communities. Indeed, an apt observation in this volume is that when White feminists, media outlets, and others fail women of color, women of color have found it necessary to rely on their own technical and social capital by turning to what Williams (2015) calls a "digital defense" to band together or create enclaves.

The authors here also strive to complicate our epistemologies, inciting us to reappraise from within who engenders our interventions, thus meriting the utilization of digital social capital. *Women of Color and Social Media Multitasking* interrogates questions of capital, as well as our survival and thriving, our social networks and acts of citizenship, our agency and identity work, and having our voices heard and our bodies seen. The authors in this book ask that we allow them to inform our explorations and critical analyses of the uses of social media by women of color.

REFERENCES

Brock, André, Lynette Kvasny, and Kayla Hales (2010). "Cultural Appropriations of Technical Capital." *Information, Communication & Society* 13:7, 1040–1059. doi: 10.1080/1369118X.2010.498897.
Nakamura, Lisa (2014). "'I WILL DO EVERYthing That Am Asked': Scambaiting, Digital Show-Space, and the Racial Violence of Social Media." *Journal of Visual Culture* 13:3, 257–274. doi: 10.1177/1470412914546845.
Ticktin, Mariam (2011). *Casualties of Care: Immigration and the Politics of Humanitarianism in France.* Oakland, CA: University of California Press.
Williams, Sherri (2015). "Digital Defense: Black Feminists Resist Violence with Hashtag Activism." *Feminist Media Studies* 15:2, 341–358. doi: 10.1080/14680777.2015.1008744.

Introduction

Keisha Edwards Tassie

The anonymity afforded by the online experience creates the opportunity for people to be free from the bounds of certain perceptions (and labels) of group characteristics associated with race, gender, class, and sexuality—providing online users with the opportunity to be "seen" as an individual. Given this unique opportunity, why do some women of color choose to use social media to align themselves with "the group" by intentionally self-identifying and seeking other women of color?

Unlike our professional networks, social networks like Facebook, Instagram, Twitter, blogs, chat rooms and the like are "locations" where women of color choose and/or build their own communities. These virtual spaces are both intentionally and unintentionally created for multiple purposes in order to achieve a variety of goals that include, but are not limited to, locating professional networks, "safe spaces," resources for support, entertainment and relaxation, and relatability. Social media provide women of color with easily-accessible tools for developing and/or honing one's strategies for managing the serious pressures that often come with the life experiences of being, at minimum, a double-minority in society.

In a manner that is accessible for all, and relatable for many, the poignantly-intellectual chapters in this book explore and critically analyze the motivations for and uses of social media by women of color, as well as the social, psychological, and political contexts for which social media multitasking is not only evident in the lives of women of color, but, more specifically, provide extended communities for those who share particular experiences, interests, and concerns that are exclusive to women of color. This book focuses on the uniqueness of the social media multitasking experience of women of color.

Our book examines not only the varied uses of social media by women of color in various contexts, but also how social media tools affect the manner in which women of color make use of social media as social, personal, and/or political tools for navigating the world. In unique, yet connected, ways, the chapters address several key components of the nature of "virtual community," and the motivation(s) and pathways for establishing these communities by, and for, women of color.

This volume specifically speaks to various contexts for the social media uses of women of color: chapter 1 analyzes how women of color use social media as a tool to create and strengthen social networks and communities, as a tool to share information, and as a positive force for agency; chapter 2 addresses how women of color use social media as a tool for feminist consciousness-raising and feminist hashtag activism, as well as providing analysis of the contentious relationship between women of color and white women within the realm of feminist activism; chapter 3 examines the uses of social media by Arab women as a tool for (e)Revolution, cyberactivism, and digital reverberation of feminism through the Arab Spring; the focus of chapter 4 is on women of color as bloggers and online community creators, on the black millennial woman, and on the connection between themes that emerge from black women's social media uses and historical black rhetoric; chapter 5 explores how women of color use natural hair blogs as a form of bell hooks's "homeplace" that challenge/counter dominant "ideals" of beauty and professionalism; chapter 6 investigates how women of color use social media as a tool for transnational feminism and the shaping of street harassment discourse; chapter 7 explores how women of color use social media, specifically, Instagram, as a tool for identity construction and self-presentation/niche identity; and the focus of chapter 8 is on examining the differences in blogging intent by bloggers of color (using blogs about race as a form of resistance of dominant culture and solidarity of minority culture) and white bloggers, as well as a focus on the content and impact of the chapter author's own blog within the context of racial identity development. This edited volume incorporates analyses and explorations of various, important issues relevant to gender studies, feminist/women's/womanist studies, race studies, communication studies, mass communication/media studies, cultural studies, sociology, psychology, counseling, and other related disciplines.

Whether an undergraduate or graduate student, a scholar/academic, a professional, a clinician/practitioner, or simply an individual with a genuine interest in the issues relevant to women of color, this book will substantively contribute to your discussions concerning gender, race, class, sexuality, and uses of social media through chapters that will, individually and collectively, reflect the unique experience of women of color and their uses of social media for the construction of both "self" and "community."

Chapter One

Women of Color Cultivating Virtual Social Capital

Surviving and Thriving

Linda Charmaraman, Bernice Huiying Chan,
Temple Price, and Amanda Richer[1]

Early theorists on computer-mediated communication before the rise of social media focused on the potential of web-based communication to mini-
mize or equalize status and power differentials, where disenfranchised
groups, such as women, could be liberated from their overlooked or stigma-
tized status (Seigel, Dubrovsky, Kiesler, & McGuire 1986; Turkle 1995).
Much has changed since that male-dominated cyberspace such that women
are now surpassing Internet usage when it comes to social media use. In
2014, the Pew Research Center (Duggan, Ellison, Lampe, Lenhart, & Madden 2014) reported that 77% of women (compared to 66% of men) are using
Facebook, and this roughly ten-point gap has been found to be a significant
gender difference in recent years. Specifically, women tend to dominate
Facebook, Pinterest, and Instagram, whereas there are no significant gender
differences in Twitter or Tumblr use. Partially explaining this gender gap is
the fact that women rank social communication as their number one reason
for going online, whereas males rate entertainment as their top motivation
(Jones, Johnson-Yale, Millermaier, & Perez 2009). The racial digital divide
is also disrupted when it comes to social media use, showing 67% of Black
adults and 73% of Hispanic adults using Facebook. Their motivations for
going online, however, differ: Black and White adults tend to use Facebook
primarily for social communication whereas Hispanic adults use it for entertainment purposes. Twitter is rising in popularity in disenfranchised racial
groups with 27% of Blacks and 25% of Hispanics using it, significantly

higher than White users (21%). Given the recent trend in social media communities providing space for disenfranchised cyber users, such as people of color and women, to engage in these digital technologies fully, little is still known about how and why women of color in particular utilize social media networks in this age of expedient online connectivity across geographic boundaries.

One reason for the scarcity of research on women of color using social media is that empirical investigations into racial or gender differences in social media use have revealed inconsistent results (see DiMaggio, Hargittai, Celeste, & Shafer 2004; Hargittai 2008; Junco 2013; Muscanell & Guadagno 2011). Often there are inconsistent ways of measuring social media use, such as engaging in activities on a site vs. the amount of time spent on a site. For instance, past research on gender differences in blogging did not show a significant difference between 31% of males and 34% of females who blog in a college context, however female bloggers tended to update their blogs with more frequency than males (Jones, Johnson-Yale, Millermaier, & Perez 2009), which could be a meaningful difference in how and why these women interact with their blog reader audience. In terms of racial differences, significantly more Black students (36%) kept blogs than White students (31%), and Hispanic students were the least likely to keep a blog (27%). Attempting to go beyond differences between racial or gender groups as if they were mutually exclusive categories of experience, our study explores how to understand the intersectionality (Crenshaw 1989) of race and gender in order to tease apart the historically subordinate and oppressed position of women of color compared to other groups, such as White women and men of color.

Given the recent trends of women dominating Facebook and Black and Hispanic users dominating Twitter, it becomes critical to understand if and how social media networks can liberate these disempowered groups to increase their social capital online and engage with their racial group identities. The current study utilizes mixed methods, analyzing both closed-ended survey questions and open-ended interview questions, to tease out how women of color have been strategically using social media.

THEORETICAL GROUNDING

Using dynamic interactionism frameworks, social psychologists Snyder and Ickes (1985) argued that technology, social context, and personal characteristics can be dynamic in their influences, such that an individual's choice of group membership online is dependent on their idiosyncratic values (for example, liberal-leaning folks will seek out affiliations with like-minded people online). Continued exposure to such similar-thinking environments can increase a person's predisposition to that particular interest or identity and influence future behaviors, such as contributing as an activist in that community, and so on. Sociologist Swidler (1986) described less formal, less individualistic, and often unconscious ways in which individuals seek mastery over their lives through the use of technologies available to them— referring to these practices as "strategies of action." These behaviors are not a result of rational decision-making but rather a taken-for-granted knowledge of how the world works through their relationships with other people and where they are located in terms of status, gender, racial/ethnic group, geography, socioeconomic status, etc. For women of color who encompass double-minority status, who consciously or unconsciously select particular virtual spaces to explore their social identities, their strategies of action may be in concert or in conflict with one or more of their identities. For instance, a feminist online social group may not be as inclusive of racial/ethnic minorities or a racial/ethnic-affiliated interest group may be dominated by male perspectives, with women's issues taking a sideline.

The concept of social capital describes how resources are embedded in one's social networks that can be accessed or mobilized through connections or ties within one's network (Lin 2008). Prior research maintained that since Internet use decreases face-to-face time with others, an individual's social capital can be diminished (e.g., Nie, 2001). However, other research demonstrates that online interactions can supplement in-person exchanges and even build stronger community connections, involvement, and social capital (Hampton & Wellman 2003; Kavanaugh, Carroll, Rosson, Zin, & Reese 2005). Social capital is often thought of as either "bridging" (connecting to novel information resources across interconnected ties, e.g., "friend of a friend") or "bonding" (generating support and trust through intimate ties) (Putnam 2000; Williams 2006). Ellison and colleagues' recent study (2014) found that women are more likely than men to engage in relationship maintenance behaviors such as responding to good or bad news posted on their Facebook networks, offering advice to others when asked, and posting birthday messages on a Facebook timeline. Little is known about how the intersection of race and gender can influence minority women in engaging in social media behaviors that can increase their social capital.

Resnick (2001) pointed out that social media sites can establish new forms of social capital through technical tools like distribution lists, search capabilities, and photo directories. Social media sites enhance one's capability to maintain a network of both strong and weak ties (beyond close friend and family relationships) without much effort or cost (Donath & Boyd 2004), thereby keeping the potential for opening doors to novel sources of information and resources. The strong linkages between Facebook use and maintaining high school and college connections showcase how social networking sites help maintain relationships as people move from one geographic location to another. This could potentially mean critical payoffs in terms of jobs, internships, and other benefits of networking with strong and weak ties. In our study, we wanted to understand how women of color motivate and are motivated by their networks to create spaces that increase information sharing, resources, and safe forums to voice their opinions.

This chapter will primarily focus on qualitative interview findings with 34 women of color from across the country to investigate the research questions below, with additional quantitative survey data to illustrate differences between women of color and other groups, namely White women and men of color.

RESEARCH QUESTIONS

1. Compared to White women and men of color, how central is social media use in the daily lives of women of color? What are the motivations driving this use? (Survey and Interviews)
2. How and when do women of color reach out to their online friends for social or psychological needs, such as when times are tough? (Survey) Do women of color feel psychologically supported by their online networks on Facebook, Twitter, and Tumblr? (Interviews)
3. How are women of color participating in virtual spaces that are safe spaces? Do they report joining social media groups that are tied to their race/ethnicity and/or gender? Do women of color believe they have potential social, political, or professional impact on others' lives through their activities on social media sites? (Interviews)

METHODS

Participants and Procedures

The Media & Identity Project (Charmaraman 2014; Charmaraman & Chan 2013) is a mixed-method study of over 2,300 individuals, which included (a) a purposive online survey that targeted hard-to-reach adolescents and emerging adults across forty-seven U.S. states and twenty-six countries and (b) 60 to 120 minute follow-up in-depth interviews with thirty-four participants from the larger survey. The survey contained items regarding young men and women's beliefs and attitudes about televised media, social media networking, and civic engagement through media. Our survey sample consisted of 776 women of color (504 Asian American, 85 Hispanic, 109 Black, and 78 Multiracial), 786 White women, and 194 men of color from 47 different U.S. states and over 140 schools across the country. Average age was 19.37 (SD = 2.12), ranging from 12 to 25. Average level of education for participants' mothers was 3.69 (SD = 1.21), which represents between "not completing college" and "completing college." After obtaining active parental consent from participants under the age of eighteen, the survey was piloted through middle school and college-aged focus groups to attain adequate item readability and age-appropriate wording. We recruited the study sample from schools and community organizations through electronic (e.g., emails from teachers/professors, Facebook advertisements, listservs) and traditional recruitment methods (e.g., psychology department subject pools, flyers), and repeated efforts one week later. Before starting the survey, participants read and electronically signed study disclosures and informed consent, a process approved by Wellesley College's Institutional Review Board. As part of our targeted recruitment strategy to oversample hard-to-reach populations, two institutions in each collegiate category (two-year community college, four-year college, and doctorate-level university) were randomly selected from each state using a national database. From each pair, the institution having the most racially diverse students was identified. By the end of the eight-month recruitment period, we had reached out to 273 institutions from middle school to college level, over 90 student clubs, and over 100 non-school organizations. Each completed survey entry with a voluntarily provided valid email address was entered into a raffle drawing for a $25, $50, or $100 Amazon.com e-gift certificate. Duplicate and incomplete surveys were identified by tracking IP addresses with multiple entries in a short period of time and were discarded from the dataset.

Survey participants who indicated interest in a follow-up interview were selected via stratified sampling in order to maximize representativeness of the original survey sample in terms of race/ethnicity, age, and region of the country. Our final interview sample comprised of thirty-four women of color (eight African American, four Latina, fourteen Asian American, and eight biracial), aged eighteen to twenty-six, from eleven different states representing all major regions of the country.

Survey Measures

I can't stop checking my email or Facebook. Participants indicated on a four-point scale (1 = not at all like me to 4 = a lot like me) how well this statement reflected their behavior. *Written a blog.* Participants were asked whether they had ever written a blog. *Notify friends about bad day.* Participants were asked whether they used Facebook to notify friends about having a bad day.

Interview Themes

After piloting the interview themes with three female college students, we followed a semi-structured interview guide. Interviews were audio recorded and transcribed verbatim. Qualitative themes centered on strategic uses of social media sites and identity development. Subthemes included behaviors and motivations behind using different social media sites, involvement in online social identity groups, supportive and unsupportive interactions within networking communities, "friending" and "unfriending" activities, and expectation of social media's impact on others through the exchange of information between network members.

Analysis Plan

Our analytical approach was a sequential mixed-method design (Creswell & Plano Clark 2011), which began with a quantitative survey dataset, followed up by qualitative interviews to help explain the processes underlying the preliminary findings, and then a quantitative analytical follow-up to explore the resulting insights from the qualitative analyses. The multiple "points of interface" (Morse & Niehaus 2009) occurred in the data interpretation stages, when the results of the surveys were compared with results of the interviews and vice versa.

During the quantitative analyses, linear and logistic regression models were conducted to explore group differences in reports of social media usage comparing White and minority women, and minority men and women. Models were conducted individually for each social media or Internet usage outcome and effects were compared separately for White and minority women, and for minority men and women. The demographic category "minority women" was created using participants' self-identification as a female and as any race/ethnicity other than White; all other female participants were coded as "White women." The category of minority men was created based on participants' identifying themselves as male and as any race/ethnicity other than White. Participants self-reported their age (range from twelve to twenty-five years) and mother's education (ranging from 1 = some high school or less to 5 = school beyond college (master's, doctorate). Age and mother's education were used as control variables in the models. Only models with significant Likelihood Ratio Chi-squares are presented (see Table 1.1).

	I can't stop checking my email or Facebook.			Written a blog			Notify friends about bad day on Facebook		
Model 1—Minority Women										
Likelihood Ratio Chi-square (df = 3)[a]	12.36 **			32.05 ***			24.66 ***			
	B	SE	Wald (df = 1)	B	SE	Wald (df = 1)	B	SE	Wald (df = 1)	
Intercept	2.85	0.03	7717.10 ***	-0.11	0.08	2.08	-1.09	0.09	158.64 ***	
Minority Women (vs. White Women)	0.15	0.05	9.56 **	0.48	0.11	18.85 ***	0.44	0.12	13.26 ***	
Age	0.01	0.01	0.78	0.10	0.03	17.15 ***	-0.07	0.03	6.50 *	
Mother's education	-0.02	0.02	0.61	0.03	0.05	0.55	-0.02	0.05	0.11	
Predicted Values	Mean	SE		Mean	SE		Mean	SE		
Minority Women	3.00	0.03		0.59	0.02		0.34	0.02		
White Women	2.85	0.03		0.47	0.02		0.25	0.02		
Model 2—Minority Men and Women										
Likelihood Ratio Chi-square (df = 3)[a]	8.21 *			44.09 ***			11.84 **			
	B	SE	Wald (df = 1)	B	SE	Wald (df = 1)	B	SE	Wald (df = 1)	
Intercept	2.79	0.07	1815.44 ***	-0.63	0.16	15.98 ***	-0.89	0.16	29.32 ***	
Minority Women (vs. Minority Men)	0.21	0.07	8.05 **	1.00	0.17	33.51 ***	0.22	0.18	1.44	
Age	0.00	0.01	0.07	0.10	0.03	8.68 **	-0.10	0.03	8.89 **	
Mother's education	0.01	0.02	0.07	0.08	0.05	2.27	-0.04	0.05	0.64	
Predicted Values	Mean	SE		Mean	SE		Mean	SE		
Minority Women	3.00	0.03		0.58	0.02		0.34	0.02		
Minority Men	2.79	0.07		0.34	0.04		0.30	0.03		

* p < .05. ** p < .01. *** p < .001.
[a] Only models with significant omnibus tests are shown in this table.

After developing a codebook to set up themes and subthemes for the interview analyses, we used NVivo 10.0 to organize the interview data into meaningful units, assign attributes to understand themes across demographic categories, and to visually map the data in order to reveal underlying processes while coding. To assure reliability during content analysis, all themes were coded by one investigator and at different stages of the coding process reliability checks were made by another investigator. Any differences in coding schema were identified, evaluated, and discussed until consensus (Strauss & Corbin 1998).

RESULTS AND DISCUSSION

Research Question 1: Compared to White women and men of color, how central is social media use in the daily lives of women of color? What are the motivations driving this use? (Survey and Interviews)

Social Media Frequency and Motivation

Survey respondents were asked whether they felt like they couldn't stop checking their email and Facebook throughout the day. Significant group differences were found between minority women and White women, where minority women reported feeling significantly more like they couldn't stop checking their email and Facebook ($M = 3.00$) compared to White women ($M = 2.85$; Wald $= 9.56$, $df = 1$, $p < .01$). Similarly, minority women were significantly more likely to report being unable to stop checking their email or Facebook ($M = 3.00$) compared to minority men ($M = 2.79$; Wald $= 8.05$, $df = 1$, p $< .01$). In order to test whether the *perception* of checking frequently was related to frequency of logins, we demonstrated a significant positive correlation between frequency of Facebook checking and feeling unable to stop checking email and Facebook for all survey respondents ($r = .50$, $p < .001$), further supporting associations between perceptions of behavior and actual social media use.

A majority of the Black, Asian American, Latina, and biracial interview participants described the consuming nature of social media and difficulty to stop checking social media sites, supporting the survey findings. For example, a Black participant said, "I have a slight addiction. Why do I like Facebook? I don't really even like Facebook any more. It's kind of just a chore but I can't help but not check it. It's how we keep in touch nowadays." Many participants specifically described the "fear of missing out" if they did not constantly check their social media sites, such as this Black participant:

> I make sure to check it every day to see if anyone has tried to contact me. Sometimes friends and family from home will send me messages and posts

from overseas, so I want to make sure I don't miss anything. Also, I am in a work-related group on Facebook so I want to make sure I stay up-to-date on any new announcements that may be posted.

Some participants specifically mentioned checking social media sites for stress relief to engage with their inner circle without physically meeting up, or as a distraction technique to get away from school or work-related obligations: a biracial Latina/White participant said,

So it is very difficult for me to stop checking the site so much. And I think that's because I've been stressed out mostly, and also because I use it as a way to communicate with my friends or to see what my friends are doing as well.

Our interview participants were in networks that relied heavily on Facebook for communication, and viewed checking-in online as crucial for actively maintaining strong community ties. At the same time, the community building was only part of the picture—social media use was also an important distraction technique away from stressors outside of participants' social circle, such as school obligations. Leaning on their social circle online was a highly motivating factor in using social media sites, and at times, a stress-relieving part of their daily lives.

Blogging

Minority women were significantly more likely to report having written a blog (59%) compared to White women (47%) (Wald = 18.85, $df = 1$, $p <$ .001). Similarly, minority women (58%) were significantly more likely than minority men (34%) to report ever having written a blog (Wald = 33.51, $df =$ 1, $p < .001$).

Several of our Black and Asian American interviewees said they had started online blogs at some point. The microblogging platform Tumblr was popular among participants, such as with this Asian American participant: "[Tumblr] is a place that's supported my learning in terms of my identities— ethnic identity, racial identity, gender identity, and all that stuff." Tumblr provided a social media site where one could learn about different identities in greater depth that other social networking sites did not necessarily provide. One biracial Black/White participant explained her Tumblr use,

You make a blog and then you can post things on it or repost things that other people have posted, and a lot of the times things other people have posted build up large amounts of commentary and you can comment on what they said. And it's like a little community.

When asked about what she posted, a biracial Black/White participant said, "It's generally just things that I find amusing, but I'll also reblog things about news issues and I guess like social justice issues." Another Black participant stated, "I had a blog about my time abroad . . . the first summer after I graduated. And I currently have two—one is movie reviews and the other is beauty product reviews."

One Latina participant distinguished Tumblr from Facebook because it provided deeper interpersonal engagement and "bridging" social capital through the ability to re-blog content:

> It's a cool interaction because you're saying, "You like this thing, I also like this thing, and I like it enough to claim it as my own and let people identify me with that." So you build friendships based on genuine interests, I think, more than you would on other sites.

Several Black participants described Facebook and Tumblr as "bridging" resources for information about everything from current events to hair styling techniques. When asked about which social media pages she followed, a Black participant responded: "A lot of beauty blogs. Feminism, a few feminist blogs." By "liking" topical pages, young women can join large communities filled with people that they may not know in real life, but who share common interests, which can increase access to new information outside intimate circles, thereby increasing "bridging" social capital.

Research Question 2: How and when do women of color reach out to their online friends for social or psychological needs, such as when times are tough? (Survey) Do women of color feel psychologically supported by their online networks on Facebook, Twitter, and Tumblr?

Minority women (34%) were significantly more likely to report using Facebook to tell friends about a bad day compared to White women (25%) (Wald = 13.26, $df = 1$, $p < .001$), while this comparison between minority men (30%) and minority women (34%) showed no significant differences (Wald = 1.44, $df = 1$, ns). This suggests that people of color regardless of gender are equally as likely to reveal their stress online, whereas White women do not reach out to their networks as often as women of color do.

Interview participants felt that they had garnered support from network friends and family near and far by posting about difficult moments, such as during relationship turmoil: A Black participant recalled, "After my last breakup actually, you post a status and people are just like, 'it's gonna be okay.' Stuff like that. Just people liking your status more than they used to."

Even when one Latina participant was physically separated from others when she was upset, having an intimate online network to bond with provided her with the space to release her frustrations, and a safe space to blog and express her thoughts: "When I've been physically isolated, [it] has been a great place for me to vent any sort of mental struggles that I'm having, any emotional stuff that's going on, because that's oftentimes hard for me to do." In this way, social media sites provide ample opportunity to developing "bonding" social capital, despite geographic distance.

Several Latina participants described the support they created by liking each other's posts, especially if they were upset or stressed: "It makes you feel better about yourself if you have somebody who's publicly saying that they're supportive of your stuff or they like your photo or whatever." Another Latina participant described social media to be a space where people can show their support:

> I think just to know that people are there and that they care—that they actually took the time to sit there and write something. It made me feel like I had a support system even though I felt alone in that moment—seeing people's faces, little pictures, and seeing their comments—it made a connection.

"Liking" statuses and comments were described as ways to show and receive affirmation from one's inner and outer circle of friends.

A few participants described their online posts that would lead to contact with friends in offline contexts, such as this Latina participant:

> I have one friend who is like a little over-reactive on these things, but if I post something on Tumblr that sounds vaguely sad she'll immediately text me and be like, "Hey, what's going on? How are you doing? Saw that. If it's nothing let me know, but like just thought I'd check in." So it's a way for me to tell people that something's going wrong without have to like call them up and say it.

Participants also used Twitter to tell their friends about a bad day: "If I just don't feel like exactly sharing what the situation is, then I'll just be like, 'Oh, this day sucks.' Or, 'This is the worst day ever.' Or something to that nature." Both Tumblr and Twitter were spaces where some participants felt they could share their feelings and they would receive acknowledgement and support from their online networks, cultivating more bonding social capital. Others talked about the self-improvement aspects of social media networks, such as "how-to" guides and checklists that offer advice when times are tough:

> I just read something about how to be happy and it's just like, "Don't care what other people think about you, cut out the criticism, cut out negativity and anger," and all that kind of stuff. And it was really good advice. It's like impossible to do, but it's inspiring.

Not only did these women of color report how they reached out for help during times of distress, but they also revealed their desire to search for insider tips and strategies to improve the quality of their lives.

Research Question 3: How are women of color participating in virtual spaces that are safe spaces? Do they report joining social media groups that are tied to their race/ethnicity and/or gender? Do women of color believe they have potential social, political, or professional impact on others' lives through their activities on social media sites?

EXPLORATION OF SAFE RACIAL AND GENDERED SPACES

In terms of Internet sources for exploring their racial and gender identities, participants reported joining or following websites such as Racialicious.com and Colorlines.com, which focus on race, popular culture, and current events. Groups on Tumblr about feminism were popular with Black and Asian American interviewees. Almost half of the Asian American interviewees reported writing or re-blogging social commentary on racial, gender, and/or sexual identity issues, demonstrating that these were considered pertinent topics that deserved a wider audience. Latina participants also described joining social media groups on Facebook and Tumblr for online communities related to their social and personal identities. For our Latina participants in college, some of these groups were university-related and directly tied to their race, such as a group for Hispanic students or racial minorities at their colleges.

Strategically "Friending" and "Unfriending" for Safer Virtual Spaces

Many of our women of color interviewees talked about their "tipping points" in deciding when to friend or unfriend someone in their online networks. Black women participants seemed to edit or cull their spaces to push out those whose opinions were oppositional to them. For example, several participants reported "unfriending" their Facebook friends who made bigoted statements on the site. The information that their friends posted was useful in determining who should be included in their social networks. Acquaintances revealed their true colors on social media by posting tasteless "jokes" or opinions that were offensive to some of the Black interviewees:

> I mean there's always the people that post things that are like "funny," but it's actually not because it's a joke about women or people of color—it's the whole get back to the kitchen thing. It's like can you *not*? If it's a regular thing for one person I'll just unfriend them.

By deleting those people from their online spaces, our participants were able to create safer social media environments, rather than holding on to weak ties with those acquaintances that did not help these women thrive online. When asked if she ever unfriended individuals, a Black participant asserted, "Oh yes, lots of times, because they were offensive, because they were harassing me, because they were trying to find out information about me and violating my privacy for the most part." Another summarized her reasons for breaking away from friends: "I've unfriended people because they were homophobic. And sometimes I've unfriended people just because I don't feel like I'm friends with them anymore." The majority of the Latina participants described unfriending Facebook friends they did not know well, or who became distant over time. By having these informal rules to friending and unfriending people on Facebook, participants were able to control who had access to their feeds and whose content they followed. One biracial Latina/White participant said, "I have unfriended a couple of people who've made me feel uncomfortable and so who I don't want to have to deal with on Facebook if they decide to Facebook message me." Taking these steps allowed these women to cultivate and tailor their online spaces in order to enhance their online experience rather than just tolerate unwelcome messages.

For at least half of the Asian American interview participants there was a similar weeding process of "unfriending" and unsubscribing from offensive posts as well as when they did not want to read things they found to be "junk." Two Asian American participants mentioned specifically unfriending someone after having an online disagreement with them: "I'll post something and they'll comment and they say things that are problematic or really condescending or they're wrong. . . . there is just no dialogue going on. And I don't want to talk to them in the future." By unfriending people, these Asian participants were able to create a more intentional virtual space where they could share political posts without arguing with people they did not know well, and to stay in contact with people they cared about. One participant said: "We'd had disagreements or I would end the friendship or I just don't talk to this person on Facebook so I don't see why we should be friends or I should know about your personal life and vice versa." Where there were weaker ties as well as many disagreements in values, our participants chose to end the connection and not include toxic individuals in their social capital circle of support.

STRATEGIC ENGAGEMENT THROUGH SOCIAL MEDIA GROUPS

A large number of Asian American interview participants reported academic social media groups that were tied to courses they were taking or groups they were members in, such as Women in HealthCare Leaders. One interviewee talked about the use of a course-based social media group to facilitate shared information and resources:

> I have one for my department which is Health Management and Policy. . . . So there's like eighty of us in this Facebook group and we share information about what's going on in our classes and there's this specific group, like a small group from it of twenty people and we all study together. So we'll share notes and study guides.

Latina interview participants also described utilizing a Facebook group to help with academic work and career aspirations: "If I needed to interview somebody for journalism class, I would throw out a question over the dorm Facebook group because I know they live near me." Access to Facebook allowed her greater ease in collecting responses and increased intellectual resources for her academic work. Some participants shared they were also influenced by the Facebook posts they read that addressed feminist issues such as girls in STEM (Science, Technology, Engineering, and Math), or being a better feminist. A Latina participant shared a link about engaging girls in engineering: "I posted something about Goldieblox and how those are important for girls to be introduced to because they teach girls about engineering. Or they teach girls more about how to problem-solve, which they aren't exposed to enough." The examples above highlight how these women of color were engaging in online social groups aimed at academic and career exploration, often tied to increasing access and social capital to women in underrepresented fields.

Besides utilizing social media to build community within known networks, Twitter was described by some Latina participants as a social media site that allowed for direct following and messaging, or "tweeting," at celebrities and meeting new people outside of real-life friend groups. One Latina participant followed the NBA All-Star celebrities and was able to befriend other fans and message the celebrities through Twitter:

> I met a lot of new people because they're part of the All-Star Weekend fandom and if it wasn't for Twitter, I don't think I would have met them. And I can communicate with celebrities a little easier. I have talked to some celebrities through Twitter and that's pretty exciting.

This illustrates a finding from a previous study that demonstrated that Hispanic online users primarily focus on entertainment purposes, rather than strengthening ties within their social circles (Jones et al. 2009). In addition, several of the Asian American participants joined groups for commercial or economic purposes, such as getting a group discount on events, which demonstrates the power of numbers to increase one's access to cultural capital and shared resources through social media.

SOCIOPOLITICAL DISCOURSE

Our women of color interviewees described multiple ways to engage with the web in a sociopolitical way. Several participants described sharing news articles and political cartoons to raise awareness on important issues. One biracial Latina/White participant described being challenged and made more aware by her college peers who were interested in social justice issues such as race and class. One Latina participant joined a group not related to her identity, but to environmental issues she cared about: "It's basically a page where they post quotations or pictures about environmental issues and it's of a more liberal—definitely a more liberal mindset than I have." The Facebook group was not entirely in line with her own views, but she joined it because it challenged her own thinking. Asian participants described using Facebook to share articles to make others more aware of an issue: "I kind of use it to make people more aware, I think of what's going on and issues that I see come up." One participant shared "an article about Kate Gosling doing 'Asian slant eyes.'" This post was political in nature and related to her Asian identity.

Black participants used social media to address specific social justice issues or events. One interview took place shortly after the George Zimmerman trial in 2013. The participant described seeing many reactions to the trial, saying, "I think just a couple of days ago with the Zimmerman trial, people were kind of taking sides and sometimes it was kind of hurtful with what they said about African Americans." Another timely issue for participants was abortion legislation in Texas. One Black participant explained, "With the whole abortion debate in Texas there were a bunch of people that were standing up on Facebook and saying things, which felt nice because sometimes it feels like you're the only one." Other Black participants mentioned social justice in a more general sense. When asked about what she chose to post to her Tumblr, one participant said, "I have a Tumblr, which is also sort of feminist-y, social justice-y I guess."

"Preaching to the Choir:" Welcoming and Resisting Change

Latina interview participants were more likely to believe that it is difficult to change people's set beliefs through Facebook posts and less likely to feel that a post can influence people's attitudes. Yet, even those who described the difficulty of changing people's beliefs could pinpoint a previous post that influenced the way they thought. Of the participants who said it was difficult to influence people through a Facebook post, most said it was because people come with their own strong beliefs when they approach reading a post:

> I think people are pretty set in their ideas. I think when you post something, it's more to gain support from people who already agree with you. . . . I think

people will enter discussions with the intention of changing your mind, not to have *their* mind changed.

In terms of their social networks making an impact on their own beliefs, Asian American interviewees felt that they were more informed and made aware of more political issues, such as current events, different parts of the world, disabilities, sexual orientation, saying that they would not have paid attention without a friend posting an article. On the other hand, several Asian American interviewees were skeptical of the potential to make an impact on others through social media, mentioning that the networks they were a part of attracted like-minded folks in the first place, so there wasn't much need for converting or convincing:

> Now I get pessimistic because like attracts like, you are going to follow things that you kind of agree with, right? So maybe what social media ends up doing is creating all of these different factions or little networks that don't necessarily talk to each other and you end up getting the same kind of thing that you have in life. I don't know. Just because the way that it's structured is that you end up getting content or seeing content from your own network, there isn't a lot of cross network opportunity. I mean there is obviously. But then again like attracts like and I see that play out in a lot of social media.

Many participants seemed willing to "debate" with people online about topics that were important to them. At times, there were tensions within a network and there was a harsh reminder that not everyone was likeminded politically and/or culturally:

> There was a high school friend who posted something about getting raped by an exam and I very quickly but politely told him that using "rape" in such a context is just really wrong on so many different levels and he removed it. I've seen people post things like, "Oh all these certain demographic of people do this. . . ."

This illustrates incidents where network members reveal their "true colors" and can either distance other members or incite others to call them out for chauvinist or racist remarks. In the end, the stress that came from an insertion of challenging and sometimes offensive ideas was offset by the opportunity to connect with like-minded individuals who shared a common political, cultural, or personal bond. The few who were hopeful about making an impact in their networks focused on rallying their known friendship circle and making a dent from inside rather than from the outside perspective. In some respects, this observation is a testament to the desire of women of color to provide support for each other, rather than trying to recruit others to join them.

CONCLUSIONS AND IMPLICATIONS

To summarize, we took an intersectionality lens for analyzing our quantitative survey data, separating the potential unique contributions of racial and gender background to one's daily experiences and perceptions. We demonstrated that women of color tended to rely on their social networks more heavily than both White women and men of color, through online outlets such as Facebook and blogging. In addition to our finding that women of color reported more venting of problems when having a bad day on Facebook than White women, men of color also used Facebook as a forum for frustrations, suggesting that people of color may be using online social networks in a unique and strategic way. Social media sites seemed to be useful for having their marginalized voices heard through blogs, sharing articles, and joining affinity identity groups online, perhaps in attempts to balance out their lack of power and status in offline contexts. Perhaps these online communities served to combat the lack of representation and difficulties of community formation in real life. At times preferring online "confessions" over real life encounters, the women of color we interviewed found psychological empowerment and social support on social media sites like Facebook, Tumblr, and Twitter, which offered spaces for the development of comfort and trust necessary for giving and receiving social support without the need for connecting in person. Our interviewees reported being sensitive to their close-knit friendship networks and could take cues when someone was in trouble, resulting in online and offline offers of social support. Our findings demonstrate the value of social media sites for voicing emotional needs and avoiding isolation in women of color networks, pointing to the need for more mental health initiatives that will target this often invisible double minority segment of the population. Health organizations are beginning to use social media sites such as Facebook and Twitter to conduct health campaigns and interventions, relying on peer networking to help push change related to norms, beliefs, and stigmas in the same way that off-line peer networks make a difference (Valente & Davis 1999). Researchers and educators wishing to get the attention of hard-to-reach population such as women of color can capitalize on the interconnected, intimate nature of this community to galvanize toward positive psychosocial and behavioral health outcomes through online interventions and prevention programs.

Furthermore, it is important for educators to take note of the women's engagement with political and social justice issues on social media sites. Some women used these sites to share articles and read others' posts in hopes of raising awareness and knowledge. Even when they did not believe that they could use social media posts to change others' opinions, some women reported being influenced themselves by posts they saw. This speaks to the power of social media as a platform to disperse information with different viewpoints. Educators may look into using social media platforms for engaging in sociopolitical conversations that may be more difficult to have face-to-face as compared to taking place in online forums with self-enforced rules that can garner respect for tolerating conflicting perspectives.

By unfriending weak network ties that did not serve to help them thrive, the women of color we interviewed were empowered to strategically shield themselves from triggering and offensive online content—an option that is not always available in real life. For instance, when online friends have revealed themselves to be bigoted, these women could just eliminate those voices from their screens in a relatively safe fashion, exercising control that may be denied to women of color in other spaces. Our interviewees described ways to successfully use social media as a tool to cull and strengthen their social circles. Counter to the mass media sentiment of online networking being full of negativity or "cyberbullying," our findings demonstrate the power of encouragement and resilience within women of color networks that yearn to improve access to information that could help them better understand themselves, the world, and their own communities.

NOTE

1. Publisher's Note: The interviews used as supplemental research in this text were all conducted with the participants' knowledge and agreement that these interviews would be used in a later publication.

BIBLIOGRAPHY

Charmaraman, L. (March 2014). *Adolescent social media communities: A mixed-method exploration of racial and gender differences in seeking social support*. Paper presented at the 2014 Society of Research on Adolescence Meeting, Austin, TX.

Charmaraman, L., & B. Chan (October 2013). *Televised images and social networking: Asian American media habits and attitudes*. Poster presented at the Diversity Challenge, Boston College, MA.

Crenshaw, K. (1989). "Demarginalizing the intersection of race and sex: A black feminist critique of antidiscrimination doctrine, feminist theory and antiracist politics." *University of Chicago Legal Forum* 140: 139–167. Retrieved from http://politicalscience.tamu.edu/documents/faculty/Crenshaw-Demarginalizing.pdf.

Creswell, J. W., & V. L. Plano Clark (2011). *Designing and conducting mixed methods research* (2nd ed.). Thousand Oaks, CA: Sage.

DiMaggio, P., E. Hargittai, C. Celeste, & S. Shafer (2004). "Digital inequality: From unequal access to differentiated use." In K. Neckerman (ed.), *Social inequality* (pp. 355–400). New York: Russell Sage Foundation.

Donath, J. S., & D. Boyd (2004). "Public displays of connection." *BT Technology Journal* 22(4): 71–82. doi: 10.1023/B:BTTJ.0000047585.06264.cc.

Duggan, M., N. B. Ellison, C. Lampe, A. Lenhart, & M. Madden (2014). "Demographics of key social networking platforms." Retrieved from http://www.pewinternet.org/2015/01/09/demographics-of-key-social-networking-platforms-2/.

Ellison, N. B., J. Vitak, R. Gray, & C. Lampe (2014). "Cultivating social resources on social network sites: Facebook relationship maintenance behaviors and their role in social capital processes." *Journal of Computer-Mediated Communication* 19: 855–870.

Hampton, K., & B. Wellman (2003). "Neighboring in Netville: How the Internet supports community and social capital in a wired suburb." *City & Community* 2(4): 277–311.

Hargittai, E. (2008). "Whose space? Differences among users and non-users of social network sites." *Journal of Computer-Mediated Communication* 13(1): 276–297.

Jones, S., C. Johnson-Yale, S. Millermaier, & F. S. Perez (2009). "U.S. college students' Internet use: Race, gender, and digital divides." *Journal of Computer-Mediated Communication* 14: 244–264.

Junco, R. (2013). "Inequalities in Facebook use." *Computers in Human Behavior* 29: 2328–2336.

Kavanaugh, A., J. M. Carroll, M. B. Rosson, T. T. Zin, & D. D. Reese (2005). "Community networks: Where offline communities meet online." *Journal of Computer-Mediated Communication* 10(4): article 3. doi: 10.1111/j.1083–6101.2005.tb00266.x.

Lin, N. (2008). "A network theory of social capital." In D. Castiglione, J. W. van Deth, & G. Wolleb (eds.), *The handbook of social capital* (pp. 50–69). London, England: Oxford University Press.

Morse, J., & L. Niehaus (2009). *Mixed method design: Principles and procedures.* Walnut Creek, CA: Left Coast Press.

Muscanell, N. L., & R. E. Guadagno (2011). "Make new friends or keep the old: Gender and personality differences in social networking use." *Computers in Human Behavior* 28(1): 107–112.

Nie, N. H. (2001). "Sociability, interpersonal relations, and the Internet: Reconciling conflicting findings." *American Behavioral Scientist* 45(3): 420–435.

Putnam, R. (2000). *Bowling alone: The collapse and revival of American community.* New York, NY: Simon & Schuster. doi: 10.1145/358916.361990.

Resnick, P. (2001). "Beyond bowling together: Socio-technical capital." In J. Carroll (ed.), *HCI in the new millennium* (pp. 647–672). New York, NY: Addison-Wesley. doi: 10.1145/358916.362079.

Siegel, J., V. Dubrovsky, S. Kiesler, & T. McGuire (1986). "Group processes in computer-mediated communication." *Organizational Behavior and Human Decision Processes* 37: 157–187.

Snyder, M., & W. Ickes (1985). "Personality and social behavior." In G. Lindzey & E. Aronson (eds.), *Handbook of social psychology* (3rd ed.). New York, NY: Random House.

Strauss, A., & J. Corbin (1998). *Basics of qualitative research: Techniques and procedures for developing grounded theory* (2nd ed.). Thousand Oaks, CA: Sage Publications.

Swidler, A. (1986). "Culture in action: Symbols and strategies." *American Sociological Review* 51: 273–286.

Turkle, S. (1995). *Life on the screen: Identity in the age of the internet.* New York, NY: Simon and Schuster.

Valente, T. W., & R. L. Davis (1999). "Accelerating the diffusion of innovations using opinion leaders." *Annals of the American Academy of Political and Social Science* 566(1): 55–67.

Williams, D. (2006). "On and off the 'net: Scales for social capital in an online era." *Journal of Computer-Mediated Communication* 11: 593–628. doi: 10.1111/j.1083–6101.2006.00029.x.

Chapter Two

Hashtagging from the Margins

Women of Color Engaged in Feminist Consciousness-Raising on Twitter

Caitlin Gunn

Launched in 2006, Twitter is an online social networking platform that allows users to post 140-character "tweets," real-time messages that create a micro-blogging experience. Though anyone can read public Twitter accounts and feeds, users are required to make accounts in order to tweet and join Twitter conversations. Several different methods of communication are possible on Twitter, from public or private direct messaging between users, public general tweets for one's followers to consume, information sharing, and participating in trending topics bound by the use of a hashtag (#), a feature which works to consolidate dialogue surrounding a given topic or theme. Through the use of hashtag conversations like #SolidarityIsForWhite-Women, #Ferguson, and #BlackLivesMatter, black women, indigenous women, and other women of color have utilized the Twitter platform to express their lived experiences and move their voices from the margins to the center of public feminist discourse. These conversations can be viewed as a consciousness-raising technique, rooted in radical feminist understandings of the second wave, and taken to the digital landscape. Despite the precedent for consciousness-raising activity among feminist groups, there has been significant pushback against hashtags with an intersectional focus created and propagated by women of color on Twitter. These hashtags and conversations have been labelled toxic and damaging to an overall sense of unity in the feminist movement by some mainstream white feminists. For many, the intersectional—and often radical activist—nature of the conversations on Twitter are threatening and overrule the need for consciousness-raising among women of color. Proponents of intersectional feminist hashtag activism[1] as well as those who consider the dialogue detrimental to a unified feminist movement all utilize a variety of online platforms to engage the topic.

The academic literature surrounding Twitter and the communities it encompasses is currently evolving. Relatively few academic articles and books have been written about the way people of color are engaging with social media websites like Twitter, though social media and hashtag activism are increasingly becoming topics of scholarly attention. There are a multitude of places, mainly news websites, feminist and race-related blogs, where these conversations are taking place. Many of the prominent writers who focus on Twitter, identity, and the power of hashtag activism are not academics, but bloggers, journalists, writers, and activists.

This chapter covers the concepts of consciousness-raising in a feminist historical context, and the way feminist consciousness-raising can look on the Twitter platform. There is discussion of "Black Twitter," and the way activism is fostered and organized in online space. Lastly, a discussion of the more recent debates about the activities of women of color on Twitter are outlined, with attention drawn to the way a feminist consciousness-raising framework can highlight racist and hostile responses to women of color speaking their truths and lived experiences on Twitter and other social media platforms.

LIVED EXPERIENCE AND FEMINIST CONSCIOUSNESS-RAISING

However recent the emergence of feminist hashtag activism and cyber-feminism, the concept of speaking to individual lived experiences as political action is not new. Rooted in the radical consciousness-raising efforts of the Women's Liberation Movement, tweeting about experiences of oppression can be considered a modern response to what is frequently considered a second wave feminist notion that the "personal is political." One of the first to explore politicizing personal experiences in a women's liberation context was Carol Hanisch, who wrote the prolific essay "The Personal is Political," originally appearing in the book *Notes from the Second Year: Women's Liberation; Major Writings of the Radical Feminists*, in 1970. "The Personal is Political" was a defense against the charged and misogynistic critiques of feminist consciousness-raising practices and groups. Rejecting the idea that discussing personal issues related to one's womanhood and the lived experiences of women was simply a kind of "personal therapy," Hanisch claims that consciousness-raising does not do the work of solving personal problems on an individual level, but rather is a political action with a group solution (Hanisch, "The Personal Is Political"). In the 1960s and 1970s, feminist consciousness-raising was a controversial idea; many within and outside of the feminist movement considered consciousness-raising a practice without substance or true activist impact. Proponents of consciousness-raising argued that there was in fact a radical and political motivation for sharing one's experiences with oppressive patriarchal structures.

Consciousness-raising was also addressed in Kathie Sarachild's essay "Consciousness-Raising: A Radical Weapon." Adapted from her talk given on consciousness-raising in 1973, the essay addresses the necessity of consciousness-raising to the success of the Women's Liberation Movement. Embracing radicalism as the desire to seek the true roots of problems, Sarachild considers consciousness-raising as "studying the whole gamut of women's lives," working to see women's liberation as not only a collective fight or a fight for the benefit of other women, but also as an individual undertaking (Sarachild, "Consciousness-Raising: A Radical Weapon"). Though the personal nature of consciousness-raising was considered by some frivolous, therapeutic rather than political, or downright dangerous and divisive, Sarachild emphasizes the political nature of radical feminist "bitch sessions." She does clarify that consciousness-raising does not require one particular method, and that it should not be considered an "end in itself" towards the goal of liberation.

A link between cyber-feminism and the radical consciousness-raising work done by second wave feminists was made explicit in an article written by Tracy Kennedy: "The Personal Is Political: Feminist Blogging and Virtual Consciousness-Raising." Kennedy makes the connection between the "personal is political" understandings of the feminist movement and the modern feminist Internet experience, claiming that feminist blogging provides spaces for consciousness-raising and community building. She notes that the exclusionary attitudes prevalent in the second wave feminist movement may not have carried over into online feminist spaces, where traditionally marginalized voices have more opportunities to be heard in the center of feminist discourse:

> Feminism has changed considerably over the last thirty years; the days when groups of women met in person to discuss their personal experiences of social inequities are now few and far between. Consciousness-raising groups were pivotal to the feminist movement of the 1960s and 1970s, despite the exclusionary tendencies many of them displayed—particularly toward women of color, lesbians, and disabled women. (Kennedy 2007)

Like the feminist blogging experience Kennedy reflects upon, Twitter has served a similar purpose for a multitude of different communities and groups. Framing the actions of women of color on Twitter as feminist consciousness-raising serves a specific purpose: to contextualize this kind of activity within feminist discourse, to make it legible to those more familiar with feminist studies and feminist studies concepts and terminology. Women of color do not need to think of their collective dialogue and activism on Twitter as "consciousness-raising" in order for it to be valuable or effective. Rather, this is a grammar that aids mainstream feminists in seeing how critiques of Black Twitter and women of color on Twitter frequently carry the same racist, exclusionary, and othering language and attention from white, mainstream feminism and predominantly white media coverage. In consciousness-raising groups of the past, women of color often felt more than simply "excluded," as Kennedy suggests; they were silenced, dismissed, belittled, and treated with violence once they gained entry into consciousness-raising groups. The racism and violence rampant in consciousness-raising groups of the second wave is echoed in the reactions of many white feminists to the consciousness-raising efforts of women of color on Twitter.

HASHTAG ACTIVISM

Since the beginnings of hashtag activist efforts, there have been many who see this type of engagement as a lackluster tactic that does more for the egos of individual social media users than it does on a macro level. The origin of the term "hashtag activism" is debated, but the first widespread usages of the phrase were associated with the #Occupy movement during the Occupy Wall Street protests, and with social media use and restriction in the Middle East during the Arab Spring. Similar to the discussion of the value of consciousness-raising efforts among feminists, the debate over digital activism is primarily concerned with the concrete results of online campaigns. As Dennis McCafferty mentions in "Activism vs. Slacktivism," his article in *Communications of the ACM*, "No one disputes that activists' online efforts draw greater attention to a cause, but opinion varies with respect to whether they make a significant, lasting impact" (McCafferty 2011). For women of color engaged in consciousness-raising on Twitter, two major responses to the "slacktivist" label are relevant. The first response realizes that people of color have in fact been able to use Twitter campaigns to make real-world changes. Secondly, the motivation of sharing lived experiences on Twitter, to center the experiences, lives, and voices of women of color in the public setting of Twitter is not always explicitly to enact immediate offline political or social change. It is not even intended in all cases to raise awareness of any particular issue or societal concern, but rather to do the work of raising one's own consciousness, and to be in dialogue with other women of color engaged in similar pursuits.

TWITTER, WOMEN, AND COMMUNITIES OF COLOR

Twitter has become an online cultural nucleus for people of color in many ways. In a report from the Pew Research Centers Internet American Life Project, statistics on Twitter users were released. As of August 2013, 18% of online adults were on Twitter, rising from just 8% in November 2010. As opposed to just 14% of White Internet users who are on Twitter, 27% of Black Internet users have active Twitter accounts (Brenner & Smith 2013). Those statistics reflect a phenomenon that has been labelled "Black Twitter." Black Twitter, as described by popular Black feminist and Black Twitter figure Feminista Jones, "can be described as a collective of active, primarily African-American Twitter users who have created a virtual community that participates in continuous real-time conversations" (Jones 2013). In her article for the news website *Salon*, "Is Twitter the Underground Railroad of Activism?" Jones addresses the increased interest in Black Twitter following the events of the George Zimmerman trial in 2013, noting that Black people had utilized the platform as both a place to voice personal reactions to the events of the trial, and to mobilize physical protests. In support of Black Twitter organizing efforts, Jones writes "When they work together, this collective is proving adept at bringing about a wide range of sociopolitical changes. It doesn't take much effort to get users to rally together behind causes that may have an impact on their lives" (Jones 2013).

Soraya McDonald, writing for *The Washington Post*, also considers Black Twitter a movement for both personal consciousness-raising and social organizing. She promotes the idea that Black Twitter helps to move conversations about the Black experience from the margins to the center of the public sphere in her article "Black Twitter: A Virtual Community Ready to Hashtag out a Response to Cultural Issues." McDonald notes the significance of those centered conversations:

> Perhaps the most significant contribution of Black Twitter is that it increases visibility of black people online, and in doing so, dismantles the idea that white is standard and everything else is "other." It's a radical demand for acceptance by simply existing—or sometimes dominating—in a space and being yourself, without apology or explanation. (McDonald 2014)

Black Twitter, however, is not a stable or universally accepted concept. Engaging more deeply with identity and race on the Internet, Sanjay Sharma complicates ideas about Black Twitter in his article "Black Twitter? Racial Hashtags Networks and Contagion," written for *New Formations* (Sharma 2013). He claims that Black Twitter is a difficult entity to define, and that "It has become apparent that online race is complex and mutable" (Sharma 2013). He is invested in unpacking the technosocial production and performance of race, looking specifically at hashtags that rise to popularity on Black Twitter. Acknowledging that race is a difficult concept to research online, Sharma writes "The rapidly expanding digital landscape poses a challenge to researchers, as the 'real-time' speed, propagation, and irruptions of race online create a presentism that seemingly resists critical analysis" (Sharma 2013).

Even among those who do explicitly endorse hashtag activism, hashtag feminism, and cyber-feminism as a type of radical consciousness-raising, there is controversy surrounding the way women of color have organized on Twitter. Many have openly critiqued what they consider divisive arguments, name-calling, and attacks on mainstream or "white" feminism as damaging to the feminist cause. One notable example was the article published by Michelle Goldberg, writing for *The Nation*: "Feminism's Toxic Twitter Wars." Within, she notes that pushback against feminist hashtags, particularly #FemFuture, coined by a small group of women attending a gathering at Banard College to discuss the "online revolution" of feminist activity in the blogosphere, was silencing women who would otherwise speak if not for fear of harassment, presumably from women of color via Twitter (Goldberg 2014). Within, she notes the emotional toll that comes from one's feminism being attacked on Twitter:

> Even as online feminism has proved itself a real force for change, many of the most avid digital feminists will tell you that it's become toxic. Indeed, there's a nascent genre of essays by people who feel emotionally savaged by their involvement in it—not because of sexist trolls, but because of the slashing righteousness of other feminists. (Goldberg 2014)

Despite Goldberg's attempts to reinforce concepts of frightening, bullying minorities tormenting white feminists whose unintentional racial aggressions are met with seemingly disproportionate rage and hostility throughout her article, she does acknowledge the history and lived reality of the racism in mainstream feminism when she writes, "There's a shorthand way of talking about online feminist arguments that pits middle-class white women against all the groups they oppress. Clearly, there's some truth here: privileged white people dominate feminism, just as they do most other sectors of American life" (Goldberg 2014).

Despite criticism from those who dismiss Twitter activity as superfluous, or those within the mainstream feminist movement claiming women of color have created a toxic environment on Twitter, many appreciate feminist and womanist consciousness-raising efforts for which women of color have created space. Suey Park, Twitter icon and creator of #NotYourAsianSidekick and #CancelColbert awareness campaigns on Twitter, frequently took on the critics of hashtag feminist efforts through her own Twitter feed and through her writing. In dialogue with Michelle Goldberg's piece on the divisive nature of what she considers racially motivated "Twitter wars," Suey Park and David Leonard pinpoint the racist underpinnings of Goldberg's critiques and move towards a more positive and holistic understanding of what feminists of color are doing with social media in their article "In Defense of Twitter Feminism" published on *Model View Culture*, writing: "In a world where the voices of white middle-class heterosexual men and women are privileged, it is striking that Twitter, one of the few spaces that allows for counter-narratives and resistance, is now facing a barrage of criticism" (Park & Leonard 2014). Further suggesting that some white feminists fear what women of color are discussing, Park and Leonard write:

> In a world where whiteness means presumed innocence, safety, and entrance there is born a fear of anything contrary to unquestionable authority. The reaction white feminists are having to women of color feminists entering Twitter tends to problematize those who point out racism rather than question the integrity of the framework being critiqued. (Park & Leonard 2014)

Mikki Kendall is a popular black feminist on Twitter who was described as "both famous and feared in Internet feminist circles," in Michelle Goldberg's article in *The Nation* (Goldberg 2014). Kendall, who is also an online writer, blogger, and activist, created the #SolidarityIsForWhiteWomen hashtag out of what she calls a "moment of frustration" (Kendall 2013). That moment spawned a worldwide trending discussion about the way that women of color have felt oppressed, marginalized, and subjugated by mainstream feminism, historically and in daily life. In an article for *The Guardian*, "#SolidarityIsForWhiteWomen: Women of Color's Issue with Digital Feminism," Kendall writes:

> It appeared that these feminists [on Twitter] were, once again, dismissing women of color in favor of a brand of solidarity that centers on the safety and comfort of white women. For it to be at the expense of people who were doing the same work was exceptionally aggravating. (Kendall 2013)

> Admittedly, this isn't a new problem: white feminism has argued that gender should trump race since its inception. That rhetoric not only erases the experiences of women of color, but also alienates many from a movement that claims to want equality for all. (Kendall 2013)

Kendall articulates both the usefulness of Twitter conversations for women of color, and acknowledges the frequently tense relations between mainstream feminism and women on the margins of feminist dialogue when she writes:

An honest conversation between feminists about feminism and its future is happening, and like every truly honest discussion of differences, it has been incredibly contentious. Hopefully, it will also be productive: despite the natural brevity encouraged by Twitter, any conversation that can span a full day must generate some change. (Kendall 2013)

There is a significant gap in academic writing about hashtag activism and women of color, most likely a result of the current, fast-paced, and ever-evolving nature of Twitter activity. Twitter is a platform being used by women of color in complex and powerful ways, many of which are positive and consciousness-raising, and draw negative attention and resistance from a variety of sources, frequently including mainstream white feminists. Twitter conversations aid in moving marginalized voices to the center of feminist discourse to the public sphere, despite the challenges presented by critics of their frameworks, language, and methods.

Women of color on Twitter tend to engage with consciousness-raising and activism in three major, frequently overlapping, ways: hashtag campaigns, expressions of lived experiences, and online mobilization for offline action. All three serve specific roles in the feminist Twitter experience for women of color, and utilize different tools and techniques to facilitate dialogue and consciousness-raising.

HASHTAG CAMPAIGNS

Hashtag campaigns are large-scale conversations on a single topic unified symbolically and practically by the use of a hashtag (#). Most frequently, they emerge as a response to stimuli either online or as a reaction to current events. Women of color are responsible for creating and "trending" many hashtags that sought to raise consciousness of different feminist issues in different feminist groups. One such example is #SolidarityIsForWhiteWomen, created by Mikki Kendall as a response to her frustrations with the frequently racist mainstream feminist concept of solidarity. A moment of Kendall's frustration turned into a nationwide trending topic, with thousands of tweets submitted using the hashtag. Some of Kendall's tweets on the subject are listed below, with references to the ways the notion of feminist solidarity is only functional within a white feminist context. Specifically, she mentions excluding Native American women from conversations about rape culture, the concerns over police brutality in the black community, and an incident in which young black actress Quvenzhané Wallis was called a "cunt" in a crass attempt at humor on popular satirical news source The Onion's twitter feed the night of the 2013 Oscar awards and was defended against the criticism of women of color by white feminists:

I know #SolidarityIsForWhiteWomen when NDN women can't get so much as a mention in discussions of rape culture. (Mikki Kendall, Twitter Post, August 12, 2013)

I know #SolidarityIsForWhiteWomen when the murder of #RekiaBoyd doesn't merit so much as a mention in the press. (Mikki Kendall, Twitter Post, August 12, 2013)

I know #SolidarityIsForWhiteWomen when Big Name Feminism thinks it's funny to call a nine year old black girl a cunt. (Mikki Kendall, Twitter Post, August 12, 2013)

Hashtag campaigns can take on many different tones and attitudes. The most serious tweets and Twitter conversations, like those relating to recent deaths and tragedies in communities of color, specifically of Trayvon Martin, Rekia Boyd, Renisha McBride, Eric Garner, and Michael Brown, are frequently striking and dark, using radical language to illicit a response or express the devastation of racism. Hashtags that use a humorous or satirical tone are no less striking, powerful in their ability to use laughter to underscore delicate points about oppressive power structures. Usually using this type of poignant humor, hashtag campaigns have been a highly effective method of "calling out" celebrities and public figures for racist, sexist, or otherwise troubling comments or behavior. Paula Deen, Robin Thicke, Don Lemon, Josh Zepps, Morgan Freeman, and Justine Sacco have all been targets of this type of campaign following their statements that were perceived as racist, sexist, or both by those affiliated with Black Twitter and other facets of people of color on Twitter. For example, in December of 2013, black feminist Twitter users responded to singer Ani DiFranco's plans to hold her feminist songwriting "Righteous Retreat" at the site of a former slave plantation with harsh criticism. Due to the outcry about the lack of consideration for black women's history and historical traumas, an initially reluctant DiFranco cancelled the retreat and issued an online apology (McDonald 2014).

Hashtag campaigns do not need to trend or gain vast popularity to support feminist consciousness-raising effectively. The hashtag #NotYourStockMuslim, for example, worked on a much smaller scale to illuminate stereotypes about Muslims prevalent in American culture. In a tweet posted by Eeman Cheema, she comments on the way Islam has been made to seem incongruent with feminism, and how those around her have considered her feminism a form of rebellion against her religious tradition: "Feminism is not my 'rebellion.' My parents raised me this way. #NotYourStockMuslim" (Eman Cheema, Twitter Post, March 24, 2014).

Another recent use of Twitter for consciousness-raising was seen in August of 2014, following the results of the trial for Renisha McBride's homicide. McBride, a young, unarmed, black woman, had sought help after crashing her car and made her way onto the porch of a nearby home in a suburb of

Detroit. The homeowner opened the door and shot her in the head. Many suspected that the murder charges would be dismissed as they were in the Zimmerman trial, and felt justice had been served when a guilty verdict was issued. The Associated Press issued this tweet following the verdict: "MORE: Suburban Detroit homeowner convicted of second-degree murder for killing woman who showed up drunk on porch" (Associated Press, Twitter Post, August 7, 2014).

Offended by the flippant tone and percieved prejudice of the Associated Press' response, people of color responded with the satirical hashtag campaign #APHeadlines. The tweets that followed, sent in by a multitude of people regardless of race or gender, reflected the historical prejudices leveled against people of color. Satirical in nature, the darkly humorous tweets call upon historical events and people like Rosa Parks and the Montgomery Bus Boycott, the Tuskeege medical experiements on black men, and the ongoing police brutality against men and women of color. As an example of this darkly humorous and critical satire, Twitter user Afro State Of Mind tweeted: "Officer's fists bloodied by aggressive black face belonging to innocent bystander. #APHeadlines" (Twitter User @Afrostateofmind, Twitter Post, August 7, 2014).

#BlackLivesMatter is another hashtag campaign which emerged in 2014 as a response to social, political, and legal events surrounding the murders of Michael Brown and Eric Garner at the hands of police officers. #BlackLivesMatter has become a rallying cry for a movement arguably born on Twitter and on black social media outlets. The hashtag was originally created by three queer women of color: Alicia Garza, Patrisse Cullors and Opal Tometi, and it is associated with hashtags #Ferguson, #HandsUpDontShoot, and #ICantBreathe. #BlackLivesMatter encompasses critiques of police violence, white supremacy, and personal and systemic experiences of racism in the United States. A multi-media approach proved incredibly valuable for people participating in those hashtags, as images, music, poetry, videos, and historical documents were shared, frequently in order to draw comparisons between black historical moments in the country, particularly during the Civil Rights Movement, and the kinds of trauma and activism occurring in Ferguson and nationwide.

MOBILIZATION TOWARD OFFLINE ACTION

Feminist Twitter and Black Twitter frequently use the social media platform to take online consciousness-raising and activism to the offline world. This is done by both direct planning for offline action, and by responding to offline political and social conditions or events. Women and people of color are using Twitter in large numbers to express a variety of responses to offline events. Protests, rallies, demonstrations, and logistics of on-the-ground action have all been organized via Twitter, especially during the #BlackLivesMatter movement. One such incident of Twitter affecting offline change was shortly after the George Zimmerman trial. Women of color contributed to a campaign to eliminate the possibility of a book deal for juror B37 in the Zimmerman trial, resistant to the idea that someone would profit from the death of unarmed black teen Trayvon Martin. Within hours of the initial Twitter activity, the book deal was called off (McDonald 2014).

Alicia Garza writes of the movements and contributions that took #BlackLivesMatter beyond a simple hashtag in an essay written for *The Feminist Wire*:

> We were humbled when cultural workers, artists, designers, and techies offered their labor and love to expand #BlackLivesMatter beyond a social media hashtag. Opal, Patrisse, and I created the infrastructure for this movement project—moving the hashtag from social media to the streets. Our team grew through a very successful Black lives matter ride, led and designed by Patrisse Cullors and Darnell L. Moore, organized to support the movement that is growing in St. Louis, Missouri, after eighteen-year old Mike Brown was killed at the hands of Ferguson police officer Darren Wilson. We've hosted national conference calls focused on issues of critical importance to Black people working hard for the liberation of our people. We've connected people across the country working to end the various forms of injustice impacting our people. We've created space for the celebration and humanization of Black lives. (Garza 2014)

LIVED EXPERIENCES

A common way of tweeting, expressing lived experiences as they relate to systems of oppression is another way women of color work to raise consciousness on the social media platform. This form of tweeting may or may not include hashtags, but generally aim to promote ideas and topics that people of color grapple with in their lives and communities. Personal experiences, critiques, and reflections upon the experiences of people of color are all considered "lived experience" tweets in this context. Tweets posted by women of color that speak to lived experience can look like the following sample of Twitter posts, but are not limited to these expressions:

> Bretastical: My grandmother is in tears. Tears. She said they marched because she didn't want us to have to. And now look. (Twitter User @_MissBre, Twitter Post, December 3, 2014)

> Ijeoma Oluo: Until people stop ignoring the high rate of sexual and physical abuse that black women face everyday. (Ijeoma Oluo, Twitter Post, February 11, 2015)

Ayesha Siddiqi: After a certain point helping people survive white supremacy is far more worthwhile than explaining it to white people. (Ayesha Sidiqqi, Twitter Post, November 1, 2014)

Elle La Negra: The women I follow on here have been my life's blood. How do I explain how strangers have inspired me with their struggles + triumphs? (Twitter User @FireInFreetown, Twitter Post, December 29, 2014)

Being able to express the daily realities of moving through the world as a woman of color is a worthy enough consideration in assessing the value of Twitter for consciousness-raising. That value is further increased as women of color communicate with one another directly, coming to view fellow Twitter users as a support system. Artist, writer, and sociocultural critic Zahira Kelly, known on Twitter as @bad_dominicana, communicates this sentiment in her tweet: "that is what we do here on twitter too. it often becomes a group therapy/discussion/theorizing session on the fly. u don't generate that" (Zahia Kelly, Twitter Post, December 1, 2014).

TWITTER: A TOOL FOR CONSCIOUSNESS-RAISING AND ACTIVISM

Twitter is a social tool deserving of more scholarly attention as it continues to serve as an open platform for centering the frequently marginalized voices of women of color. Beyond the value that feminist consciousness-raising discussions can have for theoretical and personal engagement, we also see Twitter being used to mobilize offline activism and serve as a catalyst for real-world feminist and anti-racist community engagement. The events in Ferguson and across the country have illuminated a vibrant online community able to transform consciousness-raising efforts into powerful offline action. In the midst of a social movement, Twitter is a driving force in the current discourse about race and gender in this country. The efforts of women of color engaged with consciousness-raising have created the scaffolding and community for supporting a social movement for this unique historical moment.

NOTE

1. Hashtag activism being here defined as activist efforts that take place online, or utilize online networks to promote communication, action, or awareness.

REFERENCES

Berlatsky, Noah. "How Sex Workers Are Using Twitter to Tell Their Own Stories." *Salon*. May 13, 2014. Accessed July 12, 2014. http://www.salon.com/2014/05/13/how_sex_workers_are_using_twitter_to_tell_their_own_stories/.

Brenner, Joanna, and Aaron Smith. "72% of Online Adults Are Social Networking Site Users." Pew Research Centers Internet American Life Project RSS. August 5, 2013. Accessed July 10, 2014. http://www.pewinternet.org/2013/08/05/72-of-online-adults-are-social-networking-site-users/.

Carr, David. "Hashtag Activism, and Its Limits." *New York Times*. March 25, 2012. Accessed July 12, 2014. http://www.nytimes.com/2012/03/26/business/media/hashtag-activism-and-its-limits.html?pagewanted=all&_r=1&.

Dewey, Caitlin. "#Bringbackourgirls, #Kony2012, and the Complete, Divisive History of 'Hashtag Activism.'" *Washington Post*. May 8, 2014. Accessed July 12, 2014. http://www.washingtonpost.com/news/the-intersect/wp/2014/05/08/bringbackourgirls-kony2012-and-the-complete-divisive-history-of-hashtag-activism/.

Eudey, Betsy. "Civic Engagement, Cyberfeminism, and Online Learning: Activism and Service Learning in Women's and Gender Studies Courses." *Feminist Teacher* 22, no. 3 (2012): 233–50. Accessed July 12, 2014. doi: 10.5406/femteacher.22.3.023.

Garza, Alicia. "A Herstory of the #BlackLivesMatter Movement by Alicia Garza—The Feminist Wire." The Feminist Wire. October 7, 2014. Accessed February 14, 2015. http://thefeministwire.com/2014/10/blacklivesmatter-2/.

Goldberg, Michelle. "Feminism's Toxic Twitter Wars | The Nation. Feminism's Toxic Twitter Wars." January 29, 2014. Accessed July 12, 2014. http://www.thenation.com/article/178140/feminisms-toxic-twitter-wars?page=full.

Grinberg, Emanuella. "Why #YesAllWomen Took off on Twitter." CNN. May 27, 2014. Accessed July 12, 2014. http://www.cnn.com/2014/05/27/living/california-killer-hashtag-yesallwomen/.

Hanisch, Carol. "The Personal Is Political." In *Notes from the Second Year: Women's Liberation; Major Writings of the Radical Feminists*. New York: Radical Feminism, 1970.

hooks, bell. *Feminist Theory: From Margin to Center*. Cambridge, MA: South End Press, 2000.

Jones, Feminista. "Is Twitter the Underground Railroad of Activism?" *Salon*. July 17, 2013. Accessed July 12, 2014. http://www.salon.com/2013/07/17/how_twitter_fuels_black_activism/.

Kendall, Mikki. "#SolidarityIsForWhiteWomen: Women of Color's Issue with Digital Feminism." Theguardian.com. August 14, 2013. Accessed July 12, 2014. http://www.theguardian.com/commentisfree/2013/aug/14/solidarityisforwhitewomen-hashtag-feminism.

Kennedy, Tracy. "The Personal Is Political: Feminist Blogging and Virtual Consciousness-Raising." *The Scholar and Feminist Online Journal* 5, no. 2 (2007). http://sfonline.barnard.edu/blogs/kennedy_01.htm.

McCafferty, Dennis. "Activism vs. Slacktivism." *Communications of the ACM*, November 2011, 17–19. doi: 10.1145/2043174.2043182.

McDonald, Soraya. "Black Twitter: A Virtual Community Ready to Hashtag out a Response to Cultural Issues." *Washington Post*. January 20, 2014. Accessed July 12, 2014. http://www.washingtonpost.com/lifestyle/style/black-twitter-a-virtual-community-ready-to-hashtag-out-a-response-to-cultural-issues/2014/01/20/41ddacf6-7ec5-11e3-9556-4a4bf7bcbd84_story.html.

Opam, Kwame. "Black Twitter's Not Just a Group—It's a Movement." *Salon*. September 3, 2013. Accessed July 12, 2014. http://www.salon.com/2013/09/03/black_twitters_not_just_a_group_its_a_movement/.

Park, Suey, and David J. Leonard. "In Defense of Twitter Feminism." Model View Culture. 2014. Accessed July 12, 2014. http://modelviewculture.com/pieces/in-defense-of-twitter-feminism.

34 *Caitlin Gunn*

Sarachild, Kathie. "Consciousness-Raising: A Radical Weapon." In *Feminist Revolution*, edited by Redstockings, 144-50. New York: Random House, 1979.

Sharma, Sanjay. "Black Twitter? Racial Hashtags, Networks and Contagion." *New Formations* 78, no. 1 (2013): 46–64. doi: 10.3898/NewF.78.02.2013.

Sowards, Stacey K., and Valerie R. Renegar. "The Rhetorical Functions of Consciousness-raising in Third Wave Feminism." *Communication Studies* 55, no. 4 (2004): 535–52. doi: 10.1080/10510970409388637.

Taibi, Catherine. "Fox News Panel Slams #BringBackOurGirls Hashtag Activism." *The Huffington Post*. May 11, 2014. Accessed July 12, 2014. http://www.huffingtonpost.com/2014/05/11/fox-news-bringbackourgirls-hashtag-activism-brit-hume-george-will_n_5305749.html.

Zinn, Maxine Baca, and Bonnie Thornton Dill. "Theorizing Difference from Multiracial Feminism." *Feminist Studies* 22, no. 2 (1996): 321–31. doi: 10.2307/3178416.

Chapter Three

The Arab Spring between the Streets and the Tweets

Examining the Embodied (e)Resistance through the Feminist Revolutionary Body

Fatima Zahrae Chrifi Alaoui

CONTEXTUALIZING THE GENDERED (E)REVOLUTION

On January 18, 2011, Egyptian female activist Asmaa Mahfouz posted a video blog (vlog) on Facebook urging Egyptian citizens to protest in Tahrir Square for Egyptian dignity. A founding member of the Egyptian April 6 protest movement, Mahfouz was well-versed in social networking and media sites. She blogged, tweeted, and posted on Facebook daily. In the video, a veiled Mahfouz directed her message at Egyptian citizens—specifically male citizens. She attacked Egyptian masculinity and challenged the men, stating, "If you think yourself a man, come with me on January 25th. Whoever said women shouldn't go to protests because they'll be beaten, let him have some honor and manhood and come with me on January 25th." Posted one month after protests erupted in Tunisia, Mahfouz's video has been credited with inspiring Egyptian citizens to mobilize and protest in Tahrir Square on Friday, January 25, for what has come to be known as the "Day of Rage." She connected her activism with the Tunisian protests and the self-immolation of Tunisian street vendor Mohamed Bouazizi on December 17, 2011:

> Four Egyptians have set themselves on fire, to protest the humiliation and hunger and poverty and degradation they had to live with for thirty years. Four Egyptians have set themselves on fire, thinking maybe we can have a revolu-

tion like Tunisia, maybe we can have freedom, justice, honor, and human dignity.

In the days following her post, Egyptians, many of whom supported or participated in the April 6 movement, responded to her Facebook post with comments, re-shares and likes. Mahfouz issued another vlog on Thursday, January 24, the night before the scheduled protest, reiterating her message to protest.

Since January 25, numerous news sites have uploaded and translated Asmaa Mahfouz's vlog, extending its reach through thousands of likes, reposts, and shares. Her message articulated multiple identities, resisting both President Hosni Mubarak's authoritarian regime and Egyptian and Islamic gender roles. She claimed the right to stand in the streets next to her fellow Egyptian citizens—male and female—transgressing the boundary between cyberspace and physical space. By using YouTube and Facebook to upload a vlog, she signified that her body was a symbol to rally around. This revolutionary embodiment mirrored the symbolic images of Khaled Said's battered and bloodied body on the "We are all Khaled Said"[1] Facebook page, and the self-immolation of Tunisian street vendor Mohamed Bouazizi memorialized in a viral YouTube clip. However, unlike the symbols of male martyrs expressed in the media, Asmaa Mahfouz performed as a female symbol, calling herself the "daughter of Egypt" (binti masr).

This book chapter examines a subset of Egyptian female cyberactivists who participated in the so-called Arab Spring revolutions. Asmaa Mahfouz exemplifies the integral role these female cyberactivists played in the protests that began in Tunisia in December 2010 and spread across the Middle East and North Africa into late 2011. When the dust settled, three presidents for life—Egyptian President Hosni Mubarak, Tunisian President Zine El Abidine Ben Ali, and Libyan President Muammar al-Gaddafi—had fallen and new governments and constitutions allegedly granting greater freedoms rose in their place. The reverberations of these revolutionary movements continue to be felt today in ongoing protest movements throughout the region. Female cyberactivists such as Asmaa Mahfouz inhabited virtual and physical space simultaneously during the Arab Spring revolutions, demonstrating the importance of digital media for articulating multiple, conflicting identities and remaking the self. This research proposes the term female reverberations to encompass the influence and scope of Arab women online during the height of the protests in Egypt from December 2010 to late 2011. In renowned feminist scholar Joan Wallach Scott's recent book *The Fantasy of Feminist History*, she writes that the word reverberation "carries a sense both of infinite regression," thus female reverberations are "subsequent echoes, succession of echoes—and of effect—reverberations are also repercussions" (Scott 2011, 79). Borrowing her conceptualization, I substitute the digital media theoretical term "connectivity," which maps online networks and measures influence of digital technologies, with the term "reverberations," gendering my analysis of female activism and presence online. In this way, this research explores how the revolutionary movements in Egypt offered opportunities for resistance, in particular cyber resistance, to be deployed in new ways and spaces.

The theoretical framework of this book chapter works at the intersection of feminist critical theory, social movement theory and digital media studies. Using a subset of female cyberactivists from Egypt, it seeks to understand how these protests gave birth to diverse networks of female cyberactivists, expanding female reverberations online. In doing so, these female subjects problematized stable categories of "women," "citizen," "Arab," and "feminist." Thus, this research investigates the liberating possibilities of digital technologies and social media and examines how these female cyberactivists performed their gender and articulated their identities online.

Throughout this research, I pose the following question: Did digital technologies facilitate women's participation in the Arab Springs in new ways and with greater agency than they had previously experienced? In response to this question, I argue four main paints: 1) flows of information connected female cyberactivism with physical protests, allowing female cyberactivists to live blog, tweet, and film their participation in street protests and upload these documents online; 2) female cyberactivists deployed different languages (MS, colloquial, English, French, etc.) at specific moments to reach and build alliances with select local, regional, and international audiences; 3) during and after the protests, female cyberactivists established new networks online to connect with fellow protestors, reach out to international journalists, document their experiences, demand gender equality, and mobilize female networks against gender violence; and 4) female cyberactivists performed a multiplicity of femininities online, from modern Western constructions of femininity to the intersection of Islamic piety with feminist values. Ultimately, I argue that women in the 2010–2011 Egyptian protests used digital technologies in diverse ways to participate in and lead protests, carving new spaces to articulate claims for political, social, and cultural gender parity.

Locating the Revolutionary Micro-Blogging Social Media Sites

Launched in 2006, Twitter founders Jack Dorsey, Evan Williams, Biz Stone and Noah Glass intended the microblogging[2] site to function as a social network, similar to Facebook. To use the site, members post status updates limited to 140 characters using various websites, mobile internet devices and SMS (that is, text messages) (Murthy 2011). These updates could be anything from what someone ate that night to a message to communicating a public emergency. Twitter also connects to other websites through widgets hosted on sites that post directly to twitter. Members can also add photos, upload videos, and paste links to their messages. Twitter facilitates interaction and connectivity between users through the "reply," "retweet," and "favorite" buttons. These functions extend Twitter's reach far beyond the original member and her/his followers.

Twitter's usage soon expanded and transformed into an information network instrumental to numerous protests and revolutions throughout the world. In 2009, two revolutions occurred which thrust Twitter and social networking into the spotlight. First, civil unrest began in Moldova in April 2009 as the results of the 2009 Moldova parliamentary election were tallied. Protestors claimed election fraud and demanded a recall election. Dubbed the "Grape Revolution," demonstrators used Twitter to organize themselves and coordinate protests. Several months later, in June 2009, disputed Iranian elections led to mass youth protests, which came to be known as the "Green Revolution" (Mungiu-Pippidi & Munteanu 2009). Both social movements later came to be known as "Twitter Revolutions." The Moldova and Iranian uprisings informed how Egyptian activists would deploy digital technologies and social media networks during the 2011 Arab Spring revolutions.

Twitter, Facebook, Flickr, YouTube and other social networking and information network sites can be understood as a physiological charged space (Naghibi 2011). For instance, in the Iranian post-election protests, Twitter acted as a tool to share information, creating a sense of belonging and a virtual space perceived as removed from physical violence. Twitter organizes information and categorizes themes using a "hashtag," for example, Iranian diasporic activists tweeted #green to symbolize their support for the protests. By searching for the hashtag #green, Iranians could access a stream of tweets relaying information about the protests as they unfolded. During the Arab Spring revolutions, protestors employed similar tactics. They used Twitter hashtags such as #ir7al (leave), #Jan25, and #tahrirsquare to create a sense of solidarity and momentum and to disseminate information about when and where demonstrations would be held.

Moreover, social networking sites can be seen as an enabling space that transforms identification and belonging to political action and thought. Contemporary female bloggers bring private matters into the public domain, transgressing the virtual and physical realms (Sreberny & Khiabanny 2010; Dabashi 2007; Bayat 2007). Hence, social networking sites allow for embodied discussions and "the articulation of a more abstract 'body politics'" (Sreberny & Khiabanny 2010). Similarly, Arab female cyberactivists have employed digital technologies and social media networks to transgress offline gender divides and issue claims for gender parity in the new governments.

Therefore, micro-blogging social media sites like Twitter and Facebook serve as gateways into other virtual networks hosted digitally. In addition to their rising importance in political revolutions and protest movements, they have been used to advocate for gender equality throughout the world. Although the impact of these technologies depends on the awareness of advocates using them, the political, social, and socioeconomic circumstances surrounding them, and the existence of civil society, these technologies provide unique spaces for marginalized populations, such as women, people of color, to articulate and transmit oppressed ideas and identities. In Latin America, women's organizations and movements employ information and communication technology (ICTs) to create transnational networks that advocate for gender equality (Friedman 2005). These gendered networks sometimes reasserted traditional societal divides along race, class, etc. A closer examination of online gender activism, in Latin America, for example, leads to questions of whether ICTs have liberating potential. Does the Internet give rise to a "nomadic" subject—capable of transcending digital divides and physical boundaries? As demonstrated above, there is a strong connection between the proliferation of digital technologies and cyberactivism with political and social protest movements worldwide. Micro-blogging sites enable citizens to produce user-generated content that bypasses the biased state media and government censors. Using mobile phones to connect to online sites, take photos, and upload videos, protestors can challenge the power dynamics in their country and mobilize protests along informal, user-generated information networks. The following section argues that these technologies and their usage should be analyzed through a gendered perspective; asking, does the internet provide liberating potentialities for female activists? Or are gender divides reasserted online? I contend that a gendered perspective of digital activism during the Arab revolutions elucidates how Egyptian women used digital technologies and social media networks to participate in lead protests, inserting their marginalized bodies and empowering voices into the public domain.

Gendering the (e)Revolutions: Reviewing the Feminist Digital Subject

As stated in the introduction, this research looks at the intersection of protest movements and digital activism in Egypt. It answers the questions of how do digital technologies and social media, create diverse subjects? What are the liberating potentialities of digital media technologies? How can we theorize gender activism and agency in virtual spaces? The research applies a gendered analysis in order to unpack the intricate processes in which Egyptian female cyberactivists construct their subjects online. By looking at specific instances of protest and resistance, this book chapter deconstructs how these women strategically deployed their identities through digital media technologies. Social networking and digital technologies enabled Egyptian females to participate in political protests in new ways, operating in a virtual "third space." Thus, this research examines whether these spaces ensured women's safety or exposed them to violence, asking: does cyberactivsm produce new modalities of agency?

Contemporary feminist scholarship finds that Arab women have participated in the online and political activities of Arab feminism. Some, such as Sahar Khamis, argue that this prolific engagement contributes "to a new chapter of both Arab feminism and the region" (2011). Arab women use online activism for political engagement and resistance, challenging hegemonic and patriarchal norms and political oppression. Social networking sites such as Twitter, Facebook, Wordpress, Blogspot, etc., have opened spaces for women to articulate multiple points of resistance. Activists in the Middle East and North African employed cyberactivism to connect, organize, and mobilize resistance to the authoritarian regimes. Female activists also used cyberactivism to respond to constructed gender norms, rules, and laws in their society. To understand how feminist reverberations spread online through the Arab Spring, this research applies Saba Mahmood's reworking of Judith Butler's performative theory.

Employing Saba Mahmood's theoretical reasoning in *Politics of Piety*, this research argues that transgressing gender norms may not only take the form of challenging or affecting change in the "system of gender" (2005), but can also be realized by how female cyberactivists inhabit certain norms or gender roles. Furthermore, agency can be seen by how these subjects navigate discourses appropriating marginalized languages and creating new spaces for diverse forms of resistance to flourish. In particular, this research demonstrates how Arab bloggers and female cyberactivists embodied resistance online during the Arab uprisings. It is important to note that this research does not negate female cyberactivists who performed agency through resistance to oppressive gender norms; rather, it argues that female cyberactivists from the Arab revolutions deployed multiple modalities of agency—sometimes inhabiting conservative gender roles and sometimes resisting these roles.

In applying theories of performativity, it is important to reinforce that the performance of gender is also the performance of the political. When using the category of "Arab" "woman" and "Islamic" "feminist," this research brings into play certain political theorizations, representations, and power dynamics that these words signify. It would be remiss not to mention postcolonial theorist Edward Said's text *Orientalism* (1978). Enacting a Foucauldian understanding of how power functions through discourse, Said reveals the historical production of Western representation of the Arab world. He unpacks how stereotypical caricatures of Arabs as "backwards, ignorant, suppressive" became constructed as "truth" and informed scholarly work and political policy today. In the feminist movement, third wave feminist critical theory problematizes the imperial emancipatory project of first and second wave feminism that essentialized women's struggles into universal categories. Thus, speaking of Arab women and Islamic feminists brings to the forefront the historical production of their subjectivation. In order to have a more nuanced understanding of how the Arab Spring offered an opportunity to articulate new, diverse identities, this paper proposes a theoretical model that does not seek to "give" agency or impose an emancipatory narrative on Arab women's actions. Instead, it examines the connection between online female activism to offline protests, looking at how they used this transition to embody multiple points of resistance. Viewing internet connectivity through a gendered perspective and terming it "reverberations" allows this paper to reveal how the unstable category of "Arab woman" is written online in the Arab world.

By examining a diverse range of female cyberactivists in the Arab Spring—such as Egyptian activist Mona Seif protesting and tweeting from Tahrir Square amidst violent confrontations with the Egyptian police from January 25 to February 14, 2011, this research unpacks how women deployed diverse identities and articulated agency through digital technologies. It argues that female reverberations online expanded and transformed during the Arab Spring protests, increasing Arab women's participation online. This research, specifically, highlights how these women used digital technologies in the Arab Spring protests, creating new spaces to perform their gender in the process. In order to do so, it is necessary to first step back and assess the wide range of scholarship informing my understanding of social movements, digital technologies and feminist critical theory.

Feminist Critical Theory and Performative Actions

The following paragraphs survey notable scholarship on feminist critical theory, from landmark texts analyzing the intersection of Western feminism and neocolonialism to more contemporary works that pursue different modalities of agency for women. Several feminist scholars and activists have challenged the Arab Spring's impact on promoting women's rights and gender equality in the Middle East and North Africa (Newsom & Lengel 2012). They cite as evidence street harassment and sexual assault of women protestors and the absence of women participating in the political transformations. In response, the purpose of this section is to examine feminist theories on gender relations and performative action, using them to contextualize women's participation in the Arab Spring. Specifically, these articles consider questions of agency, noting that transnational and feminist scholars must analyze their role in contributing to essentialism to have a more nuanced understanding of the impact of the Arab Spring on Arab women (Newsom, Cassara, & Lengel 2011). Chandra Mohanty addresses the role of imperialism of Western feminist thought in her now classic generative text "Under Western Eyes: Feminist Scholarship and Colonial Discourses" (1984). Mohanty critiques the political project of Western feminism and its construction of a hegemonic "Third World woman" in the essay. She argues that feminist scholarship (reading, writing, critical, or textual) is inscribed in relations of power, "relations which they counter, resist, or even implicitly support" (334). Her work draws from Michel Foucault's theories on power and sexuality, outlined in *The History of Sexuality Volume I* (1976). She writes:

> This mode of defining women primarily in terms of their object status (the way in which they are affected or not affected by certain institutions and systems) is what characterizes this particular form of the use of "women" as a category of analysis. (338)

Since Mohanty published this article, feminist scholarship has shifted to acknowledge the existence of these reductive, hegemonic categories. However, many in the public sector and media have not followed the fight against reappropriation. For example, within the humanitarian and non-governmental organization sectors, the "Third World woman" still exists. In recent years, Western powers such as the United States have appropriated feminist discourse, using "the role of women" to justify military interventions in Afghanistan and Iraq (see also Lila Abu-Lughoud, Jasbir Puar).

Michel Foucault articulated revolutionary theories of sexuality and power relations in *The History of Sexuality: An Introduction* (1976). In his book, Foucault argued that the subject is discursively constructed through social practices and problematizes the assumption that power exists only in an oppressor/oppressed hierarchy (Foucault 1976). Feminist theorists have since taken his theories and applied them to a diverse array of issues. Judith Butler, renowned sociologist and Foucauldian scholar reworks Foucault to interrogate the gender binary and pursue the processes of biopower and performance theory, arguing gender is something that is performed and thus constructed (Butler 1990). Recently, Saba Mahmood and Allison Weir have engaged Foucault and Butler's work, applying their theories to a study of Islamic women's piety. Their writings further problematize Foucault's paradox of subjectivation, wherein the subject's capacity to action is enabled and created by specific relations of subordination (Foucault 1976; Mahmood 2005; Weir 2013). They explore different modalities of agency, unhinging it from an oppressor/oppressed hierarchy.

Politics of Piety: The Islamic Revival and the Feminist Subject (2005) by Saba Mahmood unpacks the motives and practices of Egyptian women participating in the mosque or piety movement. In the beginning of the text, she reflects on the contentious role the piety movement holds in feminist scholarship, a position she also held before beginning her research. Muslim women and the piety movement have been termed fundamentalist, conservative, and reactionary and associated with the subjugation of women. However, as her writings demonstrate, normative liberal assumptions of human nature, in particular the unquestioned ideal of individual freedom, must be interrogated and questioned when applied to questions of religious and cultural difference. Engaging Foucault's analysis of ethical formation and Butler's work on performance theory, she looks at how women in the mosque movement inhabit norms and practices. While acknowledging that a lens of resistance to norms can be applied to the mosque movement, she argues that such a reading is reductive. Her ethnographic interviews demonstrated how women negotiated competing norms in their piety, navigating male opposition to their movement and their desire to be active in their participation in Islamic studies. Mahmood's text lays out a new way of approaching agency in assumed marginalized subjects. Her work provides insight into how to study female subjects who adhere to patriarchal norms without assuming their freedom is restrained or that they can only exhibit agency by resisting these norms. In particular, this ethnographic and philosophical study offers a framework for analyzing agency in terms of the different ways it manifests and the conceptual language it employs.

Responding to *Politics of Piety*, Allison Weir critiques Mahmood's claim that feminist scholarship needs to question the ideal of freedom (2013). A social and political philosopher at the University of Western Sydney, Weir's work focuses on the intersection of gender, sexuality, class, ethnicity and religion in the development of individual and collective identities and the relation of identity to agency, freedom, power and solidarity. Her article, "Feminism and the Islamic Revival: Freedom as a Practice of Belonging" (2013), explores various conceptions of freedom, using the framework Mahmood applies to theorize on different modalities of agency. She critiques Mahmood for looking at only one type of relation: the relation to the self. In contrast, she argues that "the analytical framework of relation to the self must be supplemented with an analytical framework of other kinds of relations, in this case in particular a relationship to God" (2013, 328). Thus, for Weir, freedom can be found in submission to God or when experiencing the sacred. She also examines positive freedom, communitarian freedom, and what she terms a feminist re-conception of freedom. Combined, Weir's and Mahmood's work challenge existing paradigms of liberal-secular thought, arguing for a more diverse and nuanced application of feminist critical theory in order to understand the question of the subject's construction posed by Foucault in 1976.

Turning from the theoretical writings of feminist scholars, I now look at the Moroccan sociologist and feminist Zakia Salime's recent works. Salime's work examines the feminist movement in Morocco, analyzing its political, social and religious influences and its role in the Arab Spring protests. "The

War on Terrorism: Appropriation and Subversion by Moroccan Women"
(2007) draws correlations between Moroccan feminist discourse and neoliberal discourse. Using the 2003 Casablanca bombings by an Islamic terrorist
group al-Salafiya al-Jihadiya, she demonstrates that feminist organizations
(both liberal-secular and Islamist) appropriated the neoliberal agenda to advocate for women's rights and greater equality in the Moroccan family legal
code. Interestingly, Islamist women, rather than liberal-secular groups, faced
greater hostility and government resistance after the attacks. They had to
fight to prove their moderation and religious authority as a defense against
Islamic extremism. This article shows an active feminist movement in Morocco, which has an influence on Morocco's political, religious and social
processes.

Salime demonstrates the Moroccan feminist movement's influence further in her article, "A New Feminism? Gender Dynamics in Morocco's February 20th Movement" (2012). Salime utilizes Butler's theory of performing
gender to argue that gender equality demands in Morocco's February 20
movement exist in the virtual and bodily presence of women at all levels of
mobilization and organization. Although feminist organizations were not at
the forefront of the movement, Salime states that the movement appropriated
feminist discourse. She cites the equal participation of women and men in the
movement articulate a new feminism, one that moves out of feminism as a
strictly female project. Her analysis of gender demographics in Morocco's
Arab Spring give rise to questions of comparison with the movements in
other countries. How does Morocco's movement differ from others? Do
other movements exhibit similar feminist thought? This article provides a
framework for similar studies to be applied throughout the Arab Spring.

The above paragraphs have surveyed recent scholarship analyzing the
questions of agency and subjectivation in feminist critical theory. In conclusion, the final section of this review presents three authors who have published articles at the intersection of revolution, digital activism, and Arab
feminism: Courtney Radsch, Sahar Khamis, and Aimy Aisen Kallander.
These demonstrate the different perspectives and dominant trends a gendered
lens to cyberactivism in the Arab Spring reveals. Courtney Radsch and Sahar
Khamis have published several articles since 2011 reflecting and theorizing
on the role of female cyberactivists in the Arab Spring. Their work covers the
entire Middle East and North Africa (MENA) region and relies on data
collected leading up to and during the protests from December 2010 to late
2011. Courtney Radsch argues that women mapped new territories for blogging and online activism during the protests. In an article for Muftah, an open
source journal online, Radsch notes that digital media technologies empowered women, enabling more women to engage in cyberactivism (December
2013). Her article focuses on the actions of female cyberactivists throughout
the MENA region, bringing in cyberactivists from Bahrain and Saudi Arabia

as well as North Africa. Another recent article published jointly by Sahar Khamis and Courtney Radsch, "In Their Own Voice: Technologically Mediated Empowerment and Transformation among Young Arab Women," expands Radsch's argument in her December 2013 Muftah article. The authors use in-depth interviews with female cyberactivists to posit that these women used social media to express themselves freely and enact new forms of agency and empowerment (2013).

In opposition to Radsch and Khamis, Amy Aisen Kallander argues that scholars need to reconsider the implications of cyberactivism in the Arab Spring protests (2013). Kallendar interrogates the role blogs had during the protests and problematizes their reach. Her article focuses on the role of what she terms "tech-savvy, middle- and upper-class, bilingual professionals" bloggers in Tunisia and their effect on the Tunisian uprisings from December 2010 to February 2011. Kallander challenges Radsch's and Khamis' understanding of the impact of digital technologies in the protests, contending that, "an in-depth examination of the Tunisian case supports the skeptical position of the limitations of online activism" (2013). The diverse positions of Kallander, Radsch, and Khamis reflect the confusion that still surrounds theorizing the connection between digital activism and protest movements. How do we measure the impact of digital activism on physical protests? What is the relationship between social media and social networking sites and revolutionary events? Do digital technologies empower women (and all marginalized peoples) or reassert unequal gender binaries? This paper shares similarities with Radsch and Khamis' arguments, refuting Kallander's main points. However, it is important to note that this research does not purport to claim that digital technologies and female cyberactivists caused the revolutions; rather, it seeks to understand how the political uprisings in Egypt created new networks of female activists and enabled women to translate online activism to offline protests. Therefore, this research operates at the intersection of the vast array of scholarship on the Arab Spring revolutions, digital media technologies and social media, and feminist critical theory presented above. It applies a gendered lens to the 2011 revolutions in Egypt, examining how female activists deployed digital technologies to claim greater agency during the protests. The following section analyzes examples of Egyptian female cyberactivism.

EXAMINING THE EMBODIED (E)RESISTANCE THROUGH
THE EGYPTIAN FEMINIST REVOLUTIONARY BODY

In May 2010, a group of fifteen Arab female bloggers met through two workshops in Cairo and Amman.[3]

I walked the streets with men and women, of all sorts of backgrounds. Never have I felt a sense of belonging like then, like now. I was happy just to be in the streets sitting in close proximity with thousands of strangers, snuggled in a warm cocoon, liberating Tahrir Square, marking it as ours. (Mona Seif, January 30, 2011)

They agreed to each write one post under the same theme each month.[4] For the first post titled "My City," Egyptian journalist and cyberactivist Mona Seif wrote about Cairo on her blog *ma3t*. On July 23, 2010 she wrote, "I wanted to walk you through the streets of crazy downtown, share with you my music as i blur out everything on our way and turn it down into hazy spots of colors." But, she continued, "I can't do this now. My city is different, my city is mourning, and I can only share this with you. Khaled Said, a young Egyptian, was tortured and murdered by the police." Six months later, Seif joined millions of other Egyptian women and men in the streets of Cairo chanting in the streets and demanding the end of the regime, "Ash-shab yurid isqat an-nizam."[5]

The evening before the protests, Mona Seif posted, "We participated in January 25th." Her blogpost, written in Egyptian colloquial, urged Egyptians to take to the streets, invoking the memory of Khaled Said and countless other Egyptian citizens humiliated, beaten and killed by the police. At the bottom of the post, Seif provided links to the #Jan25 page on Twitter, the Egyptian Google executive, Wael Ghonim's appeal posted on the "We are all Khaled Said" Facebook page, and to the mission statement of the Front to Defend Egyptian Protester.[6] She encouraged her followers to follow her and other activists on Twitter (@monasosh) for updates on the protest and its locations in Alexandria and Cairo. Mona Seif continued to blog, tweet, post on Facebook and participate in the revolution.

During this time, her followers increased and she drew the attention of international journalists who began following her twitter for updates on the events occurring in Tahrir Square. Her actions online and offline demonstrate how online activism multiplied and grew to occupy the heart of Cairo in Tahrir Square. The actions of Mona Seif and her fellow female cyberactivists during the Egyptian Revolution from January 25 to February 14, 2011 elucidate questions into the relationship between digital technologies, protest movements, and gender in the Arab Spring. This research seeks to understand how Egyptian female cyberactivists deployed digital technologies, asking: What was the influence of their digital activism. And, did social media networks and digital technologies facilitate Egyptian women to claim greater agency in the public sphere?

This section examines the role of Egyptian female cyberactivists in the Egyptian revolution. Through a qualitative analysis of female reverberations online, I conduct close readings of six Egyptian female cyberactivists' online profiles during the height of the Egyptian revolution from January 2011 to March 2011. In doing so, I locate the actions of Egyptian female cyberactivists within the theoretical framework and argument of this research, examining how female cyberactivism in Egypt reflected female participation online during the uprisings. This section begins with a brief background of the gender relations and the growth of the feminist movement in Egypt, unpacking the gender binary. Then, it turns to a discussion of women's participation online leading up to the revolution. Finally, it concludes with an analysis of six Egyptian female cyber activists who participated online and offline in the Egyptian protests beginning January 25, 2011. These close readings ask: how did female cyberactivists utilize digital technologies? Did online activism transition to offline protests, and if so, how? What identities did these female cyberactivists perform and on what digital platforms? Did digital technologies and social media networks create liberating potentialities for Egyptian women during the revolution and after? In response to these questions, this section argues that during the Egyptian revolution of dignity from January 25 to February 14, 2011, Egyptian female cyberactivists transcended gender divides online and offline and carved new spaces to articulate agency in the public sphere through their online activism. Specifically, I contend three main points: 1) Egyptian female cyberactivists inhabited multiple digital platforms to articulate specific gendered messages using English, Modern Standard Arabic and Egyptian colloquial Arabic; 2) Egyptian female cyberactivists used digital technologies to share information between cyber space and the protests in the streets, connecting online activism to physical demonstrations; and 3) Egyptian female cyberactivists used virtual space to simultaneously mobilize followers to protest and reflect on their own experiences of revolution.

Unfolding the Egyptian Gender Dichotomy

Judith Butler argues that gender is discursively constructed in and through language (Butler 1990). Thus, when examining the gender binary and roles in Egypt, it is important to unpack the intersecting discourses constructing Egyptian masculinity and femininity. Egypt's Sunni Muslim population follows the Hanafi school of thought with a minority of Muslim Egyptians identifying as Shi'a or Sufi. Islamic values shaped Egyptian culture and women's place in society. British colonialism in the 1800s challenged Islamic values and displaced Islamic gender roles with a British understanding of masculinity and femininity. Colonial hegemonic masculinity dislocated Egyptian men, Muslim and Christian, creating an opposing narrative that reasserted Islamic masculinity. This narrative reified the "Muslim woman" as a symbol. On one hand, colonial powers fetishized the "Muslim woman" and saw her veil as sign of Islamic oppression, barbarism, and intolerance. In contrast, Islamic forces saw the "Muslim woman" as a symbol of piety, a barrier to the corruption of secularism. An Egyptian lawyer Qasim Amin, considered by many in the Arab world to be the first feminist, wrote several influential texts including *Liberation of Women* (1899) at the beginning of the twentieth century. His work outlined the position that President Nasser and later President Mubarak would adopt in their state feminism, believing that the political rights of women were necessary to "bringing the nation out of darkness" (Ahmed 1992).

Even though Egypt achieved independence in 1956, the question of "Egyptian women's rights" and oppression under Islam continued to be shaped by the conflicting discourses of secular Western thought and Islamic thought (Ahmed 1990). Women gained political emancipation at independence in 1956 under the rule of President Abdel Gamal Nasser and his Arab Socialist Union party. Nasser also attempted to reform the Egyptian Personal Status Law (PSL) to give women more rights; however, Islamic clergy opposed his moves and saw this as the further erosion of Western colonialism and secularization. Over time, this tension between liberal-secular and Islamic discourse in Egypt constructed a gender binary that blends Western patriarchal thought and secularizing values with Islamic piety and traditional ideals. Postcolonial Egyptian nationalism further complicated this binary, making a model Egyptian citizen-woman. The valued Egyptian femininity evolved to be a middle- to upper-class, pious, respectable university student or mother-worker employed in the country's export industries (Johansson-Nogues 2013). Thus, under Nasser and subsequent Egyptian presidents, the intersection of Islamic thought and the Egyptian government's so-called secularism created a valued femininity that merged Islamic and neoliberal values. This combination of Islamic patriarchal values with Western patriarchal norms subjugated women, yet at the same time, expected them to participate in the economic workforce.

Egyptian feminism negotiated these conflicting yet intersecting discourses, often reasserting the gender binary in this process. Until the last thirty years, feminism remained an elite discussion. Starting in the first decade of the 1900s, the dialogue between the Egyptian Feminist Union and the Muslim Women's Association reflected the struggle to articulate a cohesive Egyptian feminism. Influenced by Western feminists, Huda Sharwai founded the Egyptian Feminist Union in 1923, a political feminist organization that advocated secular reforms and women's political enfranchisement. Zeinab al-Ghazali formed the Muslim Women's Association in 1935 after disagreeing with many of Sharwai's views, specifically in her preference of Western secular thought over Islamic practices. Al-Ghazali opposed Sharwai's embrace of Western culture as superior to Islam, searching for an alternative feminism that articulated female subjectivity and affirmation within a native, vernacular, Islamic discourse (Ahmed 1992).

These two organizations shaped Egyptian feminism until the 1940s, when a new generation of young Egyptian women challenged the elitism of the Egyptian Feminist Union. It is important to note that this divide paralleled socioeconomic lines, with upper-class, educated Egyptians supporting secular reforms and Western ideals and lower class women choosing a path of female subjectivity within Islam. In 1951, Doria Shafik, who was one of the first women to receive an education at the Sorbonne in 1920s paid for by the Egyptian Ministry of Education, led a demonstration of over a thousand Egyptian women into the Egyptian parliament (Ahmed 1992). Once there, she stopped proceedings and implored parliament to consider the issues and demands of Egyptian women. Her actions caused the Egyptian government under British protectorate to grant women the right to vote and run for parliament in 1951 (Nelson 1996).

Since the 1970s, the secular-liberal/Islamic binary and the gender binary have been challenged in the theoretical and political project of feminism.[7] While some political feminist activists continue to pursue their goals in opposition to Islam, many Egyptian feminist activists and scholars have problematized the unquestionable universality of Islamic patriarchal oppression. Contemporary feminist scholarship examines how feminist projects have adopted religious discourse to achieve gains for political and legal equality (Abu-Odeh 2004). The Islamic Revival[8] changed the dialogue surrounding women's role in Islam, as Muslim women from Iran to Morocco took more active roles in their religious traditions. In the last three decades, Egyptian feminist organizations have turned to Zeinab al-Ghazali's vision of female subjectivity formed through Islamic practice. Many Muslim women now practice what they term "Islamic Feminism" or the marriage of Islamic ethics to feminist discourse and ideals. A prominent Egyptian NGO, Women and Memory Forum, aims to reread Arab tradition and cultural history in order to create a new cultural and social awareness that supports women's social roles. It conducts research, programs and events such as a conference held in spring 2012, *Feminism and Islamic Perspectives: New Horizons of Knowledge and Reform*. This conference sought to merge women's demands with the Islamic perspective, as the founders write on their website, "The main incentive behind Islamic feminist research is the activation of Islam's 'just' and 'fair' principles for the production of gender-sensitive knowledge within an Islamic frame of reference."[9] Women and Memory Forum is one of many examples that erode the division of liberal-secular and Islamic, through the creation of new modes of feminism and understanding of Egyptian woman's gender roles.

On the eve of the 2011 Egyptian protests, the constructed roles of Egyptian masculine and feminine identities in society remained divided between notions of what it meant to be an Islamic Egyptian versus a secular Egyptian. Despite Egyptian men's assertion of Egypt as a modern state, they still treated women's presence in the streets as a transgression. Gendered violence, in particular street harassment and sexual assault, reminded Egyptian women of this supposed transgression daily. Men owned the street; women were allowed to do business in the street but not to linger. Controversial feminist writer and journalist Mona Eltahawy attacks rape culture and sexual harassment in Egypt on her twitter (@monaeltahawy) and in her articles.

Digital technologies such as social networking sites and mobile phones have offered a way for women to protest and combat these issues. For example, the organization, Harrasmap, devised a method to use crowd source[10] technology from mobile phones to map sites of sexual harassment. They identified highly trafficked spots, contacted business owners around the area, and constructed a safety network for women. The following section examines the proliferation of digital technologies and social media in Egyptian social movements over the past decade. It asks, how do Egyptian gender relations manifest online? Do Egyptian women enjoy greater agency and freedom of movement through their usage of digital technologies and social media networks? In response to these questions, the following section argues that Egyptian female cyberactivists have used digital technologies and social media networks to engage in discourse online and create new spaces for women to perform their gender and express agency in the public sphere.

Gendering Online Activism in Egypt: We Are All Laila

Under President Hosni Mubarak's thirty-year rule, government censorship silenced political protest against the regime; however, in the past decade several social movements emerged online and offline that created an active and engaged protest culture by the eve of the so-called Arab Spring revolts. Social networking sites served as a space semi-removed from state violence and censorship. The grassroots coalition for change Kefaya,[11] the April 6 Movement, "We Are All Khaled Said" Facebook page, and other civil society organizations laid the foundation for the revolution through their discursive activism online. Egyptians have cultivated one of the most prolific web presences in the Middle East. Twelve million Egyptians subscribe to Facebook using an Arabic interface launched in 2010 (around 15 percent of the population). An estimated 37 percent of the 80 million population have internet access (30 million people), and Egyptians represent 13 percent of MENA twitter users (Internet World Stats 2012; Arab Social Media Report 2013). Social media enabled opposition leaders to shape their discourses of contention, frame issues, and distribute unifying symbols (such as the image of Khaled Said) and transition protests from virtual spaces to physical spaces (Lim 2012). Wael Ghonim, the Egyptian Google executive who created "We are All Khaled Said" Facebook page and movement, highlights the importance of online activism for organizing and mobilizing the #jan25 protests in his autobiography Revolution 2.0 (2012). With these social networking tools, and the decades of activism that preceded the #jan25 protest, Egyptian activists united under one demand, "The people demand the end of the regime."

As early as 2006, female bloggers gathered on the Egyptian blogosphere to interrogate the nature of feminism, cultural and religious gender roles, and to discuss how to transform traditional notions of femininity and masculinity in the virtual and physical world. Egyptian bloggers created the "We Are All Laila" campaign in 2006 to dedicate one day each year to raising awareness and discussing the concerns of women in Arab society. The name "Laila" comes from the landmark novel *The Open Door* (1960) by Egyptian writer Latifa Al Zayat and represents all contemporary Egyptian women and the struggles they endure in a repressive society that elevates the dreams and desires of men over women.[12] A 2007 study conducted by Dr. Mohamed Hossan Ismail has labeled the participants of the campaign as "cyber-feminists," a term many of the bloggers identify with. Members of "We Are All Laila" discuss a range of topics each year, from practicing Islamic feminism to a critique of previous feminist projects (Ismail 2007). In 2007, the study showed cyber-feminists focused on strengthening solidarity and relations between bloggers, rather than mobilizing the masses. The Arab Spring protests shifted the purpose of women activists, from looking at creating feminist new networks to urging all Egyptians—men and women—to protest.

The shift from static web pages to dynamic or user-generated content and the growth of social networking has provided liberating possibilities for Egyptian women to perform their gender, challenge the hegemonic Egyptian construction of femininity, and demand gender parity. Egyptian cyber forums and online chat rooms have emerged as spaces for women to challenge and transgress traditional norms regarding gender and sexuality. Howard and Hussain argue that digital media in the Arab world allows citizens to learn about gender relations in other countries, debate specific gender issues, renegotiate and restructure gender relationships, and support women-only online communities (2013). This is particularly true for Egypt and its prolific history of feminism. Courtney Radsch notes that digital media also fostered connectivity and solidarity for women, providing them a space and tools for gender politics. Specifically, the social networking sites and microblogs Twitter and Facebook enabled activists to iterate revolutionary language and protest through retweets, sharing, favoriting etc. They increased the reach of the original post, disseminating it throughout the web, at news media sites, and international journalists.

Nonetheless, digital divides exist in Egypt today. In the Arab world women represent only a third of users (Arab Social Media Report 2013), whereas worldwide women outnumber men 58 percent to 42 percent on Facebook (Internet World Stats). In Egypt, roughly one third of the five million Facebook users are female. The 2013 Arab Social Media Report produced by the

Dubai School of Government's Governance and Innovation program notes some of the factors constructing gender digital divide. The online survey conducted from mid-August to mid-October 2011 targeted men and women from all twenty-two Arab countries and received 469 full responses with 60 percent of those from women. According to their research, survey respondents in Egypt identified "societal and cultural limitations" as the top barrier, with privacy and security, ICT literacy, access to ICT, confidence in social media and education as secondary barriers. Respondents demonstrate some ambivalence in the report; 78 percent of Egyptians agreed that social media can advance women's rights yet at the same time 40 percent of respondents at the regional level believed social media can present new concerns for women at the civic level. However, the report also argues that despite the gender digital divide, social media and online activism can empower women to be active participants leading and organizing protests.

It is also important to note that Egyptian female participation online is not limited to political protest and activism. Egyptian women also use blogs as diaries to share personal stories. These sites also provide spaces for women to perform their sexuality and gender in a way physical space had not allowed them too. Young men and women bloggers often posted under pseudonyms on Facebook, skating censorship and creating new opportunities for sexual exploration that would not be traced back to them. Often, the purpose of the blog can be discerned from which networking site and what language the subject uses. For example, Egyptian women using colloquial Egyptian Arabic on a Tumblr blog generally use their blog for personal reflection and thought, including personal pictures or online images and reposts. Many of these women participate in what the blog aggregate and citizen journalist website Global Voices Online[13] has termed "Hijablogging," which is an international blogosphere movement where women discuss online veiled fashion, lifestyle, experience, and the political and religious issues surrounding veiling. Egyptian women posting in the English language participate in what Ethan Zuckerman has termed "bridgeblogging."[14] These women tend to be academics or journalists targeting international audiences and news sources. They use blogs as spaces to publish their perspectives on political issues or to act as citizen journalists circumventing the state media.

This section has argued that the proliferation of digital technologies and social media networks have blurred the boundaries between public/private space in Egypt and enabled Egyptian women to articulate diverse identities and to demand political, social, cultural, and religious gender parity. The following section examines whether this argument also applies to the actions of Egyptian female cyberactivists during the Egyptian revolution beginning on January 25, 2011. Through an in-depth analysis of six Egyptian female cyberactivists who participated in the Egyptian dignity revolution, it will contend that Egyptian female cyberactivists used digital technologies and social media to insert their voices and bodies into the public sphere, subverting the Egyptian gender divide and exhibiting multiple modalities of agency.

Embodying Gendered Resistance Online

The remainder of this section focuses on close-readings of six Egyptian female cyberactivists. These female cyberactivists represent a rich array of viewpoints, political activity, and online presence; however, they are by no means representative of all Egyptian female cyberactivists. Among the bloggers omitted include Dalia Ziada, Mona Seif and Nadia El Saadawi. Dalia Ziad is a political and human rights activist who co-founded an Egyptian political party and ran for parliament after the revolution. She has won numerous awards for her blogging from the news organizations such as the Daily Beast and Newsweek. News journalist Mona Seif braved the protests every day to capture, document and upload content online providing hourly updates of the protests. Renowned feminist writer and physician Nawal El Saadawi, seventy-nine-years-old at the time of the protests, camped out in Tahrir Square day and night, providing coverage of the protests for international news media sources such as Democracy Now. These women held instrumental roles in the Egyptian dignity revolution, mobilizing Egyptians to protest via Facebook, documenting the clashes between the police and the protestors in Tahrir via Twitter, and highlighting the incidents of gender violence and sexual harassment that occurred in blogs and news articles. However, due to space constraints, I limit the analysis to the six Egyptian female cyberactivists described below.

This section begins with April 6 activists Asmaa Mahfouz and Esraa Abdel-Fattah, examining their role as Egyptian "Facebook girls" organizing for the January 25, 2011, National Police Day demonstration (#Jan25). From Mahfouz and Abdel-Fattah's demonstration of female discursive activism online, this section will turn to an analysis of internationally renowned bloggers Zeinab Mohammed, Nadia El-Awady, and Arwa Saleh Mahmoud. Mohammed, El-Awady, and Mahmoud used their blogs to document the protests through citizen journalism, live-tweeting and blogging the revolution. Finally, it concludes with Islamic feminist and cyberactivist Fatma Emam, unpacking her experience protesting and the role of Islamic feminism in the revolt. These female cyberactivists witnessed diverse experiences protesting, blogging and posting in Egyptian colloquial Arabic, Modern Standard Arabic, and English to perform multiple identities online.

Throughout, these close-readings, I ask: How and when do these female activists use digital technologies and social media? What gendered messages do they transmit? How do these Egyptian female cyberactivists articulate agency online and offline? In response to the questions posed above, this section brings in the previous discussions of Egyptian gender relations and the rise of digital technologies to inform the analysis of these six Egyptian female cyberactivists. Ultimately, it argues that digital media technologies and social networking sites enabled women to inhabit new spaces offline and online during the Egyptian revolution, transcending the demarcation of public and private in Egypt. In these spaces, they deployed diverse identities and articulated multiple modalities of agency that inserted their presence into the public sphere.

A Call to Action: Asmaa Mahfouz and Esraa Abdel-Fattah

Many Egyptian female activists realized the significance of their bodily presence and used their presence to challenge and rally Egyptian citizens. As founding members of the Egyptian April 6 protest movement,[15] Asmaa Mahfouz and Esraa Abdel-Fattah have interacted on all forms of media—Facebook, Twitter, YouTube, blogs, etc. International media sites such as Al Jazeera, BBC, and Open Democracy dubbed Mahfouz and Abdel-Fattah "Facebook Girls," for their prolific online activism leading to the #Jan25 protest.

Their movement participated in creating the #Jan25 protest in Egypt with the "We are all Khaled Said" Facebook page. In addition, they issued their own calls to protest on Facebook, Twitter and YouTube. Asmaa Mahfouz posted her first video blog (vlog)[16] on January 18, 2011, a week before the protest was to take place on January 25. Esraa Abdel-Fattah identifies as an Egyptian political activist, although she took a brief hiatus after her detainment by the police in 2006. In an interview with *The Cairo Review of Global Affairs* on January 27, 2011, she stated, "We used social media to organize ourselves in a very active way. To publicize the event the way we want, and to make coverage for the events that happened in the street. And when we broadcast what happened, at the same time we encouraged them to join us in the street." Besides her activism, Esraa acted as a bridge between Al Jazeera and the protests, tweeting updates as the protestors moved to occupy Tahrir Square after the January 25 protests.

In her first video posted to her Facebook page on January 18, 2011, Asmaa Mahfouz appeared in the fashionably conservative attire of professional Egyptian Muslim women and wearing a hijab. Mahfouz spoke in impassioned colloquial Egyptian Arabic and challenged her audience to participate in the protests, stating, "If you think yourself a man, come with me on January 25th. Whoever said women shouldn't go to protests because they'll be beaten, let him have some honor and manhood and come with me on January 25th." Egyptian activists, including among them Wael Ghonim (creator of the "We are all Khaled Said" Facebook page) credit Mahfouz with inspiring Egyptian citizens to take to the streets on January 25 and march to Tahrir Square. In the days following, her video circulated online on

Facebook, YouTube and Twitter. Egyptian viewers from within and without the country responded to her Facebook post with re-shares, likes, comments and images of themselves, their family or even their children with the words "I will go to Tahrir on #Jan25." On January 24, Asmaa Mahfouz reiterated her call to arms in another vlog posted to her Facebook page.

By facing and speaking to the camera, Mahfouz projected a feminine image on the protests, inscribing her body as the "Egyptian revolutionary woman." Lasting four minutes and thirty-two seconds, the January 18 video shows a veiled Mahfouz holding a sign to her chest saying that she would go out and protest to bring down Mr. Mubarak's regime. In a 2011 interview with the *New York Times*, she stated that her desire to be visible and reach as many people as possible inspired her to produce the video. Importantly, her "desire to be visible" translated as her desire to be visible as a Muslim, female subject, demonstrated by her hijab. Mahfouz located her position as a girl—rather than a woman—in the opening lines of the video, "I posted that I, a girl, am going to Tahrir Square and I will stand alone." Her use of the identifier "girl" rather than "woman" can be read as both a challenge to Egyptian men and notions as well as an appeal to cultural notions of "the mother" or "daughters." By identifying as a female, Mahfouz revealed her conscious desire to transgress the separation of private "women's space" and public "men's space." Articulated via the Internet, her message transcended spatial boundaries, reaching beyond the Tahrir Square, to the rest of Cairo and all of Egypt through Facebook, YouTube, and Twitter. International news organizations such as Al Jazeera and Democracy Now took her video, translated her message into English, and posted subtitles on the video, making it accessible to English speakers as well.

Throughout the video, she directed her message at Egyptian men, using gendered language with the Arabic masculine "you." This choice of subject iterates Mahfouz's gendered message and her challenge to Egyptian men. Halfway through the video, she stated, "If you think yourself a man, come with me on January 25th. Whoever said women shouldn't go to protests because they'll be beaten, let him have some honor and manhood and come with me on January 25th." She reiterated the challenge to male masculinity in the following sentence, "If you have honor and dignity as a man, come. Come and protect other girls in the protest." These statements complicate a Western feminist analysis connecting agency with subjectivity. As Mahmood asks in *Politics of Piety* (2005), how can a challenge that reasserts traditional gender roles (such as masculinity, men as the protector) articulate the feminist subject? In many ways, the examples described above iterate a hyper-performance of Egyptian gender roles and norms. Mahfouz over-emphasized her own femininity while at the same time insinuating it has more "honor" and "duty" than male masculinity. Thus, her actions can be read as subverting the gender binary from within it.

When viewing Asmaa Mahfouz's vlogs and reading her blogposts, twitter posts, Facebook, etc., it is important to view her as responding to and inhabiting multiple discourses. She articulated resistance to state power (represented by Mubarak) through her deployment of feminist activism within the constructed Egyptian and Islamic gender binary. When she identified as the "daughter of Egypt" or as a "mother," she expressed resistance through appropriating these norms and saying "Look, here I am, in the streets" and challenging the separation of public male spaces and private female spaces. When she stated, "let him have some honor and come with me," she appropriated the religious and cultural discourse surrounding Islamic values of honor to encourage Egyptian citizens to protest. On the surface, her videos seem to only protest Mubarak's regime; however, a closer analysis reveals their embodied resistance to constructed categories of gender in Islamic Egyptian culture.

Asmaa Mahfouz and Esraa Abdel-Fattah transgressed the boundary between public/private spaces through their online activism. Employing activist language, they used digital media as a tool to inform and convey messages as well as challenge certain gender perceptions. In their activism, they articulated multiple identities, resisting both President Hosni Mubarak's authoritarian regime and Egyptian and Islamic gender roles. Mahfouz claimed the right to stand in the streets next to her fellow Egyptian citizens, male and female, in her video blogs—a claim Abdel-Fattah echoed in her Facebook posts and Twitter accounts. By using Facebook to upload a vlog, Mahfouz projected her body and marked it as a revolutionary symbol, similar to the images of Khaled Said's beaten body on the "We are all Khaled Said Facebook" page and video of Tunisian street vendor Mohamed Bouazizi self-immolation. However, she emphasized her role as a living feminine symbol, calling herself the "daughter of Egypt" or the "Facebook Girl." Esraa Abdel-Fattah and Asmaa Mahfouz claimed their place in Tahrir Square and in Egyptian society through these digital technologies, transmitting their message to all Egyptians online. The following sections introduce Egyptian female cyber activists Nadia El-Awady and Arwa Saleh, moving from calls to action issued by feminine bodies online to female experiences and narratives of protest.

Narratives of Protest: The Inner Workings of My Mind and Al Hurr

Nadia El-Awady created the Wordpress blog *The Inner Workings of My Mind* in 2009. She used it as a space to post science journal articles she had written to document her travels and to reflect on the role of Islam in her life. An Egyptian raised in the United States, El-Awady discussed the conflicting identities she navigated growing up in her blog posts. In her video blogs, she appeared in a hijab, but also mentioned that she had distanced herself from her conservative Islamic background. Her posts have ranged from discussions of faith—she wore the face veil for eight years—to asserting her independence and the independence of all women within and through Islam. At the time of the revolution in 2011, she was living and working in Egypt after attending university there. While aware of the #Jan25 event created on Facebook by the "We are all Khaled Said" page, El-Awady and her friend and fellow blogger Arwa Saleh Mahmoud of the blog *Al Hurr* doubted the turnout as well as the ability of those she describes as "privileged, educated activists" to affect change. Mahmoud reflected in English on her blog on February 20, 2011 "As I later found out, we were like many other skeptical Egyptians who were going out of a fading sense of duty. We knew there was nothing else we could do if we wanted any change." Yet, on January 25, 2011, Nadia El-Awady found herself in a taxi heading to the protests in downtown Cairo with Arwa Saleh Mahmoud.

She documented her experiences in English with photos and videos uploaded to YouTube via her blog and includes links to both her blog post and her YouTube account on her Facebook page. In addition, she also archived all of her tweets from January 25 to February 12, 2011 on her blog. Individuals from all over the globe followed El-Awady's twitter account and blog; one Filipino living in the Netherlands even wrote a blog post about the impact her twitter narrative had on him and the 8,100 other followers she had.[17] El-Awady's tweets and videos depicted the protests' escalation from January 25–29. On January 25, she uploaded a picture via Twitpic with the tweet, "Downtown Cairo now #jan25"; the image had five retweets, two favorites, one Google Plus share, and two Facebook likes. These videos compose the majority of her initial posts, with an average of several thousand views for each video by December 2013. Taken from a mobile phone, the videos captured her voice and reaction to the protests and exhibitions of violence she witnesses. A video she uploaded on January 25 at 7:02 pm depicts the women's participation in the protests; it films a crowd of people chanting [indiscernible, but something like 1, 2, the people want. . . .]. In this forty-eight-second clip, the fist of a veiled woman in front of her shoots into the sky next to blue screens from mobile phones and cameras capturing the moment. The camera shakes slightly as El-Awady's voice joins the Egyptians around her chanting in Egyptian colloquial Arabic, "Ash-shab yurid isqat an-nizam" (the people want to bring down the regime).

Nadia El-Awady's videos and posts from the Egyptian Day of Rage on January 29, 2011, exposed the rising violence of the protests, caused by police forces firing with real and not rubber bullets. El-Awady and Mahmoud first encounter tear gas on the march to Tahrir when the police use it to prevent protestors from entering the square:

> Already our faces are covered with scarfs to protest as best as possible from
> the gas. Arwa seems to yell, "RUN," I run away from the police and through

> the horrid cloud of gas forming behind us. As I run, I need to take deeper
> breaths, but I can't because that means breathing in tear gas. When I do
> breathe, it feels like acid is being down my throat. When I hold my breath as I
> run, I almost black out and faint. I continue on, my heart pounding. (*The Inner
> Workings of My Mind*, March 11, 2011)

Another time, Arwa Salah Mahmoud and she took shelter from the tear gas
and the shooting in a building with many other people. El-Awady filmed
Mahmoud in Arabic and English explaining the events going on around them
as others protestors seeking refuge add commentary, "People are taking shelter. Police and protestors are both taking shelters. Where is the enemy here? I
really don't know."[18] The next videos showed El-Awady and Mahmoud
running from tear gas and gunshots; the camera lens pointed towards the
ground and shaking back and forth as they ran down the streets amidst yells
and the ricocheting of gunshots and the sirens screeching. Although the two
Egyptian women experienced various forms of violence in the streets, El-
Awady continued to videotape and protest until street thugs broke her camera
in the first days of February.

Both Arwa Saleh Mahmoud and Nadia El-Awady emphasized their ability to slip in-between the police forces and protestors, switching identities in
order to pass through unmolested:

> Nadia and I were able to penetrate even to the side of the police, changing our
> occupations and purposes of being in the street as we went along depending on
> who asked us. One minute we were journalists, the other we were trying to get
> home. (Al Hurr, February 20, 2011)

Their freedom of movement during the daytime protests did not carry over
into the night. El-Awady wrote that it was still necessary to walk home at
night escorted by several male friends as a curfew was instated and random
acts of looting and violence began occurring in downtown Cairo. However,
those acts of violence differed from the prevalence of gender violence and
street harassment directed at women before the revolution began. The wom-
en noted the absence of sexual harassment for those eighteen days in their
blogs. In the tweet shown below, El-Awady applauds the lack of gender
violence on January 25, "Thousands of young men and no harassment to be
seen. I love you Egypt #jan25."

Nadia El-Awady and Arwa Saleh Mahmoud articulated multiple identities in their online narratives. Acting simultaneously as journalists, protestors, women, and Egyptian citizens, they witnessed first-hand the power that
the crowds gained as they marched towards Tahrir Square. Writing in her
reflection on February 20, Mahmoud recounted, "The crowds were finally
able to enter Tahrir. . . . The further the protesters advanced the more cheer-
ful they became, and soon they were joined by thousands more coming into

Tahrir from all directions. Tahrir had become theirs" (Al Hurr, February 20, 2011). Their blog posts and reflections marked the transition they underwent in those eighteen days—from skeptical observers and archivists of activism they became active participants. El-Awady's video translated into citizen journalism and kept her followers (numbering 70,000 in 2014) informed of the protestors' advances. Arwa Saleh Mahmoud acknowledges the power shift the protests engendered in the final words of her reflection, "Something very big had happened in my country. The people were no longer afraid, the regime was" (Al Hurr, February 20, 2011).

Nadia El-Awady and Arwa Saleh present detailed narratives of their participation in the Egyptian Revolution protests from January to February 2011. Their use of digital technologies while protesting enabled them to document and share the events as they were happening online. They acted as citizen journalists to move in and out of the protests and participated in the demonstration marches to Tahrir Square. For example, El-Awady's 8,100 Twitter followers used her as a source to know when and where the protests were occurring. The next section offers a different example on the use of digital technologies and social media for citizen journalism in the Egyptian revolution. Egyptian cyberactivist Zeinab Mohammed live-tweeted (@zeinobia) and blogged (Egyptian Chronicles) her participation in the revolution, documenting the events unfolding in Tahrir Square and the streets of Cairo when the state media refused to do so.

Citizen Journalism: Egyptian Chronicles (Zeinab Mohammed)

On January 19, 2011, Zeinab Mohammed of *Egyptian Chronicles* wrote, "Anyhow after a week we shall see what is going on the 25th of January 2011 and whether it will be remarkable like the 25th of January 1952." An Egyptian journalist, Mohammed's blogposts intertwined citizen journalism and discursive activism, interspersed with videos, tweets, and links to other bloggers' sites and news articles. Later on, she included the applications Twitter and Google created specifically for activists in the Arab revolutions "Speak to Tweet" and "Cover it Live." These apps uploaded a live stream of her tweets simultaneously to Twitter, Blogspot, and Facebook. She identified as, "just Egyptian girl who lives in the present with the glories of the past and hopes in a better future for herself and for her country." Writing in both English and Arabic, her blog reached a diverse audience with 80499 views as of December 20, 2014.

Zeinab Mohammed demonstrates both the importance of citizen journalism to the Egyptian Revolution as well as the necessity of inhabiting multimedia platforms to disseminate information—posting on twitter, Facebook, YouTube, Flickr, and traditional media sites. Her connectivity traced across the blogosphere and expanded into the streets, reflected by the images of protests she posted and the reception her blog posts and tweets received. By posting in Arabic and English, she appealed to international, regional, and local audiences. Her language reveals that she is conscious of the impact of the Tunisian revolution and the power structures her discourse disrupts. She wrote in English and Arabic on January 25, 2011:

> The protests have not started but I will say that the day is successful "InshAl-lah" [God willing] because it showed how much the regime is scared from the people, the regime freaked out after knowing that thousands accepted the protest invitation online not even offline. Thanks to our Tunisian brother our regime began to fear us more and more. That scared regime is actually a weak one that has no confidence in itself, sooner or later it will fail. (Egyptian Chronicles, January 25, 2011)

In the statement above, she identified a power dichotomy between the re-gime—Mubarak's government—and the "people." However, the Egyptian citizens occupying virtual and physical space disrupted the power dichoto-my—revealing that the people can and do have power. Thus, for Mo-hammed, the impending #Jan25 protest in Tahrir Square threatened the hier-archy of political and governing power in Egypt as the Tunisian protests in the cities of Sidi Bouzid and Tunis destabilized the Tunisian regime's power.

Mohammed, like many cyberactivists, believed in the power of Facebook and online activism for inciting protests. She referenced the January 25 pro-tests invite created by the "We are all Khaled Said Facebook" page several times, writing three days before protest began:

> The January 25 protest is getting serious attention more and more. More Face-book pages and groups are calling for the #25 Jan and more political groups are going to participate in the huge event. They are about 17 groups. Many are praying that it be the start of a new thing in Egypt. Now if you are interested in following the protest on twitter to know its updates then follow this hash tag [#jan25]. (Egyptian Chronicles, January 22, 2011)

In the above quote, Mohammed connected the upcoming protests to online activism and grassroots organizing, using the hashtag #jan25 on Twitter and in her blog and posting about the Egyptian Facebook pages organizing the protests. She also noted earlier in the post that thousands of Egyptians had joined the event created by the "We are all Khaled Said" Facebook page. Multiple digital media platforms appeared in each of her posts, reflecting the importance of deploying many digital technologies to reach as many people as possible.

Zeinab Mohammed live tweeted Mubarak's speech addressed to the revo-lutionaries February 10, 2011. From January 25 to February 11, Mohammed narrated the protests in Tahrir with photos and video, documenting the events as they happened on her blog, twitter, Facebook page and email. Her posts reflected the fervor unfolding events, as hundreds of thousands of Egyptians thronged the streets of Cairo, clashing with police and thugs hired by the government. She attempted to describe the sounds, smells, and passion of the people—repeating the universalizing word "we" or "ours." Her voice flowed back and forth from first person to third person as she reflected on her own experiences or appeals to the "Egyptian" "us" experience. Videos of couples marrying and famous singers performing protest songs interspersed her political dialogue. Yet, as February 11 approached her language and the frequency of her posts reveal that the revolution was approaching an apex, writing on February 10, "a possible coup in the way!!" Using the "Cover it Live" app, she live-blogged Mubarak's speech on February 10, 2011; this app includes the comments and responses to her tweets as well. Thus, when Zeinab Mohammed tweeted, "Mubarak: God bless Egypt and peace upon you #Mubarakspeech," a commenter responds, "the whole speech so far is an affront to those, who give their time, days and nights, their blood, and even their lives for this revolution. . . ." At the end of this live blog, Mohammed announced that February 11, 2011, will be a "Day of Rage" in Tahrir Square in response to Mubarak's speech and urged everyone to protest.

The actions of the Egyptian female cyberactivists Asmaa Mahfouz, Esraa Abdel-Fattah, Nadia El-Awady, Arwa Saleh Mahmoud and Zeinab Mohammed illustrate how Egyptian women used their blogs, Facebooks, and Twitter accounts to document the protests and to encourage Egyptian citizens to protest. They posted in Egyptian colloquial Arabic, Modern Standard Arabic, and English to connect with Egyptians in the country and to inform the international audience of the unfolding uprising. The final section of this research shifts from narratives of protest and citizen journalism. It introduces Fatma Emam, an Egyptian woman who blogs under the name Brownie. Emam turned to her blog to reflect on the challenges the protests placed to her identity as an Islamic feminist. Her internal struggles depict the conflicting identities Egyptian women deployed online and in the streets throughout the revolution.

Narratives of Protest, Gender, and Islam: Brownie

As stated in the previous sections, digital media can foster connectivity and solidarity for women, enabling them to inhabit private, public, and cyber space simultaneously. This final close reading analyzes Fatma Emam's blog Brownie, examining how her cyber activism during the Egyptian 2011 revolt created a space for women to perform multiple, conflicting identities and forge coalitions between secular and Islamic feminists. As a research assistant for Cairo NGO Nazra for Feminist Studies, Emam writes within the context of Egyptian feminism and gender politics. Her blog posts explore the intersection of faith and gender that shape her life. For example, on her first day Emam participated in the protests, she wrote about her experience afterwards:

> I was very self-conscious, I found it too hard to unite with the masses. One example when the prayer time came, I did not pray, because I was afraid that the prayer was led by the Muslim brotherhood, which was proved that the prayers were not political and felt annoyed by the chants of the seculars calling to the prayer because it is Islamisation of the revolution. (Brownie, February 9, 2011)

In this post, Fatma Emam expressed her sense of displacement and alienation within the protests. Her response to the protests differed from the expressions of overwhelming nationhood felt by female bloggers such as Zeinab Mohammed of Egyptian Chronicles. Emam pointed to the confusion over prayer's place in Tahrir, highlighting her uncertainty over the role of political Islam represented by the Muslim Brotherhood in the revolution. On February 9, 2011 Fatma Emam wrote in English how she believed that the revolutions in Egypt were not just a revolution against Mubarak and the status quo, but a revolution against the patriarchy embedded within the regime and reflected in Egyptian culture:

> The revolution is not only in Tahrir, it is in every Egyptian house, it is the revolution of fighting the patriarch as Hind said. In this revolution the women fought for their private and public life and this is the core of our feminist struggle as Mozn said. (Brownie, February 9, 2011)

Her post referenced the historical and cultural division of private and public life. It noted that, while no longer explicit, this division continues to permeate Egyptian society. In many ways, Fatma Emam's posts echo Asmaa Mahfouz's challenge to Egyptian masculinity in her January 18 and January 25 vlogs.

Although Mahfouz does not identify as a feminist, she employed similar language about gender parity. Both women claimed their right to protest in the streets and challenge the relegation of Egyptian women to the home. Emam implicated the Muslim Brotherhood for enshrining these patriarchal values dividing society and subjugating women, thus explaining her uneasy feelings towards their presence in Tahrir Square before Mubarak stepped down. But at the same time, she identified as an Islamic feminist, "As an Islamic feminist, I disagree with this, I believe in a secular state . . . in this state everyone express his/her beliefs" (Brownie, February 9, 2011). Consequently, she refuted the Muslim Brotherhood for their distortion of the Islam she practiced and viewed as complementary to feminist ideals.

Throughout the protests, Fatma Emam used her blog to unpack her experiences during the Egyptian revolution rather than employing it for citizen journalism, documenting human rights violations, or organizing for events. Her posts reflected her encounters with the protests in Tahrir Square as well as the participation of the women and men around her. On February 4, nine days after the protests began, she professed her surprise with the participation of women in the protests—not that they were present—but the ways in which they participated:

> I am proud to say that The Egyptian women are playing an extraordinary role in the revolution, they are fighting for private and public rights, they are claiming their rights as equal citizens in this country.
>
> When I was in Tahrir, I saw young and old women, veiled and non-veiled women, and political oriented women and non-political women.
>
> I saw them side to side to the men, they did not listen to the traditional calls that Tahrir is not a place for women. I saw the Egyptian women doing untraditional roles in organizing, strategizing. Spreading the information and leading the revolution. They were everywhere writing new line of the herstory of women. (Brownie, February 4, 2011)

In the excerpt taken from her blog above, Fatma Emam located the Egyptian uprising as a revolutionary event for Egyptian women and their "herstory." Again, she noted that women were fighting for "private and public rights" and were issuing claims for gender parity in Egyptian politics and society. Echoing Mahfouz once more, she highlighted the presence of women in a place—Tahrir Square—not traditionally demarcated for them. Emam's experience of the Egyptian revolution from January 25, 2011 to February 14, 2011 reflect the fears, anxieties, excitement, and anticipation that faced Egyptian female cyberactivists. Her posts provide an insight into the complex and conflicting emotions that guided these women in their actions. Her voice shifted in the post illustrated above on February 4, from wary of the role of political Islam in the protests to proud of and inspired by the actions of the Egyptian women protesting throughout Cairo. Fatma Emam's blog demonstrates how Egyptian female cyberactivists merged the personal and political in their lives, carving out new spaces in the public sphere to protest and voice their agency—both online and in Tahrir Square.

CONCLUSION: REVOLUTIONARY ECHOES

The above sections offer only a snapshot of the vast and dizzying array of the Egyptian blogosphere and the role Egyptian female cyberactivists played in the Egyptian dignity revolution from January 25 to February 14, 2011. These six female cyberactivists, Asmaa Mahfouz, Esraa Abdel-Fattah, Nadia El-Awady, Arwa Saleh Mahmoud, Zeinab Mohammed, and Fatma Emam, represent but a few of the myriad Egyptian women who participated in the revolution. Employing a wide range of digital technologies, they participated in diverse ways in the online and physical protests. Some, like Asmaa Mahfouz, Esraa Abdel-Fattah, and Zeinab Mohammed, were involved with the organization of the #Jan25 protest on the National Police Day. Others, such as Nadia El-Awady and Arwa Saleh Mahmoud, found themselves headed to the protest reluctantly and with the certainty that January 25, 2011 would be like any other demonstration in Egypt—crushed by the police. And many, such as Fatma Emam, wrestled with their decision to protest, inhibited by fear of the violence and suspicious of how to perform their feminist piety in the midst of secular Egyptians and political Islamists.

Despite these differences, this research has argued three main points: 1) Egyptian female cyberactivists inhabited multiple digital platforms to articulate specific gendered messages using English, Modern Standard Arabic, and Egyptian colloquial Arabic; 2) Egyptian female cyberactivists used digital technologies to share information between cyber space and the protests in the streets, connecting online activism to physical demonstrations; and 3) Egyptian female cyberactivists used virtual space to simultaneously mobilize followers to protest and reflect on their own experiences of revolution. Thus, this research concludes that the digital media technologies and social networking sites these six Egyptian female cyberactivists used enabled them to inhabit new spaces during the Egyptian revolution, transcending the demarcation of public and private in Egypt. Cyberactivism provided them with liberating and emancipatory possibilities, as Radsch notes, "cyberactivism was fundamentally about linking virtual dissent with physical protest, influencing the mainstream media, setting the media and public policy agenda, and framing the debate about political rights and civil liberties, including the role of women" (2012). Thus, through Facebook, Twitter, YouTube, Wordpress, Blogspot, etc., Egyptian female cyberactivists claimed their place to participate in the Egyptian revolutions and carved new spaces to articulate agency. These women deployed a multiplicity of femininities and identities throughout the protests, from the revolutionary woman depicted by Asmaa Mahfouz, the citizen journalist illustrated by Nadia El-Awady, to the Islamic feminist demonstrated by Fatma Emam.

Through digital technologies and social networking sites, these Egyptian women connected physical protests with online activism, bringing marginalized discussions of sexuality, gender, sexual harassment, women's political power, social, cultural, and religious gender norms to the forefront. Facebook and Twitter connected women, enabling them to share other websites and information, to organize information using hashtags (#), and to direct information towards outside sources, such as international media, journalists, etc., using the @ sign. Egyptian female cyberactivists deployed their identities online, subverting established gender roles, and embodying resistance to the regime as well as the patriarchal norms embedded within its discourse.

Inhabiting multiple digital platforms, Egyptian female cyberactivists used social media to mobilize Egyptian women and men to protest, document the demonstrations in Tahrir Square, and to reflect on their experiences protesting. For example, Egyptian April 6 activist Esraa Abdel-Fattah tweeted and posted on Facebook in Egyptian colloquial Arabic and Modern Standard Arabic to inform the Egyptians following her on Twitter and Facebook where and when demonstrations would be held, what to do when the government tried to shut down the internet, and what was happening within Tahrir Square. In addition, as Asmaa Mahfouz's vlog emphasized, these female cyberactivists used digital technologies and social media networks to issue gendered messages and subvert the gender divide demarcating private and public space in Egypt.

The actions of female cyberactivists in Egypt demonstrate that, despite the contentious results of the Arab Spring revolutions, female activists have gained new ground and claimed greater agency in the public domain. Digital technologies and social media networks facilitated the emergence of female activists online and in the streets. Egyptian female cyberactivists articulated a new body politic online that subverted established gender relations offline. They have continued to use digital technologies and social media networks to interrogate political, cultural, religious, and social gender inequalities, and they will not relinquish the spaces they inhabited during the Arab Spring revolutions.

NOTES

1. The "We are all Khaled Said" movement began when images of Khaled Mohamed Said's death at the hands of Egyptian police disseminated online, inspiring Egyptian Google executive Wael Ghonim to anonymously create the page. He posted as an anonymous Egyptian using the universal "we" to symbolize that Khaled Said's death was an injustice to all Egyptian citizens. This movement was instrumental in organizing the #Jan25 protests that began the Egyptian uprising in January 2011.

2. Murthy defines microblogging as, "an internet-based service in which (1) users have a public profile in which they broadcast short public messages or updates whether they are directed to specific user(s) or not, (2) messages become publicly aggregated together across users, and (3) users can decide whose messages they wish to receive, but not necessarily who can receive their messages; this is in distinction to most social networks where following each other is bi-directional" (2012, 1061).

3. Group of Arab women bloggers who met in July 2010 created a shared Twitter account to continue virtual interactions @women bloggers. https://twitter.com/womenblogs.

4. Pryds Helle, Merete. Transl. Bell, Andrew. "Women Bloggers Meet in Cairo." WoMen Dialogue. 7 July 2010. Web. http://www.womendialogue.org/magazine/women-bloggers-meet-cairo-0.

5. Transliterated from Egyptian colloquial Arabic, meaning "the people demand the end of the regime."

6. Egyptian Google executive Wael Ghonim was the anonymous admin of the "We are all Khaled Said" Facebook movement. In his autobiography, *Revolution 2.0* (2012), he discusses how he wrote the appeal and posted it online to encourage Egyptian citizens to protest. Egyptian youth activists created FDEP with Ghonim's support to monitor the protests and provide legal support to protestors subject to police brutality.

7. Chandra Mohanty's article "Under Western Eyes: Feminist Scholarship and Colonial Discourses" (1984) led to a shift in feminist theory and the emergence of third wave feminism that moves away from the colonizing aspects of first and second wave feminism.

8. Islamic Revival refers to a revival of the Islamic religion throughout the Islamic world that began sometime in the 1970s. It is characterized by greater religious piety and a growing adoption of Islamic culture.

9. "Feminism and Islamic Perspectives: New Horizons of Knowledge." Women and Memory Forum. March 17–18, 2012. http://womenandmemory.org/islamicfeminism/.

10. Crowdsourcing refers to the practice of obtaining needed services on texts, tweets, and emails from victims needed services, ideas, or content by soliciting to document areas where sexual harassment is prevalent and perpetrators of sexual harassment.

11. Kefaya (Egyptian Arabic for "enough") is the unofficial name for the Egyptian Movement for Change that began in 2004 and gained national attention in the 2005 constitutional referendum and presidential election campaigns.

12. Admin. We are all Laila. 10 September 2006. Web. http://laila-eg.blogspot.com/2006/09/1.html.

13. York, Jillian C. "Hijablogging in Vogue." Global Voices. 1 March 2009. Web. http://globalvoicesonline.org/2009/03/01/global-hijablogging-in-vogue/.

14. Arab female cyberactivists employed bridgeblogging to draw international attention and news media to the protests. This was a strategy to communicate and subvert government censorship and state media.

15. On April 6, 2008, Mahfouz and fellow bloggers Ahmed Maher and Ahmed Salah organized support for a workers strike in the industrial town of El-Mahalla El-Kubra. They turned to Facebook to mobilize Egyptian citizens to protest. The movement became known as the April 6 movement and continued to be active online until they collaborated with Wael Ghonim and Kefaya to hold the National Police Day protests January 25, 2011.

16. Asmaa Mahfouz vlog January 18, 2011. YouTube. http://www.youtube.com/watch?v=SgjIgMdsEuk.

17. Butalid, Carlo. "The Egyptian Revolution from Nadia's Eyes." Carol's Think Piece: Reflections of a Filipino in the Netherlands. 11 February 2011. Web. http://butalidnl.wordpress.com/2011/02/11/the-egyptian-revolution-from-nadias-eyes/.

18. El-Awady, Nadia. The Inner Workings of My Mind. "Arwa explains what's happening in building." 2 February 2011. Web. http://www.youtube.com/watch?feature=player_embedded&v=S3je0YwYlzE.

BIBLIOGRAPHY

Abu-Odeh, Lama. 2004. "Egyptian Feminism: Trapped in the Identity Debate." *Yale Journal of Law and Feminism* 16(2): 145–192.

Ahmed, Leila. 1992. *Women and Gender in Islam: Historical Roots of a Modern Debate*. New Haven: Yale University Press. Print.

Bayat, Asef. 2007. *Making Islam Democratic: Social Movements and the Post-Islamist Turn*. Stanford, CA: Stanford University Press. Print.

Butler, Judith. 2007. *Gender Trouble: Feminism and the Subversion of Identity* [1990]. New York: Routledge.

Dabashi, Hamid. @007. *Iran: A People Interrupted*. New York: New Press. Print.

Dubai School of Government, Governance and Innovation Program. 2013. "Social Media in the Arab World: Influencing Societal and Cultural Change?" Arab Social Media Report. Web.

El-Nawawy, Mohammed, & Sahar Khamis. 2012. "Cyberactivists Paving the Way for the Arab Spring: Voices from Egypt, Tunisia and Libya." CyberOrient 6.2. Web.

Foucault, Michel. 1990. *The History of Sexuality Volume 1: An Introduction* [1976]. New York, Random House.
Friedman, Elisabeth J. 2005. "The Reality of Virtual Reality: the Internet and Gender Equality Advocacy in Latin America." *Latin American Politics & Society* 47(3): 1–34. Print.
Howard, Philip N. & Muzammil M. Hussain, Muzammil. 2013. *Democracy's Fourth Wave? Digital Media and the Arab Spring* [2013]. New York: Oxford University Press.
Internet World Stats: Tunisia. 2012. Minwatts Publishing Group. Web. Accessed December 18, 2013.
Ismail, Dr. Mohamed Hossam. 2007. "Layla's Soft Screaming: A Discourse Analysis of Cyber-Feminist Resistance on the Egyptian Women Blogsphere." The International Conference of the IAMCR: Media, Communication, Information: Celebrating 50 Years of Theories and Practices. UNESCO. Paris, France. KolenLaila. Web.
Johansson-Nogués, Elisabeth. 2013. "Gendering the Arab Spring? Rights and (in)security of Tunisian, Egyptian and Libyan women." *Security Dialogue* 44(5–6): 393–409.
Kallander, Amy Aisen. 2013. "From TUNeZINE to Nhar 3la 3mmar: A Reconsideration of the Role of Bloggers in Tunisia's Revolution." *Arab Media and Society* 17(Winter). Web.
Lim, Merlyna. 2012. "Clicks, Cabs, and Coffee Houses: Social Media and Oppositional Movements in Egypt, 2004–2011 (report)." *Journal of Communication* 62(2). Print.
Mahmood, Saba. 2005. *Politics of Piety: The Islamic Revival and the Feminist Subject*. Princeton, NJ: Princeton University Press.
Mohanty, Chandra Talpade. 1984. "Under Western Eyes: Feminist Scholarship and Colonial Discourses." *Boundary* 2(12.3): 333–358.
Mungiu-Pippidi, Alina, & Igor Munteanu. 2009. "Moldova's 'Twitter Revolution.'" *Journal of Democracy* 20(3): 136–142. Print.
Murthy, Dhiraj. 2011. "Twitter: Microphone for the masses?" *Media, Culture & Society* 33(5): 779–789.
Naghibi, Nima. 2011. "Diasporic Disclosures: Social Networking, Neda, and the 2009 Iranian Presidential Elections." *Biography* 34(1): 56–69. Print.
Nelson, Cynthia. 1996. *Doria Shafik, Egyptian Feminist: A Woman Apart*. Cairo: The American University of Cairo.
Newsom, Victoria A., & Lara Lengel. 2012. "Arab Women, Social Media, and the Arab Spring: Applying the Framework of Digital Reflexivity to Analyze Gender and Online Activism." *Journal of International Women's Studies* 13(5): 31.
Radsch, Courtney C. December 10, 2012. "Women, Cyberactivism, & the Arab Spring." Muftah: Free & Open Debate from Morocco to Pakistan. Web.
Radsch, Courtney C. May 17, 2012. "Unveiling the Revolutionaries: Cyberactivism and the Role of Women in the Arab Uprisings." James A. Baker III Institute for Public Policy, Rice University. Web.
Radsch, Courtney C., & Sahar Khamis. "In Their Own Voice: Technologically Mediated Empowerment and Transformation among Young Arab."
Salime, Zakia. 2012. "A New Feminism? Gender Dynamics in Morocco's 20th of February Movement." *Journal of International Women's Studies* 13(5): 101–115.
Salime, Zakia. 2007. "The War on Terrorism: Appropriation and Subversion by Moroccan Women." *Journal of Women in Culture and Society* 33(1): 1–24.
Scott, Joan Wallach. 2011. *The Fantasy of Feminist History*. Durham, NC: Duke University Press.
Sreberny, Annabelle, & Gholam Khiabany. *Blogistan: The Internet and Politics in Iran*. London: I. B. Tauris
Weir, Allison. 2013. "Feminism and the Islamic Revival: Freedom as a Practice of Belonging." *Hypatia* 28(2): 324–340.

Chapter Four

Move, Get Out the Way

Black "Women-of-Words" Voyaging
on the Information Superhighway

Alexa Harris

Politics. Hair politics. Sexual politics. Environmental politics. Pop Culture-tics. Black women have addressed them all in the digital space. On any typical day, it is common for a Black woman to experience online communities that fulfill curiosities and satisfy her every need of escapism from a workplace where she may be the only person of color. To her co-workers, she may be "just" the Black woman that sits in the corner cubicle. For them, she may be the "anti-social" person that never ventures on coffee breaks, lunch, or happy hour. The reason? She's enthralled with her own company of friends in online communities that live millions of miles away.

Her daily online routine may be a bit like this—first, upon getting settled in at work, she may first stop by her favorite hair blog or YouTube channel to learn the latest tips of how to fight humidity and maintain a fresh "do." Next, she may scroll down a blog that provides faith-based, critical commentary on her favorite topics in popular culture. Then, she may venture to a site high-lighting the latest environmental issues pertinent to the African American community. This maybe followed by checking a website that offers a confer-ence to teach women like herself, with a dream of creating their own blogs, how to become entrepreneurs. Finally, she may round off her afternoon by watching a web show on her favorite ".tv" site, before packing her bag and heading home for the day.

For some, this could be a typical schedule of "break activities" while at work. However, for others, their "job" is to provide content for website visitors to enjoy. This chapter will highlight the creators of websites that serve as online communities providing diverse experiences for Black women in cyberspace. Their sites serve as platforms to inform, inspire and ignite critical thinking on topics relevant to the Black community and unique to Black women's experiences.

In this chapter, Black Feminism and Womanism serve as the compass to guide the discourse of Black women as participants in daily social media activities. Additionally, the rhetorical methods of thematic analysis and generic criticism serve as methods to dissect a sample of works by Black women who have created online spaces devoted to entertain and enlighten others.

The purpose of this chapter extends from the findings of a previous study I completed that investigated an African American millennial woman's communication dynamics through blogging. Specifically, the goal was to determine whether there was a connection between her words and previous studies in African American rhetoric. Theybf.com, a blog by Natasha Eubanks, was selected as the artifact for the study. Fifteen postings were selected by random from Eubanks's site and a textual analysis was conducted to determine characteristics and themes from the blog entries. Signfiyn', humor, call and response, and creative language were found as examples of the types of rhetorical devices found in her blog postings. These echoed the works of previous Black Rhetorical scholars, such as Smitherman, who described the types of unique words and phrases specific to the Black experience. Six themes, "The Black Women's Physical Image," "The Black Community," "The Black Church and Churchgoers," "Courtship and Good Loving," "Problems with Husbands and Lovers," and "Dealing with a racist and sexist America" were found based on the subjects of posts that corresponded with chapters in Dance's (1998) anthology of African American women's humor. In other words, there were similarities found between the content of Eubanks' blog and the language of Black women from the past. However, there were also additions to the way perspectives and ideas of Black women were expressed via the digital space versus traditional "kitchen table talk" settings.

Through Eubanks's creative use of slang, humor, and "text message" language, she formed a rhetoric reflective of her experience as a Black Millennial woman. This proved a new genre of performance needed to be created for "Women-of-Words" regarding the role of African American Millennial women and blogging. The idea of "Women-of-Words" in the blogosphere is comparable to Abraham's (1983) "Men-of-Words" findings in his study of Creole men and their daily communication dynamics and performance in the Caribbean. Just as their communications patterns were observed, analyzed, and reported, the addition of Black Millennial women's communication patterns were an imperative addition to the academic landscape.

The study mentioned above was completed in 2011. Now, four years later, it is important to focus on the current, multifaceted strides Black

"Women-of-Words" have made in the digital space. Are Black women still expressing their frustrations of "dealing with a racist and sexist America"? Do Black women continue to air their dirty laundry of previous "problems with husbands and lovers" if it may provide healing and encouragement to their sister billions of miles away? How have issues in "the Black community" been highlighted, tackled and addressed online? Are there Black women still writing about diverse topics in a manner "the Black church and churchgoers" can relate? Have there been sites created to express "good loving and courtship" to help young Black women understand the way they should be treated while dating and in relationships? Again, these were the themes found from the postings of just one celebrity gossip website, imagine how many individual sites may single handedly address such issues? If such themes continue to reflect the current state of topics Black women choose to use to lift their voices in the digital space, it would show continuity exists with women of today. This would also mean the powerful words of women over one hundred years ago, as reflected in Dance's (1998) anthology, remain to be consistent with contemporary experiences of Black women. Since the study in 2011, many Black women have used the Internet to not only mobilize and build communities, but also use it as a channel to fight social ills in society. Moreover, while "dealing with a racist and sexist America," Black women have created safe "homes" and online communities for other women. For this chapter, I focused not only the rhetoric of African American women creators of these online communities, but their role to inspire others to think critically, find their voices, and become change agents.

A BRIEF REVIEW OF LITERATURE: BLOGGING UPDATE

Contrary to articles in academia that leave out the contributions of diverse populations in the blogosphere, Black people, including Black women are blogging. It is important not only to research this phenomenon that has been ignored in scholarly research, but also to analyze the content of the blogs Black women are writing. Black women blog about an array of topics, from current events, social and political issues in America and around the world, to celebrities, reality television shows, and gossip. The phenomenon of Black women and blogging will be examined in this chapter with hopes to show the way blogging has enhanced intraracial connections in the Black community by bridging gaps between class, age, and academic achievements through technology and digital media.

Cummings and Daniel (2007) suggest, "there is a need to study the impact of factors such as age, education, caste, social class, and religion on specific aspects of Black Communication" (p. 457). Furthermore, Cummings and Daniel explain many studies in Black Communication have come from the perspectives of Black males who hang out on street corners and pool halls, as opposed to an array of Black voices and perspectives. This chapter answers Cummings and Daniel's call for research by seeking to discover ways Black women use new media to interpret current events, and investigate innovative elements of Black Communication dynamics.

Blogging has emerged as a form of citizen journalism, or an alternative to mainstream media, that provides a platform for diverse voices to be heard. According to Kline and Burstein (2005), blogging allows the "ordinary citizenry, on a national and global basis, to re-engage in the lost art of public conversation" (p. xiv). However, with the growth and expansion of regular citizens having access to technology, those in power in the areas of "information, knowledge, and policymaking" continue to be members of an "elite class of experts and professionals" (p. xiv), disseminating their own agendas in media platforms other than the Internet. As a result, the media that once served as a means of "checks and balances," or "fourth branch of government" (p. xiv), proving to be critical in a democracy, has proven itself to be biased and untrustworthy to some audiences. Where the "whistle blowers" of the Watergate scandal and Vietnam War have left, bloggers have raised the torch and continued on as the challengers of the status quo. Black bloggers have taken a stand and used blogging as a form of protest rhetoric by sharing their perspectives.

In the spirit of Black women and blogging, this study carries on from where Wright's (2005) text concludes about Black women using technology as a place for "diasporic discourse" (p. 56). By citing Black feminist scholars Audre Lorde and Barbra Smith, Wright explains the importance of understanding and defining "the African Diaspora as a fluid, heterogeneous collective that operates through fluid, elective affinities, defying the established heteropatriarchal norm Black Nationalism seeks to impose on diaspora studies" (p. 56). Through bringing a counter-discourse to the perspectives of mainstream news and media outlets, Black women use blogging as a way to bridge gaps between the community and technology.

CENTERING THE BLACK WOMEN'S EXPERIENCE

Allen's (2002) work on emancipatory communication research of Black women has also laid a strong foundation for this chapter. Allen encourages scholars to conduct research that places Black women at the center, as a mode to generate "practical wisdom that can help to emancipate Black women in our various public and private roles" (p. 26). An examination of the rhetoric seen in current blogs provided insight into the varied expressions of the Black female blogging community. This research also affords an opportunity to investigate and interpret the way the "identities" of being Black and female are negotiated in everyday discourse.

Allen (2002) provides a detailed guide for studying Black women in communication. By categorizing the study of Black women as "emancipatory research," with the goals of emancipating Black women, challenging essentialist notions of Black womanhood, studying a variety of Black women, studying domination and oppression, discovering Black women's skills and strategies, generating practical wisdom, using procedures and methods that honor a primary purpose as ways to enhance "rhetoric, interpersonal, organizational communication, mass media, health communication and intercultural studies" (p. 25). Allen also challenges researchers to explore the full gamut of possibilities in Black women's communication research. From documentaries and video diaries to blogs, Black women are using inexpensive alternative media forms to share stories. New communities of Black women living miles apart have been created through the Internet, serving as a space to engage in discourse while exchanging lived experiences.

The same "center" that Asante encourages to be placed in the core of rhetorical studies of African texts (with "Afrocentricity") is similar to the "center" Houston encourages for more communications scholarship on Black women. In her text with Houston and Davis (2002), a section by Brenda Allen shares,

> To place African American women at the center of research, we must move beyond work that looks at race and gender as independent variables. Rather, we need to address race, gender, and other aspects of identity as socially constructed, analytic categories. Therefore, qualitative methods such as narratives, oral histories, interviews, focus groups, participant observation, and ethnographies seem particularly appropriate. However some research questions will elicit quantitative methods, such as experiments and surveys, which also might be fruitful. Moreover, researchers might use multiple methods or multiple sources of evidence (p. 29).

Other scholars like Karla Scott (2002) examine various aspects of Black women's talk in ways to portray "more accurate representations" of Black womanhood and identity (p. 70). While Houston's 1997 study of Black women's speech found Black women characterized their language as

> Standing behind what you say, not being afraid to speak your mind; speaking with a strong sense of self-esteem "speaking out, talking about what's on your mind" getting down to the heart of the matter; speaking with authority, intelligence, and common sense "being very sure of oneself" being very distinguished and educated; reflecting Black experience as seen by a Black woman in a white patriarchal society (Houston and Davis 2002, p. 108–109).

Additionally, Houston (2002) found Black women had positive views of their speech dynamics and characteristics as opposed to negative perceptions European American women in her study had about Black women. Moreover, in the scholarship about Black women's "everyday encounters," by Orbe, Dummond, and Camera (2002), the researchers found that African American co-participants in their study "shared that their interactions with other African American women were like 'communicating at a different level'; it often involved 'comforting talk,' 'mutual respect and admiration,' 'being completely honest,' and 'a sense of acceptance'" (p. 134). The scholars went on to describe such explanations as examples of African American sisterhood, described as "unconscious, yet undeniable" (p. 135). This "sisterhood" is present between Black women across the world while also connecting discourses on blogs.

THEORETICAL FRAMEWORK

Some Communications scholars, such as Houston and Davis (2002), believe it is important to use both Black feminist and womanist theoretical frameworks in research that places African American women at its core. In their anthology, *Centering Ourselves: African American Feminist and Womanist Studies of Discourse*, both authors discuss reasons they included both theoretical frameworks in their book,

> Despite tensions between African American feminism and Womanism, they remain interrelated ideologies. Like Holloway and Collins, we consider ideological labels to be less important than the questions authors raise and the methods by which they pursue their answers. We have encouraged authors to eschew abstractions and to produce contributions that illumine how African American women use to negotiate gendered cultural identities, affirms sisterhood, build community, and confront, demystify, and overcome oppression. Such as experientially grounded approach to research is not only consistent with the traditions of Black feminist and womanist thought, but also with the tradition of "practical wisdom" in the discipline of Communication (p. 12).

Following suit with these scholars, both Womanism and Black feminism are embraced in this study as the goal is focusing on communication dynamics and characteristics of Black Millennial women and blogging. Houston and Davis (2002) reference Collins who also connected both ideologies by stating Womanism and Black feminism share a "culture of resistance," similar to the choice Black women have made use in the digital space to make their personal concerns political (Houston and Davis 2002).

Black feminist theory provides a framework for women to think outside hegemonic, patriarchal barriers that have oppressed, silenced and devalued the unique experience of marginalized groups in the world. In Black women studies, Black feminism sits at its core, sharing and embracing the lived experiences of Black women. Black feminism was created as an outcry against the White hegemony that dominated feminist organizations in the 1960s. There was a monolithic ideology that all women were the same, based on the experience of White, middle-class women (Collins 1990). In reality this idea could not be further from the truth. Black women had a different history, socio-economic conditions, lived experience and could not simply be viewed "the same" as White women. Therefore, the fight for White women's rights was not the same as the fight for Black women's rights, which also created tensions in academia.

Audre Lorde, Angela Davis, bell hooks, Beverly Guy-Sheftall, and Toni Cade Bambara are a few of many Black feminist scholars who have devoted their scholarly pursuits to share the perspectives, lived experience, and injustices that face marginalized groups, particularly Black women. Houston and Davis (2002) explain:

> To claim the label African American or Black feminist is to position oneself and one's scholarship within those global struggles, examining how the global feminist agenda, which includes multiple issues related to women's economic status, political rights, health, and partial and family status and rights, affect Black women in the United States . . . to call oneself "African American feminist" disrupts and challenges the recalcitrant racism within the feminist movement in the United States (p. 7).

Early Black feminist scholars saw the connection of issues relating to race, class and gender and incorporated the intersection point in their texts. Black feminist scholars value the lives of all women, those in academia and those who are not, with the goal to end oppression for all people. Collins (1990) theorizes, "developing Black feminist thought also involves searching for its expression in alternative institutional locations and among women who are not commonly perceived as intellectuals" (p. 14).

Alice Walker's (1983) *Search of Our Mothers' Gardens: Womanist Prose*, clearly explains Womanism as follows:

> Womanist 1. From womanish. (Opp. of "girlish," i.e., frivolous, irresponsible, not serious.) A Black feminist or feminist of color. From the Black folk expression of mothers to female children, "You acting womanish," i.e. like a woman. Usually referring to outrageous, audacious, courageous or *willful* behavior. Wanting to know more and in greater depth than is considered "good" for one. Interested in grown-up doings. Acting grown up. Being grown up. Interchangeable with another Black folk expression: "You trying to be grown." Responsible. In charge. Serious.

> Also: A woman who loves other women, sexually and/or nonsexually.
> Appreciates and prefers women's culture, women's emotional flex-
> ibility (values tears as natural counterbalance of laughter), and wom-
> en's strength. Sometimes loves individual men, sexually and/or non-
> sexually. Committed to survival and wholeness of entire people, male
> and female. Not a separatist, except periodically, for health. Tradition-
> ally universalist, as in: "Mama, why are we brown, pink, and yellow,
> and our cousins are white, beige, and Black?" Ans.: "Well you know
> the colored race is just like a flower garden, with every color flower
> represented." Traditionally capable, as in: "Mama, I'm walking to
> Canada and I'm taking you and a bunch of other slaves with me."
> Reply: "It wouldn't be the first time."
>
> Loves music. Loves dance. Loves the moon. *Loves* the Spirit. Loves love
> and food and roundness. Loves struggle. Loves the Folk. Loves her-
> self. Regardless.
>
> Womanist is to feminist as purple to lavender. (p. xi)

By sharing examples of specific communication patterns Black women use
for various situations, Walker shows the necessity of having a special area of
study for Black women, with a name that speaks to the unique experiences,
Womanism. The perspective of a Womanist in America is not synonymous
to all women, but specific to Black women, just as African American women
do not have the same experiences as Latino, Asian, or White women.

Moreover, Black women have critiqued and extended Walker's (1983)
initial definitions of Womanism throughout the years. Some, like Collins
(1998), have explained "womanism seemingly supplies a way for Black
women to address gender oppression without attacking Black men" (p. 63).

In a communication and media studies context, Hamlet (2006) shared
"within the parameters of African American rhetoric, there has always existed a rich and diverse women's rhetoric that has traditionally been devalued
if not ignored" (p. 213). Hamlet continues by explaining her understanding
of Womanist thought as,

> An area of study that combines race, gender, and class in critically assessing
> the historical, cultural, intellectual, socio-political, and spiritual consciousness
> of African American women. Its focus suggests a more holistic understanding
> of African American women, their history, culture, and lived experiences
> thereby instilling and/or enhancing a rhetoric of self-affirmation and self-heal-
> ing (p. 213–214).

Before analyzing the rhetoric of Susan L. Taylor, former editor of *Essence*
magazine, with the demographic focus of African American women, Hamlet
shares the connection Black women share despite social locations. Moreover,
she expresses the "core themes" found in the "commonality of experiences"

Black women share that "shape African American women's rhetoric and rhetorical behavior" as follows:

> (a) legacy of struggle against racism, sexism, classism and other 'isms'; (b) the search for voice as African American women battle their invisibility and fight to Erase the controlling images that denigrate them; (c) The interdependence of thought and action whereby Intellectualism and political activism are conjoined; and (d) empowerment in the context of everyday life (p. 215).

From her "womanist analysis" of Taylor's "In the Spirit" columns of *Essence* magazine, Hamlet (2006) found "seven interrelated themes," that included "spirit power; (2) harmony and balance; (3) self-affirmation; (4) cultural history and ancestral reverence; (5) love; (6) collective power; and (7) self-destruction" (p. 219). It will be interesting to determine whether similar themes will be found in a study of the rhetoric of the data selected for this project.

Patricia Hill Collins (1990) and Jacqueline Bobo (1995) suggest that Black women share collective concerns because they share a common history, yet they harbor varied expressions. Bobo states, "In the face of a commonality of oppressions, Black women do posses aspects of a common history, but there are different and varied expressions of these commonalities" (p. 205). Each of the numerous identities that comprise the Black female uniquely contribute to the holistic experience of the individual, in ways that cannot be completely or accurately informative by examining any one of the identities in isolation (Bowleg 2008). This research infuses intersectionality, by examining the discourse of the Black female blogger within its proper sociohistorical and cultural context. Collins (1990) further asserts that their varied expressions come from the diversities of class, region, age, and sexual orientation, which shape individual Black women's lives. Therefore, even though it is argued that there is a Black female standpoint, within this standpoint, Black women can harbor a diversity of expression. Research, then, on Black female expression through the rhetorical space of the blogosphere helps further identify and document the Black woman's perspective.

BLACK WOMEN AND BLOGGING

The discourse of Black women in blogging is now starting to spread to "mainstream" news outlets. On May 3, 2010, CNN.com featured an article about a White actress, Sandra Bullock, adopting a Black baby from New Orleans (France, 2010). Instead of solely offering the reporter's perspective of the story, the writer interviewed Black bloggers for their thoughts and opinions on the issue. Each of the Black bloggers who were contacted had already posted stories about Bullock adopting a Black baby before CNN contacted them. The Sandra Bullock story allowed many blog writers to share their thoughts about the trend of "White stars in Hollywood commodifying Black babies" discourse, and whether or not Bullock's adopting a baby from Louisiana is better and more "culturally" sound than celebrities like Madonna who have adopted babies from Africa. This perspective would have not necessarily been the angle of an ABC or NBC news story when it first made headlines. Consequently, Black women having a place to voice their thoughts in cyberspace becomes imperative; otherwise, it may never be heard or garner national attention.

In addition to topics such as images of Black women in popular culture, blogs by Black women have addressed other portrayals of African American women in the news. If one was to have observed the commentary of the three blogs during April 19–23, 2010, they would have found perspectives on ABC's Nightline news special entitled, "Why are There so Many Single Black Females" co-hosted by Steve Harvey and Vicky Mabrey. A counter-discourse is present in blogs that share the perspective of "real women" and not the views reflected on television by Steve Harvey sharing his "reasons successful Black women can't find a man" (Noir 2010). Readers of the blogs that post thoughts and perspectives feel comfortable in the digital space to voice concerns and exercise agency of their lived experiences.

Moreover, blogs can fill an unfortunate gap by including posts about tragedies and injustices in multicultural communities that lack the "mainstream" media attention they deserve, such as about Black women who have gone missing. Black women's blogs give clear indication that there is a yearning and need for such commentary in cyberspace to fill the "color" void national news ignores. By staying up to date with the latest in celebrity gossip, politics, and current events, these blogs provide the antidote to solve the problem of the lack of attention given to young Black women in public digital spaces. Through the bloggers' creative use of slang and text message language, they have formed a rhetoric and ideology that can transform the minds, lived experiences, and realities of young Black American women in a manner that has led one to revisit (and possibly add to) previous knowledge on African American communication dynamics.

DEFINITION OF TERMS

Throughout this study the word blogs and blogging are used. "Blogging" in this text is referring to the definition by Barker (2008), who defines weblogs as a personal web site allowing "anyone to put their point of view and through them we may learn about events from an angle previously denied to us" (p. 353). Hookway (2008) has a definition of blogs that is embraced in this study, explaining they serve "as the new guardians of democracy, a revolutionary form of bottom-up news production and a new way of constructing self and doing community in late-modern times" (p. 91). Blogs are further explained as websites with "a series of frequent updates, reverse chronologically ordered posts on a common web page, usually written by a single author" (Hookway 2008, citing Ban-Ilan 2005; Herring et al. 2005; Serfarty et al. 2008). Moreover, Hookway (2008) cites Thelwall and Wouters's (2005) definition of blogs as "characterized by instant text/graphic publishing, an archiving system organized by date and a feedback mechanism in which readers 'comment' on specific posts" (p. 92). This relatively new phenomenon is further explored in the literature review.

SUMMARY OF INITIAL STUDY

The purpose of the initial study that took place in 2011, was to investigate African American women's communication dynamics through blogging and determine whether there was a connection between their dynamics and previous studies in African American rhetoric. Theybf.com, a blog by an African American Millennial woman, Natasha Eubanks, was selected as the data for the study. Fifteen postings were selected by random from Eubanks' site and a textual analysis was conducted to determine characteristics and themes from the blog entries. Signfiyn', humor, call and response, and creative language were found as characteristics of the blog postings. Six themes, "The Black Women's Physical Image," "The Black Community," "The Black Church and Churchgoers," "Courtship and Good Loving," "Problems with Husbands and Lovers," and "Dealing with a racist and sexist America" were found based on the subject of postings that corresponded with the chapters of Dance's (1998) anthology of African American women's humor.

As an African American Millennial woman and avid reader of theybf.com, I became interested in the role and the lack of information on the topics connecting Black Rhetoric, my generation, and the digital space. In particular, I was curious about the specific characteristics of theybf.com, in a rhetorical context, and whether there was a continuity in African American Communication dynamics between African American Millennial women, blogging, and previous studies in Black rhetoric. The goal of this study was to serve as a foundation for additional studies in academic scholarship about African American women's communication dynamics in cyberspace.

A textual analysis was used to determine the characteristics of blogs by African American Millennial women and to determine if a connection existed between African American Millennial women's communication dynamics and previous Black rhetorical studies. Defined by McKee (2003), textual analysis is a methodology "for those researchers who want to understand the ways in which members of various cultures and subcultures make sense of who they are, and how they fit into the world in which they live" (p. 1). Eubanks claims her position in the digital space through her blog. By providing candid commentary using signifyin', satire, wit, slang, creative language, and "calls" as characteristics of each posting, she shares her perspectives on news and current events, particularly those involving Black celebrities. Moreover, characteristics of her blog exhibited communication dynamics unique to the African American community, as found in previous studies by Black rhetorical scholars (e.g., Abrahams 1983; Smitherman 1999). Created to fill a void in the digital landscape as well as magazines that did not cover articles and pictures of Black celebrities, Eubanks took it upon herself to create theybf.com. In the January 2010 issue of *Black Enterprise* magazine, Eubanks was featured as a young leader to watch and it was disclosed that her blog receives 15 million page views a month and received $1 million dollars in 2009, 90 percent of which was from advertisers (Robinson 2010). Eubanks mentioned her blog is prime real estate for advertisers seeking opportunities in niche marketing (Robinson 2010).

After conducting a textual analysis of the blog, the data was reviewed again in order to complete a thematic analysis based on the subject matters of each blog posting. Because theybf.com is a blog with the motto, "celebrity gossip never looked so good," Abraham's (1983) definition of gossip as a form of humor connected Eubanks's work to previous African American rhetorical studies. Because the textual analysis revealed a great deal of humor, satire, and signifyin' took place on the site, other examples of scholarly work that exhibited similar themes regarding the rhetoric of African American women were pursued. It was discovered that Dance's (1998) anthology, a compilation of essays, poems, folktales and literary works by African American women, ranging from scholarly activists like Toni Cade Bombara and Alice Walker to playwrights Pearl Cleage and Ntozake Shange to "sister Presidents" like Johnetta B. Cole, all infused with an element of humor. Like Eubanks's site, elements of satire, signifyin', and creative language were present in the anthology, which is why chapter titles from the text were borrowed and used as themes for analyzing and organizing the blog postings from theybf.com.

The first section of findings, "The Black Women's Physical Image," featured blog postings that focused on the appearance of a celebrity as the subject matter. Falling under this category were blog postings critiquing and/or celebrating the physical appearances of a former member of the international pop group Spice Girls Mel B., R &B singer and song writer Keri Hilson, and actress Halle Berry. The next section of findings, "The Black Community" featured blog postings that focused on issues and images of African Americans in media and society. Organized in this category were blog postings about YouTube star Antoine Dobson, the cast from the movie "The Best Man," Tyler Perry's burglar, the "Black Girls Rock" awards show, and an event where video vixen Melyssa Ford was in attendance. The third section of findings, "The Black Church and Churchgoers," included blog postings that focused on a religious leader or religious institution serving as the setting of the story. Organized in this category were blog postings about rapper Foxy Brown and Bishop Eddie Long.

The fourth section of findings, "Courtship and Good Loving," featured blog postings with a positive perspective of celebrities dating or in relationships. Organized in this category were postings about R&B sensation Beyoncé Knowles and rapper Jay-Z, Naomi Campbell, and R&B crooner Monica Arnold. The fifth section of findings was dedicated to blog postings showing the negative effects of a relationship in the dissolution phase, titled "Problems with Husbands and Lovers." Under this category were entries about singers Chris Brown and Rihanna, reality star Sheree Whitfield, and Mary Harvey, who is the ex-wife of comedian Steve Harvey. Finally, the fifth section of findings highlighted postings with the subject of a celebrity experiencing social injustices rooted in racism or sexism in America. Falling under this category were posts regarding R&B singer Tearra Mari and pro-football player Chad Ocho-Cinco's dating reality show on VH1.

One of the many artists featured in Dance's (1998) anthology, whose work and humor are reminiscent of Eubanks, was comedian Moms Mabley. Similar to Eubanks, Mabley "dealt with her audiences not as a professional entertainer but as a member of their community. . . . And her audiences responded as participants—laughing, commenting, urging her on to speak for them all in the cathartic, integrative ritual of laughter" (Levine 2007, p. 366). Eubanks writes to her audience in a very informal and conversational manner as if she, too, is a part of their community. The comments readers on theybf.com leave range from witty, sarcastic comments agreeing with Eubanks' notions to suggestions for future stories for her to cover. Similar to a family that takes time to laugh, critique, and disagree with each other "out of love," the same takes place between Eubanks and her readers.

Another similarity between Mabley and Eubanks is that both discussed and were aware of their social location in America, as well as the injustices present for their race and gender. While Eubanks is a member of the millennial generation in the twenty-first century, Eubanks refers to stories not spotlighting Black people as "non ybf news," which stands for news not about Black or "fabulous" people. Eubanks also raises racist and sexist issues in America, similar to Mabley's topics in her comedy shows. Levine (2007) explains of Mabley's humor,

> The ritual of insult was an important element in Moms Mabley's humor. Whether engaging in verbal battle or with her pianist . . . she utilized the folk technique superbly, as in her signifying against the old man she claimed her father made her marry when she was just a teen-ager (p. 365).

This shows how Mabley, like Eubanks, was not afraid to speak her mind while expressing her humor, especially against any authoritive figure in her life. Eubanks expresses the fact that she has no issue expressing her thoughts and could care less about people who do not agree with her.

As a comedian, Mabley touched on the vast array of topics in African American culture, similar to Eubanks's diverse postings on theybf.com. Eubanks's blog is similar to a contemporary version of a comedy show that can be accessed on an office computer, cellphone, or even at a home to reach her audience. Theybf.com connects people, with similar interests, from various geographic locations to engage and converse with each other in an online community.

THEYBF.COM AND ALTERNATIVE MEDIA

Another notable finding throughout the study of selected blog postings, is the reference made to other forms of alternative media, such as the video website YouTube. These particular postings were based with subjects rooted in social networking sites. However, these postings were still grouped by specified theme throughout the study and also included a great deal of slang, signifyin', and creative language unique to the Black community.

Twitter was commonly used as a "source" for news and information on theybf.com. Safko and Blake (2009) define Twitter as "a service for friends, family and coworkers to communicate and stay connected through the exchange of quick and frequent answers to one simple question: What are you doing?" (p. 409). "Followers" on Twitter refers to the number of people you add as your "friends" online to "follow" or get notified immediately about all the changes or status updates to a person's Twitter page. Twitter has also been used in numerous marketing campaigns, as companies pay celebrities to mention their merchandise in their mini-blog so their "followers" will purchase various products the celebrities endorse. Twitter is categorized as a "mini-blog" due to its character limit.

Eubanks utilized not only YouTube and twitter as sources of information regarding various stories, but news and public opinion websites, too! In the article published about the potential lawsuit between Steve Harvey's current and ex-wife, Eubanks quoted a "Black Voices" article. Black Voices is a website with news and commentary specifically focused on the Black community in the digital space. Black Voices is owned and operated by America Online, an Internet service provider.

Eubanks included links to these sites as her "sources," similar to a journalist that interviews "sources" for credibility of a story. She also encouraged readers to investigate and make their own conclusions about stories. This allows readers to possibly feel empowered, knowledgeable and critical consumers regarding current events in popular culture and society. This shows Black Millennial Bloggers understand the importance of a story having some sense of "creditability." Most importantly, it shows they used the resources they have access to in the digital space as their sources for information. However, like a journalist or media entity, she has also endured lawsuit threats from celebrities and negative user comments (Bland 2009).

EUBANKS AS A GLAMALECTUAL IN THE BLOGOSPHERE

"Glamalectuals" was a term created after conducting this analysis that defines young Black Americans who are not only intrigued with "glitz and glam" of Hollywood, but also like to ensure their intellectual minds are stimulated, enriched, well informed and challenged. By staying up to date with the latest in celebrity gossip, politics, popular culture and current events, these blogs provide the antidote to solve the problem of lack of attention in the public space for young Black women in the digital space. From sharing her critical perspective of Black women like Sheree Whitfield, who depend on others for financial resources as opposed to working for themselves, to referencing the 2009 Bailout and Watergate, Eubanks is aware of current events in various arenas. Eubanks mixes issues of relevance in Black popular culture with "hard news" issues in society by using creative language and signifyin' in instances such as referring to Chris Brown and Rihanna's domestic dispute as "Chriannagate." Through Eubanks' creative use of slang, humor and text message language, she has formed a rhetoric that is reflective of her lived experience as a Black Millennial woman, similar to the way Womanism has to feminism. By claiming her space and identifying as a Black woman, Eubanks captures the essence of both Black Feminism and Womanism by placing Black women in the center of her informal "conversations" with readers. Eubanks "boldly and audaciously" creates works of art each day on her blog, utilizing themes similar to the Womanist scholars that precede her in time. Theybf.com, catered to a unique audience, represents and reflects the vision and strides that have been made for a new generation to express their voices and stories of today. This proves a new genre of performance should be created for "Women-of-Words," especially regarding the role of African American Millennial women and blogging. As previously mentioned, the idea of "Women-of-Words" in the blogosphere is comparable to Abraham's (1983) "Men-of-Words" findings in his study of Creole Men and their daily communication dynamics and performance in the Caribbean. Just as their communications patterns were observed, analyzed and reported, Black Millennial women's communication patterns are just as imperative in the academic landscape.

The rhetoric of African American Millennial "Women-of-Words" is different from those in other demographics in many ways. For starters, while many patterns and themes found were comparable to those found by Hamlet (2006), Floyd-Thomas (2006), and Dance (1998), the characteristics of the rhetoric were unique and specific to the digital space. For example, the idea of an "open letter" format on the internet while identifying oneself is quite a bold move, and a dangerous one to many members of Black women in other generations. To other African American women, such as those in the silent generation, putting personal information such as a name, e-mail address and other facts such as physical location are factors that could put one in harms way. Millennials like Eubanks, on the other hand, do not think twice about voicing their opinions and including ways one can reach them if they would like to address any comments or concerns regarding her perspective.

In addition to the "open letter" format, signifyin' and slang were used a great deal in the form of alternative media analyzed. This shows there is a connection to informal speech and the Black vernacular that connects people, even in online communities. There is an understanding and camaraderie present that is not limited to the "street corner" for Millennials to communicate and share thoughts and perspectives in a unique jargon. However, they have extended the previous findings and definitions of the terms as scholars such as Smitherman have determined in previous studies.

Because the digital space is a different landscape than the street corner, the interpersonal interactions are varied, as people connect through the computer and not physical location. While "once upon a time" signifyin' or jokes directed towards another person were shared directly with that person, with a possible audience around encouraging the verbal exchange, in cyberspace, more of an "open letter" format has been adopted to express the concerns one may have with another. The "open letter" format not only gives a public forum for discussion about a person, but creates the environment for more "middle people," or readers of a blog, to become involved in the verbal insult, which is a typical characteristic of signifyin'. In addition, by incorporating "text message" language, or slang, such as "lol," which stands for "laugh out loud," or "OMG," which stands for "Oh My Gosh," signifying, in the traditional sense, expounded into new territory. By connecting forms of "digital slang," such as text messaging or instant messaging phrases, and references unique to the Black culture, a "remixed" African American rhetoric was created and resides in an entire new realm on theybf.com.

Moreover, in the traditional sense, or definition of signification, verbal exchange typically took place in a setting where the receiver of the message could instantly reply to the sender of the message. In cyberspace, however, such exchange does not always take place, nor in the traditional definition of "call and response" take effect on blogs. If Eubanks wrote an article about President Obama, for example, there is no guarantee that he would stop everything he was doing to reply back to Eubanks's blog regarding whatever comments she may have made about him. Consequently, there have been some instances on theybf.com where artists, such as Kanye West, have sent letters to reply to the assertions Eubanks declared on her blog. In instances like this one, Eubanks posted his letter in the public forum, similar to the way she exhibits her ideas for blog postings. This shows Millennials view blogs as a platform and "safe space" for communicating ideas, in a way that once may have been utilized through alternative channels such as an op-ed article in a newspaper, or the "open letter."

Additionally, while "responses" in the former sense of "call and response" were often to agree with, or share some consensus with the sender of a message, responders to the postings of theybf.com vary their replies to Eubanks's postings. Serving as "active participants" in the discourse between Eubanks and her postings, as opposed to listeners of a dialogue between two people on a street corner, are ways in which people connect through online communities to share their opinions, despite their geographic location. People in London, England, can connect with people in Atlanta, Georgia, to agree or disagree with Eubanks's thoughts about Beyoncé Knowles's wardrobe choice for an awards show, for example. In this instance, neither of the participants, Eubanks or the readers of the blog, have ever met or know each other personally; however, they can take part in conversation about another person, Knowles, they do not even know. This shows that while a "lack of personal connection" could be argued between the relationships of those on blogs, it is evident that there is still familiarity and comfort level present in online communications, which allow people to bond and feel like "friends," despite ever meeting in the neighborhood or sitting at the same "kitchen table" to discuss current events or make jokes about others.

Another interesting component to the idea of "call and response" on theybf.com, is that many replies to Eubanks postings do not always agree with her perspective, and some even express concerns through a critical lens regarding her blog postings. By making "personal" comments to Eubanks, it is evident readers feel just as familiar to express their positive or negative thoughts about Eubanks to her directly, just as Eubanks feels familiar to share her opinion about celebrities highlighted on her blog. The interesting factor here is, again, that no physical connection has necessarily been made for these interpersonal relationships to build and grow through blogging and establishing online communities via the internet.

However, celebrity blogging is not the only avenue Black women enjoy sharing perspectives and stories. Due to an ongoing study of Black women in the digital space since 2011, a purposeful sampling was used to discover whether other sites by Black women fit into the initial themes from Dance's anthology found in Eubanks site. Specifically, the homogeneous sampling technique was used to highlight a few other blogs by Black women on different topics, and share personal experiences. Articles were read, and the google search engine was used with phrases such as "influential Black Women Bloggers." Here is an overview of a few sites found that fell into the themes of "The Black Woman's Physical Image," "The Black Community," "The Black Church and Churchgoers," "Courtship and Good Loving," "Problems with Husbands and Lovers," and "Dealing with a Racist and Sexist America." Again, these are the same themes on a celeb gossip blog by a Black woman are the categories in while the multi-dimensional blogs of Black women exists, women of unique words.

BLACK WOMEN AND BLOGGING: 2015 AND BEYOND

To revisit the initial fictitious scenario of this chapter, about the lone Black woman in her workplace that finds joy, peace and contentment surfing the internet, the following reflects a sample of the vast range of websites she explores at her job. Luckily, she is the social media coordinator at a top Public Relations firm. She gets paid to seek alternative media opportunities in the digital space for clients to promote their services and products. Interestingly, many of the same websites she explores for her job correspond with the themes mentioned earlier while discussing "Women-of-Words" in the digital space.

"The Black Women's Physical Image" theme is reflected through blogs she often partners with to promote the work of "up and coming" fashion designer clients at her firm. She makes it her personal mission to seek websites created by women of color such as Claire Sulmers's popular blog, http://www.fashionbombdaily.com and Gabi Gregg-Young's site, http://www.gabifresh.com. Her firm also represents health experts, hair care professionals, nutritionists, and trainers. Moreover, she often pitches stories to blogs catered to Black women such as Ericka Nicole Kendall's blog, http://www.Blackgirlsguidetoweightloss.com, Nikki Walton's natural hair care site, http://www.curlynikki.com, as well as Candace Mitchell, Jess Watson, and Chantel Martin's site, http://www.myavana.com.

Another one of her "hats" is to scout online talent and make recommendations for the firm to consider pitching their marketing services. Interestingly, one of her favorite online projects falls under the category of "Dealing with a Racist and Sexist America" and is a popular web series that has evolved into a stage play, "Funnelcake Flowers and the Urban Chameleons" at www.tickles.tv. She also seeks public intellectuals, activists, and writers on websites such as www.racialicious.com by Latoya Peterson, Kim Foster's www.forharriet.com, and Kari Fulton's www.checktheweather.tv. The same holds true for relationship experts, whose websites fall under the category of "Problems with Husbands and Lovers" and "Courtship and Good Loving" such as Christine K. St. Vil and Julian B. Kiganda's http://www. boldandfearless.me and Demetria Lucas's http://www.abelleinbrooklyn.com.

Additionally, she supports websites that fall under "The Black Community" theme, such as Kimberly Hines' www.soulbounce.com and Gina McCauley's website www.whataboutourdaughters.com. McCauley also is the creator of www.bloggingwhilebrown.com, an annual conference the social media coordinator frequents for networking opportunities.

Similarly, "The Black Church and Churchgoers" is reflected on innovative sites such as www.rahiel.com and www.urbancusp.com, both created by Rahiel Tesfamariam. Other sites she recommends for clients seeking spiritual guidance are www.shepreachs.com, and www.thechurchladyblogs.com.

Websites created by "Women-of-Words" serve coping mechanisms for Black Millennial women like the fictitious social media coordinator as they make it through the workday in environments they may consider to be "foreign land." As the only person of color in her entire organization, the blogosphere serves as a place one can connect with their "digital sistas," many of whom they have never physically met, yet serve as a support system. They keep her encouraged and inspired by addressing the harsh realities of "dealing with a racist and sexist America," "the Black women's physical image," "the Black community," "the Black church and churchgoers," "courtship and good loving," and "problems with husbands and lovers." The coalition of "Woman-of-Words" on the information superhighway serves as a network for Black women to connect, engage, and share contributions, despite their geographic locations. Without the internet, many would not have ever met, or had their dreams fulfilled.

BIBLIOGRAPHY

Abrahams, R. (1983). *The man-of-words in the West Indies*. Baltimore, MD: Johns Hopkins University Press.

Allen, B. (2002). "Goals for emancipatory communication research on Black women." In M. Houston and O. Davis (eds.), *Centering ourselves: African American feminist and womanist studies of discourse* (pp. 21–34). Cresskill, NJ: Hampton.

Barker, C. (2008). *Cultural studies theory and practice*. Thousand Oaks, CA: Sage.

Bland, B. (2009, December 18). "Natasha Eubanks: YBF creator chosen for *Black Enterprise*'s 'next is now' cover story." *Black Voices*.

Bobo, J. (1995). *Black women as cultural readers*. New York: Columbia University Press.

Bowleg, L. (2008). "When Black + lesbian + woman does not equal Black lesbian woman: The methodological challenges of qualitative and quantitative intersectionality research." *Sex Roles* 59: 312–325.

Collins, P. (1990). *Black feminist thought: Knowledge, consciousness, and the politics of empowerment*. Boston, MA: Unwin Hyman.

Collins, P. (1998). *Fighting Words: Black Women and the Search For Justice*. Minneapolis, MN: University of Minnesota Press.

Cummings, M., and J. Daniel (2007). "The study of African American rhetoric in Golden." In J. G. Berquist, W. Coleman, and J. Sproule (eds.), *The rhetoric of western thought: From the Mediterranean world to the global setting* (pp. 443–461). Dubuque, IA: Kendall/Hunt.

Dance, D. (1998) *Honey Hush! An anthology of African American women's humor.* New York: Norton.

Floyd-Thomas, S. (2006). *Mining the motherlode: Methods in womanist ethics.* Cleveland, OH: Pilgrim Press.

Foster, K. (2015, January 4). *For Harriet: Celebrating the Fullness of Black Women.* Retrieved from www.forharriet.com.

France, L. (2010). "Bullock's adoption of Black baby stirs debate." *Cnn.com.* Retrieved from http://www.cnn.com/2010/SHOWBIZ/05/03/sandra.bullock.

Fulton, K. (2015, January 5). *Check the Weather.* Retrieved from www.checktheweather.tv.

Hamlet, J. (2006). "Assessing womanist thought: The rhetoric of Susan L. Taylor (2000)." In L. Philips (ed.), *The Womanist Reader* (p. 207–231). New York: Routledge.

Hines, K. (2015, January 20). *Soul Bounce: Past, Present, Future Soul.* Retrieved from www.soulbounce.com.

Hookway, N. (2008). "'Entering the blogosphere': Some strategies for using blogs in social research." *Qualitative Research* 8(1): 91–113.

House, H. (2015, January 15). *Funnelcake Flowers & The Urban Chameleons.* Retrieved from www.tickles.tv.

Houston, M., and O. Davis (2002). "Introduction: A Black woman's angle of vision of communication studies." In M. Houston and O. Davis (eds.), *Centering ourselves: African American feminist and womanist studies of discourse* (pp. 1–18). Cresskill, NJ: Hampton.

Jones, N. (2015, February 1). *Rev. Neichelle.* Retrieved from www.shepreachs.com.

Kendall, E. (2015, January 28). *A Black Girl's Guide to Weight Loss—Weight Loss Blog—Losing 170 lbs and Counting!* Retrieved from www.Blackgirlsguidetoweightloss.com.

Kiganda, J., and C. St. Vil. (2015, February 5). *Bold & Fearless.* Retrieved from www.boldandfearless.me.

Kline, D., and D. Burstein (2005). *Blog! How the newest media revolution is changing politics, business and culture.* New York: CDS.

Levine, L. (2007). *Black culture and Black consciousness Afro-American folk thought from slavery to freedom* (2nd ed.). New York: Oxford.

Lucas, D. (2015, February 1). *A Belle In Brooklyn.* Retrieved from www.abelleinbrooklyn.com.

McCauley, G. (2015, January 29). *Blogging While Brown.* Retrieved from www.bloggingwhilebrown.com.

McKee, A. (2003). *Textual analysis: A beginner's guide.* Thousand Oaks, CA: Sage.

Mitchell, C., J. Watson, and C. Martin (2015, January 19). *Myavana: My Hair Nirvana Journey.* Retrieved from http://www.myavana.com.

Noir, Dior. (2010, April 22). "Hill Debate: Why Can't a Successful Black Woman Find a Man?" *Bet.com.* Retrieved from http://blogs.bet.com/celebrities/entertainment-spotlight/2010/04/22/nightline-asks/.

Orbe, M., D. Drummond, and S. Camera (2002). "Phenomenology and Black feminist thought: Exploring African American women's everyday encounters as points of contention." In M. Houston and O. Davis (eds.), *Centering ourselves: African American feminist and Womanist studies of discourse* (pp. 99–121). Cresskill, NJ: Hampton.

Peterson, L. (2015, January 10). *Racialicious—The Intersection of Race and Pop Culture: Race, Culture, and Identity in a Colorstruck World.* Retrieved from www.racialicious.com.

Robinson, T. (2010, January). "Young entrepreneurs position themselves to dominate the business landscape." *Black Enterprise* 40(6): 91–95.

Safko, L., and D. Brake (2009). *The social media bible tactics, tools and strategies for business success.* Hoboken, NJ: Wiley.

Scott, K. (2002). "Conceiving the language of Black women's everyday talk." In M. Houston and O. Davis (eds.), *Centering ourselves: African American feminist and womanist studies of discourse* (pp. 53–73). Cresskill, NJ: Hampton.

Sulmers, C. (2015, February 2). *The Fashion Bomb Blog: Celebrity Fashion, Fashion News, What To Wear, Runway Show Reviews.* Retrieved from www.fashionbombdaily.com.

Tesfamariam, R. (2015, January 10). *Rahiel Tesfamariam: Activist, Theologian, Writer, Speaker.* Retrieved from www.rahiel.com.

Tesfamariam, R. (2015, January 10). *Urban Cusp: Life. Style. Faith. Culture. Social Change.* Retrieved from www.urbancusp.com.

Victorian, B. (2015, January 18). *MadameNoire: Black Women's Lifestyle Guide.* Retrieved from www.madamenoir.com.

Walker, A. (1983). *In search of our mothers' gardens: Womanist prose.* San Diego, CA: HBJ Book.

Walton, N. (2015, February 1). *Curly Nikki: Natural Hair Styles and Natural Hair Care.* Retrieved from www.curlynikki.com.

Wright, M. (2005) "Finding a place in cyberspace: Black women, technology, and identity." *Frontiers* 26(1): 48–59.

Young, G. (2015, January 20). *Gabi Fresh.* Retrieved from http://www.gabifresh.com.

Chapter Five

Virtual Homeplace

(Re)Constructing the Body through Social Media

Latoya Lee

In October of 2013, a Missouri woman, Ashley Davis, was told that she either cut her locs[1] or risk losing her job from a finance company. Davis, who has been growing her locs for the past ten years, was employed by the company for two months before she was informed of the new company guidelines banning "dreadlocks, braids, mohawks, and mullets" (Byng 2013). The company stated, "a professional appearance is necessary for the success of the company" (Logan 2013). In the same year, an elementary school in Oklahoma sent seven-year-old, Tiana Parker, home because her loc'd hair was deemed unacceptable by the administration. The school stated that her hairstyle could "distract from the respectful and serious atmosphere" that the school strives to achieve (Klein 2013). In November of 2013, school officials told Vanessa Van-Dyke, a twelve-year-old student attending a Christian school in Florida, that her hair [shoulder-length afro] "is a distraction to other students, which is a violation of school policy" (Douglas 2013). This was in response to Vanessa reporting bullying from her peers at school. School officials told Vanessa that she either cut her hair or straighten it to avoid expulsion (Kinks 2014).

How can we explain the experiences of Ashley, Tiana and Vanessa? Can we assume that the officials at the workplace and schools were, in fact, attempting to create an atmosphere where people can feel comfortable with no distractions? If we are to believe this is true, then we must ask the question, comfort for whom—which people? Why were these females of color singled out? Why does their comfortable atmosphere go unacknowledged or get overlooked? Why were they threatened with such harsh punishment, such

91

as expulsion, for their hairstyle preference? Lastly, what makes locs and afros, on Black women, unacceptable and/or unprofessional hairstyles?[2]

These examples, among many others, demonstrate the institutional production of the unacceptability of Black women's bodies[3] in the United States. They demonstrate the policing and enforcing of standards of, not only dominant beauty aesthetics,[4] but also of "respectability," professionalism and "womanhood" on Black bodies [and, in relation, white bodies] (Brown 1992; Carby 1992; Hunter 1997).

Given the popularity of social media, I am interested in exploring the spaces that Black women create to celebrate their own bodies and also the spaces that allow Black women to (re)formulate their own ideas of the body. The body is an area that has received a lot of attention in critical feminist scholarship that have centered the bodies of women of color.[5] However, this scholarship has overlooked an area of the body, as well as a beauty aesthetic, that has been used both historically and contemporarily to control and discipline the Black body, hair. Attending to this neglected area in feminist thinking about the body, this chapter explores the importance of hair to the Black body, specifically, how hair is used as a marker of Blackness and as a tool for perpetual and inevitable persecution of the Black body in the United States.

The questions that frame this chapter are: where do women of color turn for affirmation when constantly surrounded by oppressive dominating forces? Consequently, what are the virtual spaces that are created to celebrate the Black female body? By women of color, I mean women who self-identify as Black on the social media sites under exploration, blogs that center discussions on hair. What is most interesting is that the women who engage with the blogs purposefully unite as a self-identified group, Black, for purposes of providing encouragement and affirmation for one another. Therefore, while I recognize the tension of this broad category that groups a set of people together (often based on physical appearance) without taking into consideration ethnic, cultural and class differences, I use the term because it is a category that women identify as who engage on the blogs under investigation. Inevitably, this leads to the question how one gets "made" a Black woman in these spaces.

This chapter is built on an analysis of a number of contemporary case studies that have been very popular on hair blogs. I center specific blogs and case studies to understand how Black women who visit and engage in these spaces interpret the efforts to police, discipline and oppress their bodies as well as how they frame their responses to that oppression.[6] I suggest these blogs are counter-disciplinary spaces that get created to allow one to re-envision their body within restricting and dominating forces.

The theoretical framework of this chapter extends bell hook's theory of "*Homeplace*." By placing *Homeplace* in conversation with the investigation of the blogs, I find three specific ways that hair blogs act as a *virtual home-*

place for Black women. *Virtual homeplace* is a (real or imagined) place that offers comfort and nurture, where one can seek safe harbor against the racial and sexual oppression they may face on a daily basis. In my research, I find that hair blogs operating as a *virtual homeplace* have become a site of affirmation, a space to discuss issues of concern, provide support, elevate spirits and also resist hatred; a site of networking, a space providing economic independency (and dependency); and as a site of recovery, a space of healing for Black women.

To this end, the chapter is laid out as follows: The first section sets up the problem, Black women's bodies, in the United States and twenty-first century, in their natural state, are seen as disruptive and targeted by institutions and policies. This section makes the case for the needed spaces of support and affirmation that Black women attempt to locate through social media. The second section explores bell hook's *Homeplace*. This section examines the counter-disciplinary spaces Black women have historically created to shift and rethink their body amidst dominating oppressive forces. The last section explores hair blogs as a possible *virtual homeplace* that allow Black women to reformulate their own ideas of beauty and the body. Thinking through a few case studies, I suggest three specific ways that hair blogs behave as *virtual homeplaces* for Black women.

CONSTRUCTING

Hair in the African American community in the United States has, for a long time, been a source of both pride and pain. From the shaving of enslaved African's heads, also the use of hair as a racial marker for enslavement, and the weekly social gatherings to style hair on slave plantations, hair has been a site of both struggle and joy (White and White 1998; Morrow 1973). This history of hair sets the stage for not only the importance but also the cultural and social nature of hair.[7] This section explores a few motives behind institutions constructing a narrative of the natural Black body as distracting and unprofessional.

ABSENCE OF BLACK BODIES

In April of 2014, the U.S. Army instated an update to regulation 670–1. Regulation 670–1, which regulated a soldier's appearance, banned "unkempt" and "matted" hair, which includes cornrows,[8] locs, braids, and twists (Terkel 2014). According to the U.S. Army, these banned hairstyles interfered with maintaining uniformity and proper appearance of uniforms and insignia, including headgear (Terkel 2014). While there is no mention of race or ethnicity in the updated regulations we can, however, conclude that the regulations are speaking to Black women in particular due to the specific hairstyles mentioned, such as cornrows, locs, braids and twists, and as men have to keep their hair shaved close to the scalp or as a crew cut. The regulations also stated that approved hairstyles include chemically straightened hair, weaves, wigs and cornrows (with certain spacing and size regulations) (Byrd and Tharps 2014). How do we interpret this in the midst of the institutionalized persecution of Ashley, Tiana and Vanessa?

One can make the argument that the absence of Black female bodies in these spaces has led to the establishment of appearance standards that do not accept Black bodies as they are. Also, the lack of knowledge about Black female bodies has led to an emphasis of enforcing "acceptable" hairstyles that are expensive and time consuming. For example, retired Sergeant Jasmine Jacobs of the Georgia National Guard, who started a petition on the WhiteHouse.gov website asking the U.S. Army to reconsider its regulation of ethnic hairstyles, stated twists are a popular style for Black female soldiers because they are easy to care for when in the field (Patrice 2014). Similar to Sgt. Jacobs, an army veteran, using the alias "Tonya," stated that in her experience most Black women in the military wear their hair natural[9] and therefore wear cornrows, locs and twists because they often do not have the tools needed to straighten their hair when deployed.

We can see, therefore, that the lack of Black bodies in this space as well as the lack of knowledge about Black bodies has generated regulations that seem to target Black females. While this regulation may be for uniformity of appearance and uniform, it calls into question whether these constructed standards of "appearance" and "acceptability" take into consideration Black female bodies in their natural state and the politics behind the push for "fixing" the natural Black body.

HAIR STYLES EMBODYING ANTI-AMERICAN POLITICS

Another example of the institutional construction of the Black female body as unacceptable is the assumption that certain hair styles embody a certain set of politics. Often, that set of politics includes the rebellion and/or rejection of Euro-centric standards and features. Take for example Angela Davis, who was deemed one of the country's ten most wanted criminals in the 1970s. Throughout this time media outlets used a photo of Davis with an Afro; this photo was used to construe a violent, anti-American, and Black militant identity for Davis. This racialization of the afro, during this time, allowed for the surveillance, by the state and federal government, of any Black female with an afro hairstyle (Magubane 2007).

A more recent example of ethnic hairstyles representing a certain set of politics was the New Yorker cover page, of the July 2008 issue, that satirized

Michelle Obama as an armed revolutionary. The cartoonist made a point of depicting the first lady with an afro hairstyle, army fatigues, and a machine gun strapped around her body while giving President Obama, who was dressed in Muslim garments, a fist bump[10] (*The New Yorker* 2008; Prince 2009). Thirty years, after Angela Davis, the notion that a Black female sporting an afro represents a resistant, pro-Black militant identity continues to exist.

Another example of the racialization and politicization of hair[styles] is the case of Audre Lorde who, in the 1970s, was not allowed to, cross borders, pass immigration in Tortola, British Virgin Islands (BVI), because of her loc'd hairstyle. Unknown to Lorde, there is a law in Tortola, BVI that allowed immigration officers to refuse a visitor to the island with loc'd hairstyles. In this context, loc'd hair was tied to notions of criminality and a particular brand of religion. It was not until Lorde told the immigration officers, when questioned, that she was not a follower of the Rastafarian religion that her passport was stamped for admittance. The loc'd hairstyle representing, according to Lorde, revolution and drug peddling (Lorde 2009). In this example, Lorde was being policed, on an international level, for her choice of hairstyle because it was not deemed acceptable, this aesthetic represented certain types of (undesirable) beliefs, culture and identity.

The idea of hair[styles] embodying radical, anti-American values helps us understand why the military would be invested in regulating hair[styles] and pushing an Euro-centered agenda and appearance.

CAPITALISTIC INVESTMENT IN DOMINANT AESTHETICS

If one of the pillars of American society is capitalism, then it should come as no surprise that the military would encourage such a hyper capitalistic investment, such as straighteners, weaves and wigs, in supporting American ideals. According to a Mintel[11] report, the Black hair care industry was estimated to be around $684 million dollars,[12] with more than one-third of the market belonging to L'Oreal and Alberto Culver, huge white-owned corporations that dominate and control the Black hair market (Mintel 2012; Harris-Perry 2012; Douglas 2012; Jones 1994).

Mintel (2013b) found Black women and men were aware of the role their hair plays in how people view them, as well as how corporate America perceives them as individuals. Because of the awareness and perceptions about their body, Black women and men tend to spend a great amount of time and money on their hair and hair care products. In an article published in September 2013, Mintel notes "Black women are willing to shell out top dollar on their hair" when it comes to achieving the perfect look. With Mintel's findings, it becomes clear that Black consumers represent a lucrative market for the beauty industry, making it very easy for companies to market on the weakness of Black women, their hair.

A good example of the lucrative Black hair care industry is the sales of chemical hair straighteners and/or tools that help achieve a "sleek look." In 2008, this industry was growing with estimated sales of $206 million dollars; however, in 2013, chemical hair straightener sales were estimated around $156 million dollars (Mintel 2013b). This decrease in sales is not too surprising with the emergence of women increasingly foregoing unhealthy chemical relaxers and sporting natural hair. Nonetheless, the beauty industry not wanting to miss this opportunity of consumption-oriented marketing jumped on the natural hair bandwagon and has switched gears to advertising products that will help "tame," "de-frizz," and create "manageable" natural hair. These terms, very much in line with the attempt to ban or "fix" "matted" and "unkempt" hair, are often used to describe natural hair including the afro hairstyle as the hair naturally grows up and out, not down. This has led to a steady growth in production of shampoo, conditioner and styling products for natural hair. The projected increase of the natural hair care industry is approximately $40 million dollars (which roughly makes up the decline in the chemical hair straightener sales from 2008 to 2013) (Mintel 2013a).

These examples reveal the ongoing construction of the unacceptability of Black women's bodies, and hair, in its natural state, demonstrating the continued institutionalized penalization of Black women's bodies in the push for Euro-centered beauty aesthetics. Throughout there is a common message that the natural Black body is inappropriate, unprofessional, distracting, and needs to be fixed. The consequences, of not following the dominant, constructed standard aesthetic, means loss of employment and access to the classroom, bullying, surveillance, denial to cross transnational borders, loss of economic opportunity and position in the U.S. military. With this in mind, the following section turns to an examination of the spaces that are counter-disciplinary and allow one to re-envision their body within these restricting and dominating forces.

DISMANTLING

This section explores the notion of *Homeplace* and what it can offer the larger conversation on community and resistance. In *Homeplace,* bell hooks explores a place where one can seek shelter, comfort and nurture for their soul, a place where one learns dignity and integrity, along with faith (hooks 1990, 41). When hooks discusses *Homeplace*, she is talking about a specific location, a home, which is run by women and usually a site for family and close friends to seek safe harbor. However, although hooks is thinking about it as an actual physical structure, it doesn't have to be restricted to that. While hooks is primarily concerned with Black women's senses of home and safety, *homeplace* can broadly be considered as any "place" that provides shelter, etc., for Black women.

According to hooks, Black women have made *Homeplace* possible despite the particular ways that racism marked their bodies (1990, 42). In a patriarchal sexist society, females were given the task of creating and sustaining a home environment. Whereas white women in general were given this task of creating a home, Black women, in particular, had to construct a space of care and nurturance in the face of racist oppression. Therefore, *Homeplace* is a conscious site of resistance, resistance understood here as a space for healing and recovery. *Homeplace* served to rehumanize or recreate the body, so that one could think of oneself as human instead of an object. For hooks, *Homeplace* is a site of affirmation restoring the dignity of Black women, men and children (42).

Suggestive to me are the ways in which *Homeplace* functions to (re)shape and (re)create individuals' sense of self. Here I would like to consider contemporary spaces that seem to mirror the functions of *Homeplace*. For example, to what extent can Black women's hair blogs, websites and vlogs serve as *virtual homeplaces*? To what extent do popular hair blogs, websites and vlogs allow Black women to (re)think, (re)define, and (re)create an alternative aesthetic that places their bodies at the center? Thus far the sites explored seem to offer forms of affirmation and self-definition. However, while these sites may have many similar characteristics to *Homeplace*, it is yet unclear what they have to offer in terms of "safe" spaces (Collins 2000)[13] and the kinds of resistances that are possible.

I am interested in placing bell hook's *Homeplace* in conversation with the blogs that center Black women's experiences and their bodies. Here I am exploring histories and experiences that are disregarded as well as possible sites of resistance that often are overlooked. hook's (1990) idea of *Homeplace* serves as a marker of what sites/spaces of resistance can look like within Black communities. By placing these scholarships in dialogue with each other, we will be able to 1) move away from the idea that oppressive conceptions of the body have to overdetermine our relationship to it[14]; 2) explore spaces of resistance and communities that often get overlooked; 3) shed light on a few of the ways Black women are using social media; and 4) explore sites that offer an alternative for the type of relationships Black women can have with their own bodies.

(RE)CONSTRUCTING

This section will explore the efforts to (re)construct a different narrative of the Black body, one that runs counter to the dominant institutionalized narrative, revolving around the Black body as beautiful in its natural form.

A blog is a website where the owner of the website provides information on a topic or a number of topics. It is important to note that within these virtual spaces the owner of the blog is considered a somewhat "knowledgeable" person with regard to their specific topic, thus democratizing knowledge production by giving anyone a voice on any given topic. Blogs tend to have a specialization or focus on contemporary issues, such as discussing everyday life, fashion, hair, and racial issues. People often create blogs for specific interests such as autism awareness, HIV/AIDS awareness, activism, traveling, fashion, hair and entertainment, to name a few. Those interested in creating a blog can purchase a space on the World Wide Web by purchasing a domain name or operating within a larger, already established, website. For example, Essence.com is a popular established website where people may have a blog. Naturallycurly.com is also a popular established website that has a well-liked blog called "CurlyNikki.com." WordPress.com is a site where people can create a blog for free.

The bloggers being explored are also vloggers, with videos on YouTube.[15] These bloggers, U.S. based, have been named the top "Natural Hair Bloggers" and "Black beauty bloggers/vloggers" on the web for Black "natural hair" by, Essence, Ebony, Madame Noire, and NaturallyCurly.com.[16] I monitored these sites over the course of two years, observing the blog posts and the commentator posts.[17] These bloggers stand out for a few reasons; first, they are the most popular bloggers on the web, with one site in particular receiving more than 3 million views per month. Second, the sites were created by Black women, and center and speak to Black women and their bodies. These sites also share information on social injustices encountered by Black women nationally (these injustices tend to be around the issue of hair). Lastly, these bloggers have public blogs, post regularly, and allow commentators to leave comments and feedback.

The first blogger/vlogger "CurlyNikki.com" is a blog that is under the parent company of NaturallyCurly.com. The blog owner, Nikki is a practicing psychologist who created this blog as a forum for people who are struggling to embrace their naturally curly hair. Specifically, she attempts to provide a platform for people to share "experiences, frustrations and triumphs of being naturally glamorous" (Walton 2008). This blog was created in 2008 and receives more than 3 million views per month (texturemediainc.com). As a result of its popularity, the CurlyNikki blog has been named "a leading expert in the natural hair blogosphere" by Ebony and Essence magazine (Benitez 2011; Ebony 2013; Walton 2008; Whigman n.d.).

"Afrobella, all shades are beautiful," is another popular blogger. Her blog created in August 2006 aims to fill a void she found existed in both print and on the web; a void of the celebration of "natural hair" and beautiful women of all shades. Afrobella has been featured in *Essence*, *Ebony*, and *Glamour* magazines. On this blog, Afrobella does hair product reviews, discusses fashion tips, culture, music, style, and interviews women of all shades and beauty (Afrobella.com; Ebony.com 2013).

Leila Noelliste, the third popular blogger, created "Blackgirllonghair.com" in 2009. The purpose of this blog is to create a forum for Black, Latina, and multiracial women who wear their hair naturally. This is a forum where women can discuss products, hair tips, hairstyles, and healthy living (Whigman n.d.; MadameNoire 2012).

These sites are important to this discussion on the body because they centralize Black women and their bodies, particularly by providing the space for Black women to build community around their body, but more specifically hair. These sites become affirmative spaces where self-identified Black women can visit to find people who share similar experiences and discuss not only issues surrounding their hair, or stemming from their hair, but also issues of structural-institutional oppression.

While, I have found a few preliminary ways that these blogs/vlogs operate as *virtual* homeplaces, including as sites of support, affirmation, networking and healing, there are a few limitations also found in these spaces. The following sections will explore some of the preliminary possibilities and limitations of the blogs.

The questions that drive the following sections include: how can blogs behave as a virtual homeplace and possibly redress the painful experiences of degradation in regards to Black women's bodies? What tools do the women on these blogs use to counteract the attempts to discipline their bodies, through their hair? And what are the limitations of the blogs?

SITE OF AFFIRMATION

An example of how these sites operate as a possible space to discuss issues of concern, provide support, elevate spirits and also resist hatred is in the following case of a popular matchmaker by the name of Patti Stanger. Stanger who has a popular nationally syndicated show on the cable network, Bravo, told one of her guests, a young Black woman who was auditioning to meet one of the sought-after bachelors, to weave her short afro. Stanger argued that this young lady needed to get a long weave in order to be more attractive. The bloggers were concerned with the constant negative feedback Patti gave women with naturally curly hair. Another concern for these bloggers was the invisabilized history of African American hair and the long sought after Euro-centric standard of beauty, of straight long hair through the use of hair weaves/extensions. Bloggers were concerned with how other women with naturally curly hair would perceive their own hair and beauty. But more importantly bloggers and commentators were attempting to reclaim the Black female body from white advertisements and the white beauty industry that commonly portrayed the Black body in its natural state as ugly and needing to be improved, a reinforcing of scientific racism and the Madame CJ Walker era.[18]

The sites lit up with discussions of commentators stating they were going to boycott the popular show. There was also a discussion on standards of beauty and "who" determines these standards. There was a heated discussion on how historically, Black women's hair has never been perceived as beautiful and ways to reframe that discussion so that young Black girls would celebrate their "natural hair." Lastly, many commentators shared stories of how they too struggled with their "natural hair" and had to answer to many people who did not like their hair and thought they should straighten their hair or wear a weave. As a result, the blogs turned into a place where these Black women were providing encouragement and support for each other and their choices about their body (Naturallycurly 2011). Here we see that people on this blogger's page were able to reverse the hatred and negativity towards Black hair and beauty. The blogs were used to teach and discuss the historical wounds of racial oppression, operating as a virtual homeplace, also bringing people together to enact social change, through the discussion of the boycott.

Another example, of the blogs functioning as spaces of support is the case of meteorologist Rhonda Lee, who was fired from KTBS news station in Louisiana for responding to a Facebook comment about her short styled afro. In this case a Facebook fan addressed his comment to "the Black lady that does the news" and suggested "she needs to wear a wig or grow some more hair." The "fan" went on to say that maybe "the Black lady has cancer" but regardless of why she wore her hair that way the style, "does not look good on television." Lee responded with the following,

> I am the "black lady" to which you are referring, . . . I'm sorry you don't like my ethnic hair. And no I don't have cancer. . . . I am very proud of my African-American ancestry which includes my hair. . . . Women come in all shapes, sizes, nationalities, and levels of beauty. Showing little girls that being comfortable in the skin and HAIR God gave me is my contribution to society. (Roberts 2012; Sangweni 2013)

Many bloggers posted this story on their blog (CurlyNikki.com [CN] 2012; BlackGirlLongHair.com [BGLH] 2012). The result was a huge debate with heated conversations from commentators on blogs and other social media sites about the policing of "natural hair" in the workplace. This is indeed a conversation that never gets old with previous cases of people being fired because of their choice of hairstyle. A petition on Change.org and Causes.com emerged with some bloggers urging people to sign the petition so Rhonda Lee can get her job back, an example of collective action.[19] The petitions received over 170,000 supporters (Whiteman 2012; Zayas 2013). Emerging from this was an engaging and informative online discussion between Rhonda Lee and Angela Davis on "natural hair" in the workplace (Stodghill 2012).

This is another example of bloggers and commentators being able to take something like racial oppression and the policing and disciplining of Black female bodies, for purposes of "respectability" and professionalism, and turn it into a teachable moment. Commentators were sharing stories, giving advice and creating a space of affirmation and support. This example also shows that incidences can incite collective action and solidarity in these spaces.

In a similar case, bloggers responded to Sgt. Jasmine Jacobs petition on WhiteHouse.gov, for the U.S. Army to reconsider the hairstyle regulation, by circulating the petition and information on their blog sites. The petition received over 17,000 signatures and the U.S. Army reconsidered the ban on certain hairstyles now allowing many hairstyles that were banned (Patrice 2014a; Walton 2014).

Another example of the blogs operating as a site of affirmation is in the case of seven-year-old Tiana Parker, in Oklahoma, who was expelled from school because her locs were deemed inappropriate. Many bloggers and their followers took the time to send care-packages with letters, pictures and messages of love and support, reinforcing her beauty as a person with loc'd hair in an attempt to dismiss the messages of contempt she may interpret about her body. A petition was started requesting a public apology and a change in the school's dress code. The petition received over 23,000 signatures, leading the school to reverse its ban on locs and afros (Kinks 2014).

While the Rhonda Lee and Tiana Parker cases are "smaller" examples of the institutional disciplining of the Black Body, there are continuities with larger forms of institutional violent surveillance and disciplining of the Black body in contemporary America. Take for example, Marissa Alexander, a Black woman in Florida, who was originally sentenced to twenty years in prison for shooting a gun [warning-shot] in the air to defend herself against her abusive husband at the same time Zimmerman gets acquitted of murder charges after [murdering] shooting an unarmed Black teen that "looked suspicious." Both Alexander and Zimmerman utilized Florida's "Stand Your Ground Law" in their cases. However, based on the outcome, the "Stand Your Ground Statutes" does not apply equally to all bodies. This example highlights the invisibility of violence against Black women. For instance, current national discussions of institutional violence focus usually on male bodies, leaving aside Black women's experiences.

In the case of Renisha McBride, a Detroit native who was shot in her head while seeking assistance after a car accident, her shooter claimed, he opened the door to his home and shot an unarmed Black woman, because he "feared for his safety." These examples and many more (especially in the heightened climate of police brutality and violence) demonstrate the national fear of the Black body, and thus the ongoing attempts to discipline and police these bodies by the larger society. However, these examples also emphasize the importance of the space of the blogs as an outlet for Black women, whose bodies and existence is constantly under attack. The example of Marissa Alexander was not found in any of the three blogs and the case of Renisha McBride was only found in one, this speaks to the types of concerns that these hair blogs center and the limitations of the blogs; specifically, to the types of social phenomena that are taken up by bloggers.

SITE OF NETWORKING AND
ECONOMIC FREEDOM/DEPENDENCY

In addition to support, these sites also operate as spheres of networking in a few different ways. One way these sites operate as a sphere of networking is by providing spotlights for Black-owned businesses and/or Black entrepreneurs that cater to "natural hair." For example, blogs will often feature an interview with creators of new Black hair products or provide advertisement for hair stylists and hair salons (Patrice 2013). This support of Black entrepreneurs is important for a number of reasons. The Black hair product industry is worth over $684 million dollars with more than one-third of the market belonging to huge white-owned corporations (Harris-Perry 2012; Douglas 2012; Jones 1994). However, for the past seven years there has been an emergence of successful young, Black [female] entrepreneurs creating and selling Black hair products without the support of big manufacturing and cosmetic corporations. The success of these young entrepreneurs, who often create, package and ship their hair products from their home, has a lot to do with the partnership and publicity gained through these blogs and vlogs.

For example during the exploration of the blogs, I came across a new entrepreneur in the "natural hair" care business that graduated from Binghamton University (Breyer 2006; Rubino 2012). Like many other small Black business owners, Marsha Coulton and her popular hair product, Curl Junkie, has been featured, advertised and sold on these popular hair blogs and websites, making her products available to over 240 countries. Sites like NaturallyCurly.com and other blog sites make a big difference for these small business owners who do not have the backing of large manufacturing companies such as Johnson and Johnson.

The reclaiming of some of the Black hair product production from huge white-owned corporations that dominate the Black hair market can be framed as both positive and negative. One positive aspect is the creation of the space for entrepreneurship, available for Black women [and men] who have historically been economically disenfranchised in the labor force. Another positive aspect is the production of products by Black women who understand the complexity of Black women's bodies. These small Black business owners have also, in advertising their products, created a new database of beauty. For instance, these small Black business owners advertise with women of color that you would not normally see in L'Oreal commercials. It is in these advertisements that one can see the attentiveness to the discussions on the blogs about the likes and dislikes of hair products, and also the representations of the product. Many small business owners often reach out to bloggers to be the face of their products. In return, the small business owner's product(s) gets established through the blogger's popularity and also through advertising on the blog. On the other hand, the blogger gains legitimacy by being the face of a product that has countless advertisements and is shipped worldwide.

The negative aspect here is the outrageous prices for these products created by and for Black women. While this arrangement may create economic freedom for the Black business owners, it creates economic dependency for the consumers. Black female entrepreneurs seem complicit with the established market parameters laid out by the white-owned corporations, that Black women are willing to pay large sums of money when it comes to their hair and beauty. This is an example of Black-owned businesses exploiting and taking advantage of their consumers, Black women.

Also, these small business owners have capitalized, as well as justified their high product costs, by creating an emphasis on healthier living and organic products. However, what is important in this emphasis on "healthier" living is the integration of their consumers into the "green" or organic economy. This green economy, in the past, was only accessible to the middle and upper class that could afford the higher price tags; this in return can lead to economic hardship due to the need for disposable income for Black women seeking beauty and a "healthy/natural living."

The bloggers are complicit, in many ways, with the creation of a consumer market in "natural hair" products. Many blog posts and commentators have discussed this notion of "becoming a product junkie"; this is the consuming of multiple organic/natural products because of the promises it makes towards beautifying your hair. It is a common held belief among the people that read and participate on the blogs, as well as the bloggers, that when one decides to no longer chemically straighten one's hair the products and tools that was once used on chemically straightened hair will not work for "natural hair." Therefore, many Black women are literally consumed with finding [expensive] natural and organic products that will make their "natural hair" grow and flourish.

Consequently, the blogs become the space where Black women can visit to find the hottest new hair product and the promises it has for them and their hair. But it also becomes a place that assists in the economic exploitation of Black women for the purposes of beauty.

Another point to be considered is the marketing aspect as a point of contention for many who visit the blogs, especially for those who cannot afford these expensive "organic and healthier" products. However, some may argue that the bloggers counter some aspects of this tendency with its emphasis on "Do it Yourself" (DIY) hair techniques and recipes.

Each blogger, included in this discussion, has a DIY section on their blog site. This is the section where followers can get hair recipes, ranging from inexpensive DIY shampoos, conditioners, and leave-ins, and a place where they can also share recipes. The DIY recipes often use ingredients that you may already have in your home, such as honey, avocados, mayonnaise, eggs, etc. These are the same ingredients that the expensive "organic/natural and healthier" products claim to have in them. This section of the blogs also provides inexpensive DIY techniques that mirror the expensive techniques that one would only receive at a professional hair parlor. The DIY aspect of these blogs has become so popular that many hairstylists have reached out to the bloggers and "natural hair" community to discuss their exclusion in the current hair movement.

SITE OF HEALING

Many of these sites began as a place of healing and acceptance for Black women and their bodies. It is for this reason that healing remains at the core of these sites. Therefore, whenever something disparaging is found in the news, in regards to Black women and their hair, or happens within the Black community/(ies) or a celebrity, of color, is caught saying something negative, these sites become a place for people to come, respond, discuss the issues at hand and possibly even organize a collective response.

Take for instance the case of the blogger, Antonia Opiah, who decided to present an exhibition in Union Square, New York City titled, "You can touch my hair" on June 7, 2013. According to Opiah, the purpose of this exhibition was to create a space where people of all ethnicities could come and experience African American hair. This exhibition emerged from an issue that many African American women who have "natural hair" face, namely white people wanting to touch, feel and pet their hair/explore their body without permission. Antonia experiencing this while walking down the street decided she was going to turn this issue into a teachable moment (Opiah 2013b).

The exhibition took place over two days and there were African American models standing in Union Square with different hair textures holding signs saying "You can touch my hair." After the first day of the exhibition, the blogosphere responded with fury. The reviews and comments from bloggers and commentators were mixed with some responding positively to the "teach-in" while others charged the "display" as a blast from the past, calling it a Saartjie Baartman exhibition.[20] While the charge of the exhibition as a return to Saartjie Baartman may be an exaggeration, since the conditions are not the same, what was similar is the placing of Black bodies on display for purposes of satisfying other's curiosity. On the second day of the exhibition, there were people who, opposing the exhibition, went to Union Square holding signs of their own saying, "You can't touch my hair, but you can kiss my ass" (Wilson 2013).

This sparked a huge contentious discussion on the blogs about the visibility and invisibility of the Black female body. Commentators took the time to educate younger commentators about Saartjie Baartman, and the long history of the unbridled exploration of Black bodies, and why they feel this exhibit is unacceptable (Opiah 2013a). Many shared personal stories of being put on display in their workplace or among friends because of their "natural hair." There was no final conclusion that emerged from these discussions, regarding the acceptable or unacceptable nature of the exhibition, however, the commentators and spectators walked away more educated on both Black history and/or on the present personal experiences of Black women, while also opening a space to discuss these issues. The counter-exhibition reflects the reversing of the idea of the Black female body as a place for unbridled exploration. Even with the contentious nature of the debate, the conversations on the blogs remained encouraging, and supportive, discussing the limits of such an exhibition. This example portrays the idea that not everyone on the blogs have to agree, but even in disagreement, the heated nature of the debate did not take away from this moment of Black women's hair and bodies being celebrated.

This example displays the possibility for collective action and the production of knowledge present in these spaces. The discussion on the blogs motivated people to head to Union Square the next day with signs of their own, displaying their repulsion with such an exhibition. The example above illustrates how the blogs acted as a site for the spread of knowledge and history, a particular history usually restricted to academic spaces. This spread of knowledge also demonstrates how hair is understood in different spaces and time.

A more recent example, of how these sites have operated in a healing manner, is the case of Sheryl Underwood, a Black female comedian, who during a daytime talk show discussed the act of saving your children's hair after a hair cut. Underwood stated, "why would you save afro hair? . . . you don't never see us [at the beauty supply store] looking for curly, nappy, beaded hair." After one of the white co-hosts stated that she saved her son's hair, Underwood proceeded to say that her son's hair was "probably some beautiful, long, silky stuff, [but] that's not what an afro is." News of Underwood's deprecating comments hit a number of social media sites, along with Afrobella.com, BlackGirlLongHair.com, and CurlyNikki.com. Commentators and bloggers discussed Underwood's comments as ignorance and self-hatred (BGLH 2013; Afrobella [Bella] 2013).

Outraged by Underwood's comments, blog commentators suggested boycotting her events. As a result of these deep discussions on these blog sites, Sheryl Underwood agreed to do an interview with blogger, CurlyNikki regarding the incident. In the interview, Underwood stated that she now sees how her words could be misunderstood and on another talk show Underwood apologized for her remarks, stating, "to all of you I say I'm sorry for my failed attempts at humor surrounding something that's very sensitive for us, which is our hair" (Walton 2013b). Underwood also said that she did not intend to offend her people and her community and thanked the "natural hair" community who told her she made a mistake (Walton 2013a).

This is another example of how the blog sites operate as a place of healing but also as a space for collective action with real consequences. Underwood, in some respects, was able to come to terms with her disparaging remarks and even shared with CurlyNikki that as a Black woman she also has a very difficult time working in Hollywood. Underwood promised that, in the future, she will be more aware of her reciprocating the same hatred she faces in her profession. I would define this as a moment of healing not only for the people she apologized to but also a moment of healing and self-recovery of her self and the platform she has as a professional comedian and actress in Hollywood. The bloggers and commentators spoke out against the idea of Blackness as negative and instead turned to a celebration of Black hair.

Lastly, the blog sites have also become a *virtual homeplace* for commentators to grieve over the untimely death of a couple of popular hair bloggers. Commentators went to the blogs to share stories and memories of the person. In one incident that was a suicide, bloggers and commentators made an effort to provide suicide support information (Patrice 2014; Uwumarogie 2014).

Overall these blogs seem to operate as a site of renewal and self-recovery, often providing awareness, action and consciousness. Nevertheless, I do recognize the limitations of *virtual homeplaces*, such as the limitation of scope or range. In other words, these blog spaces become a space for only those with internet access, for those who are technologically savvy and have economic/financial leverage. Recognizing that not all hair blogs behave as *virtual homeplaces* and for the hair blogs that do operate as *virtual homeplaces*, this may occur infrequently, specifically when a certain incident or situation arises. Also, the manifestations of *virtual homeplaces* on these blogs are usually up to the discretion of the blog owner and what they deem as important. These limitations have the possibility of weakening the potential of these blogs as *Homeplaces* and lead to larger questions that need to be explored. While these blogs are not without problems and contradictions, they do seem to provide a space for Black women to share knowledge, and recreate a renewed sense of self, through various counter-disciplinary actions, with the goal of accountability and a positive self-identity at the center.

NOTES

1. Loc'd, locks, or locs also known as dread locks is a hairstyle that consists of hair that is interweaved or interlocked together.

2. Take for example Bo Derek, a popular white actress, sporting cornbraids with beads in the late 1970s, making this common African-American hairstyle "trendy" in mainstream media. Whereas, on the other hand, coming off the heels of the Black power movement of the 1960s, cornbraids and afros on Black women or men were read as revolutionary (Byrd and Tharp 2001).

3. The body is a politicized material body that is produced by cultural and social forces. By cultural and social forces I'm thinking, broadly, laws and policies as well as practices people make up themselves to think about bodies in other ways. Ultimately, I am interested in a group of bodies, specifically Black women's bodies that relate within a specific set of practices.

4. I explore dominant aesthetic as a particular conception of beauty or adornment that is seen as pleasing to society, which then often times becomes pleasing to the wearer. This can include, but is not limited to, cosmetics, clothing, jewelry, the texture of one's hair, and hairstyles.

5. Black scholars who have analyzed the attempt to discipline and police Black bodies have explored how these attempts have changed within different space and time. These works are important because they explore the multiple ways women of color's bodies are policed and also the relations behind the surveillance. For this analysis, see Roberts 1997; Carby 1992; Silliman 2002; and Hunter 1997.

6. I understand "policing" of the body in the Foucauldian sense. According to Foucault (1995), policing, also known as surveillance, imposes constraints, prohibitions, and obligations on the body (136). Disciplining of the body is for purposes of domination and obedience; disciplining produces docile bodies that can be explored, broken down, rearranged and coerced (138). Surveillance and disciplining are both constructions of disciplinary power, and are closely related in the making of docile bodies (137). Consequently, docile bodies are constructed through constant surveillance (or the belief of constant surveillance) and through the internalization of the disciplining.

7. Scientific practices illustrate some of the ways in which the racialization of hair takes shape within the context of the United States, with race and Blackness being linked to hair. See Stepan 1986; Mercer 1990; Morrow 1973; Patterson 1982; Meaders 1997; Rooks 1996; and Byrd and Tharp 2001 for that analysis.

8. Cornrows, aka cornbraids, are braids against the scalp.

9. Natural hair is a term used for hair that has not been altered chemically, specifically in terms of being straightened with the use of chemicals. I use quotes around the word to mark the contentious nature of this term. Definitions of what is "natural hair" create big debates on the blogs. For example, one argument that is constantly being debated is whether permanent coloring of the hair counts as altering the hair chemically.

10. A fist-bump is a greeting where both parties touch closed fist (a variation to the handshake). This action of the fist-bump between the Obamas and the picture on *The New Yorker* is

part of a larger conversation that took place in June of 2008 when Michelle gave President Obama a fist-bump, which was televised, after he won the democratic nomination. A Fox News Anchor, E. D. Hill referred to the gesture as a "terrorist fist jab" (Corley 2008). So *The New Yorker* cover was an attempt to make fun of E. D. Hill, however what I find interesting is the militant appearance and hairstyle that Michelle received as an American Black female.

11. Mintel is a well-known company that produces marketing research reports to businesses for purposes of market forecasting.

12. The estimated Black hair care industry of $684 million dollars is a conservative estimate as it does not include weaves, extensions, wigs, independent beauty supply stores, styling tools, etc. (Mintel 2013b).

13. Collins (2000) understands safe space as a place where truthful discourse can take place among Black women, which can lead to not only resisting the objectification as Other but, also important, empowerment through self-definition.

14. Here I am thinking about women who do not let the attempt to oppress and regulate their body be more significant than the counter-disciplinary possibilities.

15. Vlogs are similar to blogs but instead consist of videos, which are usually uploaded to YouTube. YouTube is an online forum that allows people to watch and share originally created videos.

16. Popular websites and magazines that people visit for information on hair and hair care.

17. Commentators are people who frequent the blogs and leave comments/feedback on blogger's posts.

18. Madame CJ Walker was the first African American female millionaire who created her own hair-care business and line of products. For an analysis on Madame CJ Walker and her empire, see Rooks 1996; and Byrd and Tharps 2001.

19. I'm thinking of collective action as the commentators, who frequent the blogs, as well as the blog owners coming together physically, and/or virtually to support a cause or fight against an injustice.

20. Saartjie Baartman is an African woman who "agreed" to travel to England to find work in 1810. However, once in England, Baartman, linked to a primitive nature due to her body shape, was put on exhibition in the circus and displayed as a sexual curiosity where the public could pay to examine, see, and touch her body. Baartman was also at the disposal of "medical scientists." After death, Baartman's remains (her skeleton, brain, and genitals), along with a cast of her body, remained on display in a Parisian museum. It was not until the year 2002 that Baartman's remains were returned back to South Africa (Saartjie Baartman Centre for Women and Children 2013).

REFERENCES

Afrobella.com. "About me: Patrice Grell Yoursik." Retrieved on September 3, 2013, from http://about.me/afrobella.

Bella. (September 4, 2013). "How do you reach someone like Sheryl Underwood?" Retrieved on September 5, 2013, from http://www.afrobella.com/2013/09/04/reach-someone-like-sheryl-underwood/.

Benitez, Y. (August 3, 2011). "YouTube's top 5 natural hair care vloggers." Retrieved on September 3, 2013, from http://www.huffingtonpost.com/2011/08/02/-youtubes-top-black-hair-vloggers_n_916565.html#s321326title=Kimmaytube_.

Black Girl with Long Hair. (September 2, 2013). "Black comedienne Sheryl Underwood slams afro hair on national television." Retrieved on September 5, 2013, from http://blackgirllonghair.com/2013/09/black-comedienne-sheryl-underwood-calls-afro-hair-nasty-on-national-television/.

Black Girl with Long Hair. (December 11, 2012). "Black reporter fired for responding to derogatory comments about her natural hair." Retrieved on January 23, 2013, from http://blackgirllonghair.com/2012/12/black-reporter-fired-for-responding-to-derogatory-comments-about-her-natural-hair/.

Breyer, M. (May 1, 2006). "Curly hair product spotlight: Marsha Coulton." Retrieved on September 5, 2013, from http://www.naturallycurly.com/curlreading/curl-products/spotlight-marsha-coulton.

Brown, E. B. (1992). "'What has happened here': The politics of difference in women's history and feminist politics." *Feminist Studies* 18(2): 294–312.

Byng, R. (October 24, 2013). "Company policy requires Missouri woman to cut her dreadlocks to keep her job." Retrieved on October 29, 2013, from http://www.huffingtonpost.com/2013/10/24/new-company-policy-forces-woman-to-cut-dreadlocks_n_4159369.html.

Byrd, A., and L. Tharps. (April 30, 2014). "When Black hair is against the rules." Retrieved on May 30, 2014, from http://www.nytimes.com/2014/05/01/opinion/when-black-hair-is-against-the-rules.html?_r=0.

Byrd, A., and L. Tharps. (2001). *Hair story: Untangling the roots of black hair in America.* New York: St. Martin's Griffin.

Carby, H. (1992). "Policing the black woman's body in an urban context." *Critical Inquiry* 18: 738–755.

Collins, P. H. (2000). *Black feminist thought: Knowledge, consciousness, and the politics of empowerment.* New York: Routledge.

Corley, M. (2008). "Fox news anchor calls the Obamas' 'fist pound' a 'terrorist fist jab.'" Retrieved on April 29, 2014, from http://thinkprogress.org/politics/2008/06/09/24434/fox-news-anchor-calls-the-obamas-fist-pound-a-terrorist-fist-jab/.

CurlyNikki. (December 11, 2012). "Fired over Facebook posting about natural hair." Retrieved on January 23, 2013, from http://www.curlynikki.com/2012/12/fired-over-facebook-posting-about.html.

Douglas, D. (December 3, 2014). "Black females should have the right to wear an afro." Retrieved on January 5, 2015, from http://www.theguardian.com/commentisfree/2013/dec/03/vanessa-vandyke-florida-girl-threatened-expulsion-afro.

Douglas, D. (March 11, 2012). "Roots and revenue: The popularity of natural hairstyles is lucrative for local salons." Retrieved on October 2, 2013, from http://articles.washingtonpost.com/2012–03–11/business/35447619_1_natural-hair-hair-care-chemicals.

Ebony.com. (May 15, 2013). "17 Natural hair bloggers you should know!: EBONY.com high-lights some of the top natural hair bloggers everyone should know." Retrieved on September 3, 2013, from http://www.ebony.com/photos/style/17-natural-hair-bloggers-you-should-know-332#axzz2dsMaDeuT.

Foucault, M. (1995). *Discipline and punish: The birth of the prison.* New York: Vintage Books.

Harris-Perry, M. (June 10, 2012). "There's big business in black hair." Retrieved on August 23, 2012, from http://video.msnbc.msn.com/mhp/47755691#47755691.

hooks, b. (1990). *Yearning: Race, gender and cultural politics.* Massachusetts: South End Press.

Hunter, T. (1997). *To 'joy my freedom: Southern black women's lives and labors after the Civil War.* Cambridge: Harvard University Press.

Jones, L. (1994). *Bulletproof diva: Tales of race, sex and hair.* New York: Doubleday.

Kinks, K. (September 5, 2014). "The struggle continues: A timeline of natural hair discrimina-tion over the past year." Retrieved on January 5, 2015, from http://blackgirllonghair.com/2014/09/the-struggle-continues-a-timeline-of-natural-hair-discrimination-over-the-past-year/.

Klein, R. (September 9, 2013). "Tiana Parker controversy continues: Legislators say their hair policy must be reviewed." Retrieved on September 9, 2013, from http://www.huffingtonpost.com/2013/09/09/tiana-parker-controversy_n_3895149.html.

Logan, R. M. (October 23, 2013). "Finance employer wants woman to cut off dreadlocks." Retrieved on November 25, 2013, from http://newsone.com/2744625/finance-employer-wants-woman-to-cut-off-dreadlocks/.

Lorde, A. (2009). *I am your sister: Collected and unpublished writings of Audre Lorde.* New York: Oxford University Press.

Madame Noire Editor. (March 10, 2012). "Nothing but natural! Great hair blogs for natural sistahs." Retrieved on September 3, 2013, from http://madamenoire.com/144666/5-great-hair-blogs-for-the-natural-sistahs-who-need-support/.

Magubane, Z. (April 12, 2007). "Why 'nappy' is offensive." Retrieved on October 1, 2013, from http://www.boston.com/news/globe/editorial_opinion/oped/articles/2007/04/12/why_nappy_is_offensive/ and https://www.commondreams.org/archive/2007/04/12/485.

Meaders, D. (1997). *Advertisements for runaway slaves in Virginia, 1801–1820*. New York: Routledge.

Mercer, K. (1990). "Black hair/style politics." In Russell Ferguson, Martha Gever, Trinh T. Minh-ha, and Cornel West (eds.), *Out There: Marginalization and Contemporary Cultures* (pages 247–264). New York: The MIT Press.

Mintel. (September 2013a). "Hair relaxers sales decline 26% over the past five years." Retrieved on February 3, 2015, from http://www.mintel.com/press-centre/beauty-and-personal-care/hairstyle-trends-hair-relaxer-sales-decline.

Mintel. (August 2013b). "Black Haircare—U.S." Retrieved on February 3, 2015, from http://store.mintel.com/black-haircare-us-august-2013.

Mintel. (August 2012). "Black Haircare—U.S." Retrieved on February 3, 2015, from http://store.mintel.com/black-haircare-us-august-2012.

Morrow, W. (1973). *400 years without a comb*. San Diego: Black Publishers of San Diego.

The New Yorker. (July 21, 2008). Cover page.

Opiah, A. (June 18, 2013a). "You can touch my hair: What were we thinking?!" Retrieved on June 18, 2013, from http://un-ruly.com/you-can-touch-my-hair-what-were-we-thinking/#.Uk2C3iSE7fY and http://www.huffingtonpost.com/antonia-opiah/you-can-touch-my-hair-wha_b_3459578.html.

Opiah, A. (May 28, 2013b). "Can I touch your hair?" Retrieved on January 23, 2014, from http://www.huffingtonpost.com/antonia-opiah/can-i-touch-your-hair_b_3320122.html.

Patrice, C. (August 15, 2014a). "The US army rolls back regulations against natural hair after months of backlash." Retrieved on February 5, 2015, from http://blackgirllonghair.com/2014/08/the-us-army-rolls-back-regulations-against-natural-hair-after-months-of-backlash/.

Patrice, C. (April 11, 2014b). "Rest in peace: Natural hair vlogger Domineque Banks aka LHDC2011 passes away." Retrieved on May 15, 2014, from http://blackgirllonghair.com/2014/04/rest-in-peace-natural-hair-vlogger-domineque-banks-passes-away/.

Patrice, C. (August 8, 2013). "8 Incredible Black-Owned Natural Hair Businesses to Support." Retrieved on September 3, 2013, from http://blackgirllonghair.com/2013/08/8-incredible-black-ownednatural-hair-businesses-to-support/.

Patterson, O. (1982). *Slavery and social death: A comparative study*. Cambridge: Harvard University Press.

Prince, A. (2009). *The politics of black women's hair*. Canada: Insomniac Press.

Roberts, C. (December 12, 2012). "Black meteorologist in Louisiana, Rhonda Lee, touched by support after getting canned for defending natural hair from racial comments on Facebook." Retrieved on September 3, 2013, from http://www.nydailynews.com/news/national/black-meteorologist-fired-defending-hair-touched-support-article-1.1218782.

Roberts, D. (1997). *Killing the black body: Race, reproduction, and the meaning of liberty*. New York: Pantheon Books.

Rooks, N. (1996). *Hair Raising: Beauty, culture and African American women*. New Jersey: Rutgers University Press.

Rubino, K. (2012). "Marsha Coulton gets a career makeover." Retrieved on September 20, 2012, from http://www.binghamton.edu/magazine/index.php/profiles/show/marsha-coulton-gets-a-career-makeover.

Sangweni, Y. (January 10, 2013). "EXCLUSIVE: Meteorologist Rhonda Lee on Getting Fired, Being Labeled the Rosa Parks of Natural Hair." Retrieved on September 3, 2013, from http://www.essence.com/2013/01/11/exclusive-meteorologist-rhonda-lee-getting-fired-being-labeled-rosa-parks-natural-hair/.

Saartjie Baartman Centre for Women and Children (SBCWC). "Saartjie Baartman's story." Retrieved on December 3, 2013, from http://www.saartjiebaartmancentre.org.za/~sbcwcor/index.php/about-us/saartjie-baartman-s-story.

Silliman, J. (2002). "Policing the national body: Sex, race, and criminalization." In Jael Silliman and Anannya Bhattacharjee (eds.), *Policing the National Body: Race, Gender, and Criminalization*. Massachusetts: South End Press.

Stepan, N. L. (1986). "Race and gender: The role of analogy in science." *Isis* 77(2): 261–277.

Stodghill, A. G. (December 22, 2012). "Rhonda A. Lee and Michaela Angela Davis discuss natural hair on the job: 'It's the last piece in a racial puzzle.'" Retrieved on September 3, 2013, from http://thegrio.com/2012/12/22/rhonda-a-lee-and-michaela-angela-davis-discuss-natural-hair-on-the-job-its-the-final-piece-in-a-racial-puzzle/.

Terkel, A. (April 1, 2014). "Black Female Soldiers Criticize Army's New Hairstyle Rules As Racially Biased." Retrieved on May 30, 2014, from http://www.huffingtonpost.com/2014/04/01/army-hairstyle_n_5070180.html.

Uwumarogie, V. (April 11, 2014). "RIP: Karyn Washington, founder of empowering site, for brown girls, and #darkskinredlip, commits suicide." Retrieved on May 15, 2014, from http://madamenoire.com/419330/karyn-washington-founder-empowering-site-brown-girls-commits-suicide/.

Walton, N. (August 14, 2014). "The US Army reversed its natural hair restrictions!" Retrieved on February 5, 2015, from http://www.curlynikki.com/2014/08/the-us-army-reversed-its-natural-hair.html.

Walton, N. (September 4, 2013). "Sheryl Underwood Apologizes for Natural Hair Remarks on The Steve Harvey Morning Show." Retrieved on September 5, 2013, from http://www.curlynikki.com/2013/09/sheryl-underwood-apologizes-on-steve.html.

Walton, N. (September 3, 2013b). "On the Couch with Sheryl Underwood—She Explains Natural Hair Remarks." Retrieved on September 4, 2013, from http://www.curlynikki.com/2013/09/on-couch-with-sheryl-underwood-of-talk.html.

Walton, N. (October 11, 2008). "About me." Retrieved on September 3, 2013, from http://www.curlynikki.com/2008/10/my-hair-story-pt1.html.

Whigham, K. "Behind the Keyboard: 30 Black Bloggers You Should Know From politics to pop culture, from relationships to fashion and natural hair, today's bloggers are an exceedingly opinionated bunch. We like 'em like that." Retrieved on September 3, 2013, from http://www.theroot.com/multimedia/28-black-bloggers-you-should-know.

White, S., and G. White. (1998). *Stylin': African American expressive culture from its beginning to the zoot suit.* Ithaca: Cornell University Press.

Whiteman, S. (December 11, 2012). "KTBS-TV Rehire Rhonda Lee." Retrieved on September 3, 2013, from https://www.causes.com/actions/1714107-ktbs-tv-rehire-rhonda-lee.

Wilson, J. (June 7, 2013). "'You can touch my hair' explores fascination with black hair, sparks debate." Retrieved on June 7, 2013, from http://www.huffingtonpost.com/2013/06/07/you-can-touch-my-hair-exhibit-black-women-hair_n_3401692.html.

Zayas, C. (January 16, 2013). "KTBS-TV: Give Rhonda Lee her job back ASAP!" Retrieved on September 3, 2013, from http://www.change.org/petitions/ktbs-tv-give-rhonda-lee-her-job-back-asap.

Chapter Six

Epistemic Advantage and Subaltern Enclaves

Tracing Anti-Street Harassment Discourse through Social Media Usage by Women of Color

Minu Basnet

On October 20, 2011, Rueben Fernandez and Keenan Santos were stabbed multiple times when they protested against a group of men harassing their women friends on a Mumbai street in India. Keenan died the same night while Fernandez succumbed to the injuries and died two days later. The two young men had protested against "Eve teasing," or street harassment (Singh 2011). A more recent September 2014 report noted that a woman in Detroit who had refused to give her phone number and a fourteen-year old girl in Florida who had refused to have sex with a man who had offered her $200 for it were brutally killed by their perpetrators (Chemaly 2013; Ressler 2014). Lewd comments, brushing of hands, and unease felt by winking or continual gazing by opposite sex on public transportation systems like trains and buses are realities that many women encounter. Police in several nations have held the opinion that choice of clothes by the victims have resulted into sexual assault (NDTV; Lemaitre, para 8). For a young female unaware of being victim to this form of unwanted attention on the streets, it is definitely an ugly jolt out of the innocent ignorance of the issue. Street harassment entails uninvited attention in public as well as behavior that is "implicitly or explicitly sexual" in nature (Kissling 1991, 6). Kissling (1991) collected responses of women from different parts of the world, who recounted their incidents of street harassment ranging from following or "girl-watching" by men to pinching body parts and passing lewd comments on the streets (p. 14). Over time, the issue has garnered attention in the media in the form of talk shows or articles examining the perception of men and women who participate in the act. Moreover, in the recent few decades the act has gained attention as demeaning and uncomfortable to women.

As a social issue, street harassment and resistance to it is widely present online through support groups. Support groups like Stop Street Harassment, Street Harassment Project, and Hollaback! are major organizations that help victims or women in general learn to fight back or deal with such situations. Besides these organizations, several other grassroots and regional organizations actively work on generating awareness and attention to the issue. Organizations that have tackled street harassment problems globally, are Safe Cities Project and Safe and Friendly Cities for All associated with women's issues branch of the United Nations. Some regional organizations active in addressing the issue are, Young Women for Change in Asia, Egyptian Center for Women's Rights in Africa, ASH Campaign in Europe, and Can I get a Smile? in North America among many others (Online Resources n.d.).

Street harassment is considered a problem that occurs globally and affects men and women regardless of their race, class, or gender. Among the responses to street harassment, women of color find the victimization that occurs for them to be different from that of White women. This kind of altered responses can be seen in the case of social responses to street harassment. While some may feel the need to respond back to the harassers others may take a more drastic approach. The confidence with which Minnesota woman Lindsey (who prefers not to reveal her last name for preserving her anonymity) distributes cards to men who catcall her on the street was not shared by a woman in Cairo, as well as two teenagers in India who resorted to suicide, unable to stand the humiliation of street harassment. So while it is true that the Cards Against Harassment approach is drawing confident women like Lindsey to directly confront their harassers, there are other groups that are making strides by attending to the challenges that are part of dealing with street harassment. Such lesser known but equally motivated outlets like People's Girls, the Egyptian social media approach are making us aware of the necessity to pay attention to the drastic steps like suicide case in Cairo by posting on their Facebook page.

Nancy Fraser (2007) criticized the Western centric logics that comprise the theorization of public sphere. She noted that the legitimacy and efficacy of the public sphere is called into question when public opinion of a citizenry expands beyond the bounded political space that was originally the framework for theorizing public sphere as a defining component of connections between civil society and the state in a democracy. Here Fraser (2007) has sought to re-imagine public sphere by turning a critical eye towards the individuals who are affected and hence are participants in shaping the discourse to resonate with others at a transnational level. For Fraser (2007), public sphere in its transnational phase needs to move beyond considering the "how" of public sphere participation but also attend to the "who" in order to retain the critical orientation of public sphere theory. The subaltern space of social media that I examine in this chapter attends to these anxieties of public sphere theory that Fraser calls to attention. While Fraser (2007) theorized public sphere with a transnational public in mind, for this chapter, I find Fraser's attention on putting diversity at the center essential to framing the utility of the alternative spaces.

The aims to capture public opinion in diversity help to shape my argument on the usage of social media forms by women of color. We can no longer account for one public sphere made of similar voices. The availability of internet and social media forms provides a rich resourceful answer for Fraser's contention about the predominance of multiple voices. Social media experiences can be documented through sites like Hollaback! and blogging efforts like YouOkSis or People's Girls, where we can see how the reactions are governed by stories imbued through epistemic advantage. Epistemic advantage is the power to understand perspectives that arise from different experiences shared and related among people who experience it the same way. I locate the social media experiences of women of color that I examine in this chapter within the framework of epistemic privilege that accords them with "structural intricacies . . . genealogies, power relations and commitments" which then shape the "knowledge and subjectivities" that are enacted within that space (Code 2000, 226).

In this chapter, I argue that women of color shape anti-street harassment discourse by using social media to express their stance on the issue which then helps to perceive the issue as a threat to the lives of women affected by it. This chapter examines dominant and well known organizations like Hollaback! and Stop Street Harassment and juxtaposes their approach with that of minority led social media forms to identify how the approaches speak to the anxieties of being a double minority experienced by the latter group. The approach and end goals aspired by the African-American women I examine in this chapter are enabled through the social media platforms. Hence, the utility of the social media form is central to shaping anti-street harassment discourse by women of color. The efforts of Window Sex Project drawn from dance forms based in African American culture to engage with reclaiming the body on the streets shapes the discourse on anti-street harassment through a means that are different from that adopted by mainstream anti-street harassment groups. Through the social media presence, the proliferation of these alternative ways to address street harassment directs attention to how the subaltern social media space works as the means to contribute to anti-street harassment discourse at an equalizing level. Social media platforms like Twitter campaign YouOkSis as well as the two blogs Gradient Lair and No Disrespect, orient the anti-street harassment discourse by functioning as alternate/subaltern enclaves by women of color. I seek to add to the efforts by transnational feminism that urges feminist scholarship to engage a multiplicity of voices when we are turning to a feminist issue so that minority voices too find the space to shape the discourse.

IDENTIFYING AND DEFINING STREET HARASSMENT

Several studies have focused on the issue to understand why harassment occurs on the streets. Scholars have focused on pinpointing those actions that constitute as street harassment and some have examined the inclusion of racially disparaging comments within the act of harassment. Bowman (1993) identified street harassment as limiting women to "sex objects" while at the same time causing a feeling of "disempowerment" (p. 537). Davis (1994) and Fogg-Davis (2006) drew our attention to the difficulty in placing street harassment as a recognizable act of aggression against women because of the nature of the action. Street harassment occurs when it is not expected or there are no grounds for picking out perpetrator/s, as it occurs in everyday spaces such as in streets and public places. Moreover, as Fogg-Davis (2006) pointed out, young girls experience harassment on the street "at or even before puberty" which leads to recognizing and dealing with the problem just as it were part of being female and a "burden" that they have to deal with as part of their lives (p. 63).

Davis (1994) defined street harassment as "sexual terrorism" and as Fogg-Davis (2006) claimed, the term rightfully describes the act because just as terrorism occurs without warning and is difficult to define when it occurs, harassment on streets too occur without the knowledge of the victim and therefore is "hard to define and difficult to combat" (p. 63). Bowman (1993) has defined harassment of women as "ghettoization [of women] to the private sphere of hearth and home"; he further added that harassment refers to men as debilitating women and taking away their power to free movement (p. 520). Thus, Bowman (1993) identified the urgency in calling forth the attention of lawmakers to step forward and take the responsibility of creating regulations for safeguarding women who fall victim to it. On the other hand, Kissling (1991) urged that the term itself had to go through a naming phase where the triviality would give way to a graver and serious place for the term. Scholars of law as well as gender studies brought attention to the issue during the early 1990s. They too, like Bowman (1993) and Kissling (1991) identified a lack of strong laws on this issue as well as the need for people who encounter it on a daily basis as both culprit and victim to raise their voices against the crime. As seen from the scholarly work done in the area in the 1990s, scholars and academics writing on the subject, were engaged in grasping with such facets of the issue as action/s that result in street harassment. In addition, in the early 1990s, they were acknowledging the issue as a serious one but were at the same time confronted with the difficulty of seeing it reflected in social spheres as sexism that was demeaning for women. Bowman (1993) mentioned the lack of sufficient resources on the topic, which led her to recommend the "student of street harassment" to investigate "female audiences, literature, movies, plays, and letters to the editor in large city newspapers" as sources for the topic (p. 522).

The term street harassment taken together with sexual harassment masks the brutal yet fleeting nature of the harassment, thus making it hard to define. The fact that a victim of street harassment is attacked when walking alone in public places with catcalls and whistles directed by a single man or a group of men/boys makes it difficult for women to capture and place the action as concrete proof of harassment. Comparatively, in the case of sexual harassment especially in the workplace, it is possible through means of documenting and more importantly knowing the transgressor. Lesbians for their non-conformity to heterosexuality as well as non-white women because of their different race have been found to be severe targets to such harassments on the street (Bowman 1991; Davis 1994; Nielsen 2000). Several organizations have taken steps to combat the problem by employing effective strategies of empowering women with the ability to deal with the issue.

MEDIATED IDENTITIES AND RESISTANCE

Whittaker (2004) raised an important point when he posited formation of identities on the internet as where "identity and resistance" occur as the same. Borrowing from Habermas's terminology about the nature of identity as a form of resistance, Whittaker (2004) placed a mediated identity in the context of internet where asserting any form of identity would indicate the resistance to some form of power. Diaspora scholars have noted that various kinds of texts such as "books, songs, television shows, newspapers, magazines, blogs, and web sites [that] provide a wealth of messages to form a basis for studies of news media, popular culture, and politics" work as a means of asserting identity for women in diaspora (Sharma, 139). Hollaback! as an easily accessible internet organization offers space for collective resistance to street harassment. Through their mediated identities on Hollaback!, visitors and contributors to the site find the space to express their resistance to street harassment. My interests are centered on exploring street harassment beyond the element of gender as the defining factor. If mediated identity in itself can be considered a form of resistance, I find it intriguing to explore the way mediated identities aid in unpacking our understanding of anti-street harassment discourse when besides gender, race is equally at the center.

Criticism against street harassment primarily focuses on calling out how it exaggerates a simple case of harmless greetings by strangers on the streets.

Condemning groups like Hollaback! on a CNN segment about street harassment, the invited guest speaker Steve Santagati, author of a book called *The MANual*, quipped that women liked being catcalled by men whom they thought were attractive. He further went on to state that parenting and culture may be the reason why some men acted in such ways on the streets. *New York Post* writer, Doree Lewak (2014) also expressed that catcalls worked as a boost to her ego and she looked forward to walking by construction sites. This form of treatment towards street harassment as a non-issue or an issue of little importance frames street harassment as deserving less importance. In the argument against considering street harassment a real issue for women, the discourse is limited to the technicalities of social behavior where the anti-street harassment advocates are called out for exaggerating harmless compliments and that as a society we need to "let men be men" (Fox News). I find such conclusions to trivialize the problems instead of focusing on the underlying structures that create the atmosphere for objectifying women is not adequately addressed. The escalating and fatal outcomes of street harassment especially when race and sexuality are involved are completely left out in framing the street harassment discourse. Besides the efforts by major organizations like Stop Street Harassment or Hollaback!, the platform for elaborating on the levels and degrees of consequences that result from street harassment are few if not absent. Moreover, concerning issues of race and sexuality within street harassment, there is very little attention from mainstream media outlets. Social media forms present an outlet for not reaching only into complexities of race and gender but they also serve as online communities for learning how to engage with street harassment as a double-minority.

Turning to women's participation in various forms of social media shows how street harassment becomes an issue of power and female body in public space. Hollaback! contends that bringing in race as a dynamic only deflects attention from the fact that it is a gender issue and affects women all over the world. Nevertheless, as Black feminist blogger Trudy discussed, it is necessary to bring up race and class within street harassment discourse. As the social media participation of women of color shows, experiences of women vary and are tied to how their identities and representation affect the street harassment scenario. The experiences of women of color as seen in the actions of the campaigns and attempts to capture the moments of power play on the streets, suggest that victimization does not merely stop at harmless greetings from strangers. Instead, street harassment is guided by exchanges laced with racist overtones and threats that are demeaning to women. Turning to examine street harassment through perspectives grounded in individual encounters with harassment and the way context and history of male-female relationship plays a role provides us with one way in which to perceive street harassment as a serious issue. In urging for involving minority experiences within social media, a vital element is the standpoint that informs their assessment on the issue of street harassment. Addressing how standpoint theory may be regarded to promote essentialism, Fricker (2013) defended standpoint theory by noting that some common experiences based in race and class can be generalized. Fricker (2013) noted that some experiences like sexual discrimination would still relate across women in a society. However, as she pointed out, generalizing a White woman's experiences to that of a Black woman would be incomplete.

RHETORIC AND THE "EVENT" OF STREET HARASSMENT

Anti-Street harassment discourse deserves importance as the space which illuminates how non-white women use social media to manage anxieties that arise with being a double minority. Rhetoric helps to understand how various outlets of dissent ranging from traditional movements to new social movements that utilize logos, pathos, and ethos in innovative ways draw attention to pressing social issues. Besides attention to protests and sit-ins, rhetoricians have interrogated further into other ways of enacting resistance. Along with usage of language, rhetoricians explore the rhetoric at work within a wide range of "symbolic activity" such as songs and posters (Morris and Browne 2006, 9). I am interested in how rhetoricians have theorized rhetoric as response to an event. As Hauser (2002) explained, rhetoric occurs through actions—situated action, symbolic action, constitutive action, strategic action, or through transaction. Through these forms, what we can witness is the way in which "things or objects carry meaning as much as we name and constitute it through language" (34). Lloyd Bitzer (1968) too had offered a similar interpretation of rhetoric as response to an event in his theory. He suggested that "rhetorical situation" is composed of "exigence," or reason for which the response is needed, "audience" or those who will be able to react and respond to the exigence, and "constraints" or the limiting factors that need to be taken into account. Here Hauser (2002) and Bitzer (1968), both explained events in their own ways but the fundamentality in both these theories remain the same—rhetoric works through language with defining characteristics as the basis on which there is conscious effort to call for change.

   Crick (2014) used John Dewey's explanation of rhetorical event to add further to this theoretical approach. Crick (2014) suggested that while the rhetorical situation may be influenced by various extenuating circumstances that guide and frame the response, it is up to the rhetor to shape the event through his/her perspective. In this emphasis on the rhetor, I find the importance of epistemic situatedness of the rhetor central in construing the event. Crick's use of rhetoric as response to event approaches the point of rhetorical intervention as one aspect of response within a continuity of experiences. For

Crick (2014), rhetoric is a "strategically constructed" response to a disruptive event where the continual focus is on making meaning out of an event even though it may not fully capture all of the pieces of the experience. As he noted, "to construct a situation is thus to give meaning to those events which have already captured our attention, whether through direct experience or through various media, using language to thread facts, objects, agents, and events into a contextual whole in which an audience is not only affected but somehow implicated" (258). Therefore, the attention to the identity of the individual creating meaning out of events resonates with the efforts of non-white female social media users who strive to work through the meanings that street harassment carries as an event to inform the resistance strategies that they offer (262). Crick (2014) suggested that we create meanings out of a "flux of experiences for the sake of power" (270). The significance of sexism and patriarchal attitudes within the flux of experiences that occurs within street harassment is itself something that activists, advocates, and women affected by street harassment strive to explain. For women of color, the flux of experiences is further complicated by race as a factor. Through the social media platforms, women of color build and contribute to anti-street harassment discourse using their voices informed by their own experiences, thus, strategically constructing meaning to making sense of street harassment as a serious issue that needs attention.

ANTI-STREET HARASSMENT DISCOURSE: POINTS OF CONVERGENCE AND DIVERGENCE

To situate the meaning making constructed by women of color, I will first outline how the street harassment discourse has been framed. It is important to discuss how street harassment as a real threat has been questioned as a legitimate social issue because the lack of seriousness itself complicates the larger street harassment discourse or "flux of events" within which women of color seek to build a voice (Crick 2014, 269). One of the defining aspects stressed by many advocates of anti-street harassment is that women from all parts of the world are affected by it. While some feminist groups consider street harassment as an indication of universal sexism or "byproduct of global patriarchy" (Ebony.com), the dynamics of power that govern the relationship and hence the interaction between the harasser and the victim is shaped by more than just gender differences. In other words, while street harassment does occur with all women, such factors as race, ethnicity, sexuality, and physical features mark the power at play in incidents of street harassment. Backlash against advocates of anti-street harassment arose through the assertion that the resistance aggravates what is merely simple complimenting of physical features. These trivializing responses expressed through news "discussions" through various news channels on the topic understate the severity of harassment on the streets. There are no laws that define and identify street harassment as a punishable offense (Nielsen). The lack of laws against street harassment may be explained with the point that it as a fleeting experience rather than a sustained form of harassment that can be recorded and documented. For those skeptical about whether laws against street harassment would be stretching the limits of public speech too far, sociology professor Nielsen (2014) argued that catcalling could be made consistent with "First Amendment jurisprudence about other kinds of hate speech that intimidates, harasses, and perpetuates inequality" (para 3).

Projects such as the Window Sex Project or People's Girls, both work to resist disciplining of female bodies that occurs with street harassment. Offering performance and their dance as resistance and means to reclaim their bodies, Window Sex Project invites audience to perceive the situation through the experiences of the dancers who seek to convey their affective engagements with street harassment to call forth action. People's Girls, an Egyptian movement started by two women to sensitize people about street harassment, makes its presence through a Facebook page and Twitter, and primarily seeks to draw attention to the problem of street harassment in Egypt. They adopt story-telling and reaching out to Egyptian women through workshops and documentaries as a means to continue the conversations on street harassment of women.

Window Sex Project, a blog that incorporates videos and writings as well as links to other social media outlets, deals with resisting street harassment through dance performance and approaches harassment on the streets by emphasizing the body as the site which suffers from street harassment. The point that Window Sex Project seeks to make is that with participation in dance performance, the body can again be made "whole." While participants vary in the ethnicity and race they represent as dancers, the elements that they seek to utilize to represent street harassment as an exigence or an event that necessitates action. Through the dance performance, body as a site for harassment becomes the larger focus. The approach to interpreting street harassment is hence significantly influenced by the focus on the body. As Crick (2014) explained, the meaning making by the rhetor presupposes transaction with prior/past events with the aim for "leveraging change in events to come" (268). So, the dance form which takes in the bodily experience of harassment suggests that instead of making the skin color of the victim central to the discourse we need to focus on introspection in dealing with harassment. This kind of response, I argue, places the victim's physical body interpolated in the moment of street harassment, at the center of the street harassment discourse. It does not directly encourage action in the form of addressing the harasser or picking out the harasser, but it urges the victim to take a step towards addressing the harassment and seeking to do something about it.

Therefore, the dance form and celebration of body, in this instance of resistance to street harassment shows how the approach of involving dance and body comes from the realization of the double minority status. The double minority status entails that the hurdles in responding to street harassment are not only through being a female but also in the non-White experience where their racial difference is highlighted in the harassment they experience. Regardless of skin color, the act of participating in the dance form allows a means to express one's experiences with street harassment. This resistance strategy makes the process of dealing with the harassment a process of internalizing the experience with the situated knowledge of the victim, the circumstance, and the identity of the harasser intact. Hence, instead of brushing over differences, this form of approach to street harassment preserves the individuality of the identity of the victims.

Instead of attempting to challenge street harassment by calling out the harassment as a form of punishable offense, the Window Sex Project participants/dancers engage in performances that as one dancer explains in an after discussion helps to relive the affective responses of fear and anger. Hence, through reliving it through the performance, it opens up the opportunity of navigating street harassment as a woman. Instead of expressing through words, they express it through dance. The dance form puts a woman at the center of the harassment and as the creator of the Window Sex Project. Sydney Mosley discussed in an interview that she expects the efforts of Window Sex Project to generate conversations and have people express and discuss street harassment as a problem. While the activism expressed through dance aims to involve large numbers of people in the discussion about street harassment, they do not emphasize meeting an "end" with street harassment as a form of harassment against women. Instead as Mosley, the creator of Window Sex Project emphasized, to have women assert their confidence and work through the challenges of harassment in the form of humiliation experienced on the streets would be a significant step. Mosley also noted that unlike Holly Kearl and Emily May, the founders of Stop Street Harassment and Hollaback!, respectively, her approach to anti-street harassment is different. She stated that her motive is to help people perceive the incidents of catcalling or unwanted attention on the streets as harassment and to help women find the courage to stand up against it and prepare themselves from within to challenge the harassment.

In comparison to the approach that Kearl and May have in terms of dealing with street harassment by sharing stories and calling for an "end" to street harassment, Mosley's approach focuses on having women change the way they perceive the dynamics of power so that they would feel less threatened by perpetrators. Mosley's approach works as better geared towards addressing the challenges of women of color who have to work through the double minority status. The efforts employed by Kearl and May on the other hand, center on change where there is complete end to harassment on the streets. Here the difference in approach that I see at work is in the intersecting identities that contextualizes Mosley's approach to street harassment in comparison to that of Kearl and May. As the description of Mosley's profile implies, her dance form is inspired from experiences engrained within Black cultures and women's experiences (Window Sex Project, "About," para 4). Thus, Mosley's approach shows how the activism through dance performances arises from the producer Mosley's conscious efforts to mold experiences from the intersecting identities of women of color. Hence, the knowledge and context based in identities of women who have intersecting identities that posits them as minorities points to an expectation of material change which does not extend to imagining a final end to harassment. Based on these experiences, the most that Mosley finds herself working towards through her activism is raising consciousness among women.

SUBALTERN ENCLAVES AND VIRTUAL COMMUNITIES: TWITTER AND BLOGGING

Acknowledging how street harassment is raced and affects women of color differently than White women, Trudy, a blogger whose blog Gradient Lair is focused on Black experiences, has noted that diminishing the importance of race and class silences the realities of street harassment for women of color and women in low-income statuses. Unlike the efforts by Mosley whose efforts though rooted in dance forms adopted from Black cultures resonates to all women, there is conscious effort by some women of color to make meaning and frame the street harassment discourse for women of color through subaltern enclaves within social media. So, I will now turn to alternative/subaltern publics and the formation of enclaves in the virtual world of the internet.

If, as suggested by Asen and Brouwer (2001), the various combinations of "counter" and "publics" offer insightful dimensions to understanding how marginalized populations deal with power, then the possibilities for virtual community building that social media platforms offer need to be addressed. While counter publics serve as the overarching theory for tapping into alternative spaces, the purpose that counter public theorists identify for use of counter public spaces broadens how we understand social media usage by women of color within the larger framework of resistance among women against street harassment. As Park and Wald (2000) pointed out, the participation in public sphere for minorities and women can only be enabled by engaging in "patriarchal scripts" rather than moving away from it. Hence, this stands true for anti-street harassment groups like Hollaback! or Stop Street Harassment. However, as seen in the strategies that they employ and promote to impede harassment of women in the streets, the approach by social media outlets that consciously address street harassment from the dual perspective of gendered and raced perspectives differ. They are less likely to ascribe directly to engaging in the patriarchal scripts that Park and Wald (2000) urge as necessary for counter public spaces organized by minorities. Nancy Fraser (2007) has encouraged us to consider alternative publics who are excluded from the public sphere. She expands on the existence of multiple publics by distinguishing subaltern or alternate publics who find other means to engage as part of citizen bodies of a nation. In considering social media usage by women of color as counter public spaces, Catherine Helen Palczewski's (2001) discussion about enclaves created within the virtual space of the internet provides an excellent overview. Palczewski (2001) urged that tapping into the "new social movements" in the form of cyber movements gives us a rich insight into the possibilities for creation of dialogue that it enables (173).

Social media is expansive and open to people across the world as long as easy and cheap access is possible. We not only celebrate social media usage for the instant means of access to popular events going around us as well as at the national and international level but also for the space for building and developing connections on topics and interests that may pertain to particular and nuanced issues or matters of interest. Availability of social media as a platform that can be used for topics or issues that do not get exposure through dominant outlets gives minority voices a chance to be heard.

As the three year anniversary on Sweden's "social media experiment" completed in February 2015, the uniqueness of the social media form was noted by news sources for the innovative step taken by Sweden to give voice to people within a democracy. The social media experiment refers to steps taken by the Swedish government in the form of offering the official twitter account "@sweden" to be handled by ordinary citizens of the country for a week each. National Public Radio (2015) reported that over the span of three years, up to 150 citizens of Sweden have expressed their thoughts and views on issues related to Sweden. This kind of social media usage with possibilities for multiplicity of voices within a democracy to be heard is notable but here the twitter account being the official source for Sweden adds authenticity and a wider platform than individual voices would have found on their own. This social experiment functions as an important place to understand how opinions differ and converge. In the case of the Sweden Twitter page, tweets ranged from concern over local issues to that of national importance without resorting to painting a clichéd picture of the country. I find this twitter experiment to show how individuality and multiplicity together exist to give voice to people on an equalizing platform though as the NPR report mentioned, they have only been able to offer the opportunity to 150 people over a period of three years.

Similarly, turning attention to opinions on street harassment through Twitter shows how social media has shaped the discourse on street harassment by steering people to recognize what street harassment may look like. One of the problems which non-white women have identified is the minimal attention to street harassment as not only a feminist issue but also a racially charged form of harassment that needs to be perceived through a gendered, classed, and raced lens. Here is where I find the social media use by non-white women to be valuable for shaping the discourse on street harassment as a transnational feminist issue while also paying attention to individual experiences bound by dynamics of power pertaining to the context. The steps taken by Hollaback! and Stop Street Harassment involve creating a virtual space for people from around the world to share their accounts of facing harassment in public. Hollaback! recently produced a video that covered the account of an actual woman who was harassed as she walked through the streets of New York. Equipped with a camera, the female actor tracks the men who call out to her in sexist and demeaning ways. One of the points of criticism lashed out to the organization was regarding the dominant emphasis on African-Americans and Latinos as harassers. Non-white women criticized the absence of white males as harassers. In addition, the actor who was featured in the video appeared Caucasian and so this was another element that was criticized by non-white women and others who saw this social experiment to diminish the importance of street harassment on non-white women. Hollaback! on the other hand retorted by saying that street harassment runs across cultures and that to simply divide it along "race lines" takes away the purpose of the real issue. Rob Bliss who had shot the entire event stated that diverting attention to race was "distracting from real issue" ("You won't believe," para 8). The criticism against Hollaback! video claimed that it did not represent women as a whole because non-white women often face harassment for different reasons than being called out for their physical attractiveness. In a video response, two African American and two Indian-American women reflected on their experiences of being catcalled and harassed on the streets. They noted that they were called out not just for their looks or style of clothing but also for their racial distinctiveness such as skin color or hair. So, in acknowledging their experiences as different from that of White women, these non-white women establish street harassment as something experienced differently and expressed by the opposite sex on a different level through their perception of non-white women. One of the points made by a woman appearing in the video is that instead of vilifying the Hollaback! video, it would be better to continue on the dialogue through reflection about the ways in which street harassment targets women of non-white races. Such responses resonate with the point made by Fricker (2013) that engaging in criticism based on standpoint addresses the incomplete nature of discourse on such feminist issues.

In a study conducted by Kietzmann, Hermkens, McCarthy, and Silvestre (2011), they distinguished social media outlets for the types of functions they fulfill for users. For Kietzmann et al. (2011), social media carries out the functions of building relationships, sharing, generating conversations, showing presence, formulating and maintaining identity, and forming a sense of community through groups. These functions touch on the fundamental characteristics of social media use but instead of classifying the functions into neat categories that these authors identify, the experiences with social media is made richer when we consider the intertwined possibilities for influence that are enabled with social media. Therefore, while Kietzmann et al. (2011) considered the implications of Twitter to fulfill mainly the function of presence for users, they contend that blogs are more effective for generating conversations. In making these distinctions, the authors seemed to be primarily interested in placing social media usage into recognizable categories. So when we turn to a social issue like street harassment as the lens to put social media usage into perspective, the functions of social media overlap further intrinsically than the categorical divisions that Kietzmann et al. (2011) identified. Social media usage by women of color also faces the problem of less avenues for women of color to express their thought.

One of the issues that feminists outside of the West as well as non-white feminists bring to the table is regarding the problem with generalizing over experiences of women of color by using the term "feminism" when actually focusing mainly on the experiences of White women. So in the case of the social media usage by women of color for building connections about facing street harassment as a problem that is further aggravated because of race and class issues, the implications for social media usage is further complicated than the categorical usage that Kietzmann et al. (2011) ascribe to social media use.

As the YouOkSis Twitter hashtag reflects, the use of this nomenclature not only became a point for recognizing an identity but a source for weaving together elements about anti-street harassment discourse that focused on the uniqueness of experiences of women of color. The hashtag placed race at the center of the anti-street harassment discourse making people aware and sensitizing them to how street harassment for non-white women and mainly Black women differed from that of Whites. The YouOkSis campaign on Twitter specifically focuses on the experiences of Black women. The creator of the Twitter hashtag, with the Twitter username, Feminista Jones, noted that the attention is on sisterhood or males and females coming together to be there for each other to fight it. In using the colloquial everyday phrase "You Ok Sis," the motive behind the twitter hashtag is not merely to have it "trend" on Twitter but to have the social media phenomenon materialize into a concrete outcome. Jones's approach is in seeking out consciousness among people who witness the street harassment through actual action in the form of doing something for the situation.

CONCLUSION

Instead of merely trying to create and sustain their own identity or form relationships to keep up with the trends of social media usage, the women that I identify in my chapter have more at stake in turning to the social media forms. Instead of just using Twitter to feel a sense of identity, users are invested in how their identities figure as an element within the discussion about anti-street harassment. Instead of being isolated spaces that are used for different functions, each of the social media outlets become resources for placing street harassment and experiences of women of color as a discourse in itself.

The responses of women of color indicate less of confrontation that women of color choose to apply as resistance to street harassment. Two of the blogs, Gradient Lair and No Disrespect, both make the conscious effort to establish that they are African-American female bloggers before providing intricate details about how they have had experiences with street harassment. Epistemic advantage or the knowledge that results from being situated in a position is not only useful to understand what kind of change is necessary but it also gives a good idea about the level of material change that is possible. For the YouOkSis campaign that I discuss here in this chapter, the approach is less about structural change by enforcing laws against street harassment and more about how people who see and experience the issue can make a change. No Disrespect, a Boston based organization that focuses on combating street harassment that involve historically marginalized communities, notes that it is committed to a community based approach where they move away from pointing out men as harassers but instead use the system of community to raise awareness and speak up against harassment in public spaces. Here too, like the YouOkSis Twitter campaign, the approach is community based. The choice of community based approach reinforces the use of social media as forms of social media enclaves that are necessary for people to find a place where others with similar experiences and perspective converge. I do not seek to suggest that these are social media platforms exclusively for women of color. Window Sex Project also features White dancers who participate in the performances as well as the discussion afterwards that are featured in their website. Similarly, No Disrespect too involves women of other races. However, perspectives gained from experiences of people within the African-American community shape the format of both approaches.

Street harassment refers to the sexual harassment of women on the streets and while it is true that this form of harassment remains the same across race and cultures, racial identities show that there is a difference in the response to the issue. If street harassment is trivialized by arguing that males are only just "acting as males" by showing the harassment behavior, then the further fatal outcomes of street harassment in the form of rape or assault are likely to follow. However, while these perspectives are also accompanied by less confrontational but energetic moves to draw attention to the need for community based involvement as used by social media platforms offered by women of color the outlook towards dealing with street harassment is diversified. Besides the confrontational approaches that dominant groups like Hollaback! and Stop Street Harassment may adopt, the means for internalizing and confronting by celebrating one's body that Window Sex Project offers colors the rhetoric of street harassment in a more innovative way. Transnational feminism urges us to embrace the diversity and make painstaking but conscious efforts to include the myriad of feminist voices that exist. In this chapter, I point out to one such feminist issue in the form of street harassment and as transnational feminism seeks, I identify the diverse and rich resources for dealing with street harassment in the social media participation by women of color.

REFERENCES

Asen, R., and D. C. Brouwer (2001). "Introduction." In R. Asen and D. C. Brouwer (eds.), *Counterpublics and The State* (pp. 161–186). Albany: New York Press.

Bell, E., and S. H. Jones (2008). "Performing Resistance." In E. Bell (ed.), *Theories of Performance* (pp. 199–250). California: Sage Publications Inc.

Bell, E. "Introducing Theories of Performance." In E. Bell (ed.), *Theories of Performance* (pp. 5–21). California: Sage Publications Inc.

Bitzer, L. F. (1968). "The Rhetorical Situation." In William A. Covino (ed.), *Rhetoric: Concepts, Definitions, Boundaries*. Boston: Allyn and Bacon.

Boal, A. (1979). *Theatre of the Oppressed*. London: Pluto Press.

Bowman, M. S., and R. L. Bowman. (2010). "Telling Katrina Stories: Problems and Opportunities in Engaging Disaster." *Text and Performance Quarterly* 96(4): 455–461. Retrieved from http://web.ebscohost.com.proxy.lib.wayne.edu/ehost.

Bowman, C. J. (1993). "Street harassment and the informal ghettoization of women." *Harvard Law Review* 106(3): 517–580. Retrieved from http://www.jstor.org.proxy.lib.wayne.edu/stable/1341656?seq=22.

Brodsky, A. (2010, August 30). "Hollaback!: Misguided shouting for a much needed safe space." *Broad Recognition*. Retrieved from http://broadrecognition.com/politics/Hollaback!-misguided-shouting-for-a-much-needed-safe/.

Browne, S. H., and C. E. Morris (2006). "Introduction." *Readings on the Rhetoric of Social Protest* (pp. 1–100). PA: Strata Publishing Inc.

Chemaly, S. (2013, September 27). "Street Harassment: Is a Man Running Over a 14-Year Old Girl for Refusing Sex Serious Enough?" *Huffington Post*. Retrieved from http://www.huffingtonpost.com/soraya-chemaly/street-harassment-is-runn_b_4004394.html.

Code, L. (2007). "Feminist Epistemologies and Women's Lives." In Eva Feder Kittay and Linda Martín Alcoff (eds.), *The Blackwell Guide to Feminist Philosophy* (pp. 211–233). Malden: Blackwell Publishing.

Crick, N. (2014). "Rhetoric and Events." *Philosophy & Rhetoric* 47(3): 251–272.
Davis, D. (1993–1994). "The harm that has no name: Street harassment, Embodiment, and African American." *UCLA Women's Law Journal* 4: 133–178.
Fogg-Davis, H. G. (2006). "Theorizing black lesbians within black feminism." *Politics and Gender* 2: 57–76. doi: 10.1017/S1743923X06060028.
Fricker, M. (2013, July 1). "Epistemic Oppression and Epistemic Privilege." *Canadian Journal of Philosophy*, 191–210. doi: 10.1080/00455091.1999.10716836.
Green, D. (narrator) (2015, February 2). "Sweden's Social Experiment on Twitter Celebrates Third Anniversary [Radiobroadcast episode]." *Morning Edition*. Washington, DC: National Public Radio.
Hauser, G. A. (2002). *Introduction to Rhetorical Theory: Second Edition*. Waveland Press Inc.
History (n.d.). *Hollaback!.org*. Retrieved from http://www.iHollaback!.org/.
History (n.d.). *streetharassmentproject.org*. Retrieved from http://www. streetharassmentproject.org/history.html.
Irvine, J. T. (1996). "The Indeterminacy of Participant Roles." In G. Urban (ed.), *Natural Histories of Discourse* (pp. 105–130). Chicago: The University of Chicago.
Kearl, H. (n.d.). "Online resources." *Stop street-harassment.org*. Retrieved from http://www. stopstreetharassment.org/resources/online/.
Kearl, H. (2011, April 18). "Street harassment of women: It's a bigger problem than you think." *The Christian Science Monitor*. Retrieved from http://www.csmonitor.com/ Commentary/Opinion/2011/0418/Street-harassment-of-women-It-s-a-bigger-problem-than-you-think.
Kietzmann, J. H., K. Hermkens, I. P. McCarthy, and B. S. Silvestre (May–June 2011). "Social media? Get serious! Understanding the functional building blocks of social media." *Business Horizons* 54(3): 241–251.
Kissling, E. A. (1991). "Street harassment the language of sexual terrorism." *Discourse and Society* 2(4): 451–460. doi: 10.1177/0957926591002004006.
Krieg, G. (2011, June 29). "New York Anti-Street Harassment Group Asks Women to Holla-back!!" *ABC News*. Retrieved from http://abcnews.go.com/US/york-anti-street-harassment-group-asks-women-Hollaback!/story?id=13908039#.Tuf7nbIk6so.
Langellier, K. M. (1999). "Personal Narrative, Performance, Performativity: Two or Three Things I Know For Sure." *Text and Performance Quarterly* 19: 125–144. Retrieved from http://web.ebscohost.com.proxy.lib.wayne.edu/ehost.
Lemaitre, J. (2003). "Walking the Latin American City." *ReVista: Harvard Review of Latin America*. Retrieved from http://revista.drclas.harvard.edu/book/walking-latin-american-city.
Lewak, D. (2014, August 18). "Hey, Ladies—Catcalls are Flattering! Deal With It!" *New York Post*. Retrieved from http://nypost.com/2014/08/18/enough-sanctimony-ladies-catcalls-are-flattering/.
Mawson, J. (2010, July 21). "Government, NGO partners and adolescents target 'Eve teasing.'" *UNICEF Newsline*. Retrieved from http://www.unicef.org/infobycountry/bangladesh_ 55216.html.
McGinn, D. (2011, March 18). "It's fine weather for first International Anti Street Harassment Day." *The Globe and Mail*. Retrieved from http://www.theglobeandmail.com/life/the-hot-button/its-fine-weather-for-first-international-anti-street-harassment-day/article1947846/.
McIntosh, D. M. (2009). "The Forest of Performance Theories: A Review of Theories of Performance." *The Review of Communication* 9(3): 267–272. Retrieved from http://web. ebscohost.com.proxy.lib.wayne.edu/ehost.
Mosley, S. (n.d.) "About: Window Sex Project." Retrieved from http://www. windowsexproject.com/p/about.html.
Nielsen, L. B. (2000). "Situating Legal Consciousness: Experiences and Attitudes of Ordinary Citizens about Law and Street Harassment." *Law and Society Review* 34(4): 1055–1090. Retrieved from http://heinonline.org.proxy.lib.wayne.edu/HOL/Page?handle=hein.journals/ lwsocrw34&id=1069&collection=journals&index=journals/lwsocrw.
Nielsen, L. B. (2014, November 3). "Street Harassment Law Would Restrict Intimidating Behavior." *New York Times*. Retrieved from http://www.nytimes.com/roomfordebate/2014/

10/31/do-we-need-a-law-against-catcalling/street-harassment-law-would-restrict-intimidating-behavior.

No Disrespect (n.d.). brooklynmovementcenter.org. Retrieved from http://brooklynmovementcenter.org/anti-street-harassment/.

Noy, C. (2004). "Performing Identity: Touristic Narratives of Self-Change." *Text and Performance Quarterly* 24(2): 115–138. Retrieved from http://web.ebscohost.com.proxy.lib.wayne.edu/ehost/.

Pal, D. (2014, August 28). "Death over eve-teasing: What Rohtak girls' suicides tell us about how we raise our girls." *FirstPost*. Retrieved from http://www.firstpost.com/india/death-over-eve-teasing-what-rohtak-girls-suicides-tell-us-about-how-we-raise-our-girls-1685691.html.

Palczewski, C. H. (2001). "Cyber-Movements, New Social Movements, and Counterpublics." In R. Asen and D. C. Brouwer (eds.), *Counterpublics and The State* (pp. 161–186). Albany: New York Press.

Park, Y., and G. Wald (2000). "Native Daughters in the Promised Land: Gender, Race, and the Question of Separate Spheres." In M. Hill and M. Warren (eds.), *Masses, Classes, and the Public Sphere* (pp. 226–250). New York: Verso.

Perez, K., and D. B. Goltz (2010). "Treading Across Lines in the Sand: Performing Bodies in Coalitional Subjectivity." *Text and Performance Quarterly* 30(3): 247–268. Retrieved from http://web.ebscohost.com.proxy.lib.wayne.edu/ehost.

Reports (2011). *Safestreets.org*. Retrieved from http://www.thesafestreets.org/reports.

Ressler, T. C. (2014, October 9). "This Week, Two Incidents Of Street Harassment Escalated Into Violent Attacks Against Women." *Think Progress*. Retrieved from http://thinkprogress.org/health/2014/10/09/3578215/street-harassment-escalates/.

Rezaie, M. (2011, September 15). "A new generation of Afghan women demands rights." *Daily Outlook*. Retrieved from http://outlookafghanistan.net/topics.php?post_id=1868.

Scott, J. (2008). "Performing Unfeminine Femininity: A Performance of Identity Analysis of Bulimic Women's Personal Narratives." *Text and Performance Quarterly* 28(1–2): 116–138. Retrieved from http://web.ebscohost.com.proxy.lib.wayne.edu/ehost.

Sharma, R. (2011). "Desi Films: Articulating Images of South Asian Identity in a Global Communication Environment." *Global Media Journal—Canadian Edition* 4(1): 127–143.

Shome, R. (2006). "Interdisciplinary Research and Globalization." *The Communication Review* 9: 1–36.

Shome, R., and R. Hedge (2002). "Postcolonial approaches to communication: Charting the terrain, engaging the intersections." *Communication Theory* 12(3): 249–270.

Singh, V. V. (2011). "2nd Death in Amboli eve-teasing case." *The Times of India*. Retrieved from http://articles.timesofindia.indiatimes.com/2011-11-01/mumbai/30345678_1_eve-teasing-2nd-death-drunk-men.

Trudy (n.d.) "About: Gradient Lair." Retrieved from http://www.gradientlair.com/bio.

What (n.d.). objecDEFY.com. Retrieved from http://www.objecdefy.com/what.htm.

What is eve teasing? (n.d.). blanknoise.org. Retrieved from http://blog.blanknoise.org/.

Whittaker, M. P. (2004). "Tamilnet.com: Some Reflections on Popular Anthropology, Nationalism, and the Internet." *Anthropology Quarterly* 77(3): 469–498.

Chapter Seven

"Follow Me on Instagram"

"Best Self" Identity Construction and Gaze through Hashtag Activism and Selfie Self-Love

Kandace L. Harris

When I created my Instagram account in 2012, it seemed simple enough. Describe myself in 150 characters. Yet, I quickly realized that in that character limitation, I couldn't post or describe everything that I am, but instead I had to choose and give a snapshot of the things I thought represented me most. I had to ask myself, what did I want followers or visitors to know about me within those limitations? With that, I crafted my Instagram bio: "professor of 'all things media,' foodie, and life-lover." Sounds pretty awesome, huh? But I guess that is the point.

Instagram is described as "a fast, beautiful and fun way to share your life with friends and family." Yet, in the world of social media, the notion of "follower" typically expands well-passed family and friends. Inherently in being on Instagram, a visual storytelling social media platform, your goal is to have a steadily increasing "following" based on "likes." That means that the moment you open your account you are anticipating the "who" that will be following you and the "what" you would like them to see or know about your life. More importantly, you want them to like the things that you like about yourself. So, in examining my profile, are these things true about me? Absolutely. I am a mass communication and media studies professor. I enjoy food, and sharing my love of food. And the life-lover quip, well that gives me some room to photographically explore all the other things I love doing: traveling, spending time with my friends, being a social butterfly, watching Scandal. That's the beauty of Instagram.

131

Showing your best self in perfectly-coifed, and sometimes staged, pictures.

Instagram, like all social media, is about presenting the ideal version of yourself (Muenter 2014). "It's not not yourself per se, but more like, all the best parts of you displayed to the world and ignoring all the worst parts." Due to its user-friendliness and simplistic photosharing, Instagram, more so than its predecessors Facebook and Twitter, allows for strategic visual marketing of your best self. Yet, this concept of "maximized perception" (Lynch 2014) of self on social networks does not go without criticism. In the article, "Instagram's Envy Effect," Niequist (2013) argues that the Internet is dangerous in that it is easy to tell partial truths in which everyone's life looks better on the Internet than in real life. Curated images allow for the "seduction of other people's partial truths and heavily filtered photos, making everything look amazing." She suggests that this encourages comparing instead of connection and community.

Particularly for women and African Americans, who are significantly higher users of social media compared to men and whites (Pew Research Center 2013), it's also likely that they are doing more of the comparing on social media. Westring (2014) contends that social media makes it exceptionally easy to do so and there is a clear price to be paid for women comparing themselves to others. "The comparison process can backfire and cause us to judge ourselves unnecessarily harshly, particularly when we are comparing ourselves to the filtered, perfect images we see on social media." However, the affect theory of social exchange (Lawler 2001) may challenge that position. Affect theory of social exchange builds off of social exchange theory in that not only does it suggest that users choose to communicate through a context of rewards and costs, but there is a commitment to exchange relations and the effects of repeated exchange among the same users. In that, a virtual relationship is formed based on reciprocity and benefit analysis.

Harvey (2014) posits that photographic agency is an important method to connect to friends and to establish an image that is user-generated, rather than a mainstream media representation, and that self-presentation centers black participation in social media. He also suggests that for online identity construction, social media allow racial and ethnic groups to establish an online identity prescribed by them in which they can furnish a space to connect and mobilize interests in ways that were previously difficult. Moreover, belonging and community are recurring themes illustrated among black social media users (p. 1052). Also, while traditional media (print and television) and personal relationships remain the primary ways in which Americans learn about causes, African Americans are significantly more likely than Whites to believe that they can help get the word out about a social issue or cause through online social networks and look to social media as an additional source of information (Social Media Plays Greater Role in

Cause Engagement For African Americans and Hispanics, 2011). More importantly, for Black women, identity construction, offline and online, is rooted in Black feminist and womanist thought; the notion that Black women forge individual, unarticulated, yet potentially powerful expressions of everyday consciousness into an articulated, self-defined, collective standpoint (Collins 1990).

With this understanding, this chapter examines "presentation" of self and identity through the social media experience. Using affect theory of social change and black feminist and womanist theoretical foundations, it explores Instagram as an attractive social media platform for African-American women due to its accessibility, ubiquity, and influence. More importantly, it postulates that while there are criticisms, Instagram can be used as an effective social media tool to create, curate, and build congruent and integral layers of "best self" identity for African-American women; which include defining "niche" identities, distinguishing between the "authentic self" versus actual presentation, examining audience perception and gaze, and understanding the impact of visual characteristics and tone on social media.

HERSTORY: INSTAGRAM AS A PLATFORM FOR AFRICAN-AMERICAN WOMEN

With more than 300 million active monthly users, Instagram is growing, thriving, and quickly becoming the next broad-stroke social network of choice across a wide age range (Kerpen 2014). The social network is proving to be an effective tool for social engagement with a reported per-follower engagement rate 42x greater than six other popular social networks (Jung 2014). According to a 2014 Pew Research Center study on demographics of key social networking platforms, Instagram saw a significant increase in the proportion of users who are young adults (eighteen to twenty-nine), women, Hispanics and African Americans. Additionally, the most common Instagram users are young African-American women with some college education who earn between minimum wage and twice the minimum wage.

This population is important in that African-American women represent 52 percent of employed African Americans and control 43 percent of the annual spending power for the Black population (Nielsen and The National Newspaper Publishers Association 2013).

The Nielsen study further explained that the duality role of mother and manager that African-American women play provides an opportunity for connection through campaign creation that acknowledges and celebrates this duality in which social networking sites, such as Instagram, can be used to mitigate real world inequality, particularly as a large majority of African-American consumers do not fully trust traditional media (Holland 2014).

Chittal (2015) heralded 2014 as the year "hashtag feminism" reached its tipping point with trends addressing women's issues such as #YesAllWomen, #WhyIStayed, #ChangeTheRatio and #BringBackOurGirls. She argues that this type of social media activism or hashtag activism doesn't just raise awareness but generates tangible results, pressuring institutions, organizations, and companies to change. Particularly, Black women's presence on social media in 2014 demonstrated they were not just followers, but their hashtags led to tangible change in communities, and the implications of what that meant for the future of activism are far-reaching (Savali 2014). They remained leaders whether addressing intraracial domestic violence and the perpetuation of rape culture or the pervasiveness of street harassment, negative media depictions and political marginalization (para 2). For example, feminist Feminista Jones launched #YouOKSis on July 10, 2014 to bring awareness to street harassment, but specifically the importance of bystander intervention and how women of color experience violent and fatal street harassment more frequently than white women (Weedston, 2014). Beverly Gooden, the survivor of a violent marriage, started the #WhyIStayed hashtag to encourage her followers to confront the victim blaming with their own stories which trended the method of explaining why leaving an abusive relationship is never easy (Weedston 2014). The #BlackLivesMatter movement was propelled by the efforts of women of color (Pierre-Louis, 2015). Pierre-Louis (2015) explains that unfortunately "black lives matter" so quickly gets mentally translated into "black men matter" is less a product of racism than one of sexism in which the movement is often described as "leaderless," and largely framed by the bodies of slain black men and boys:

> We live in a society that frequently devalues the rights and existence of women. Issues that affect men are social issues; issues that affect women are "women's" issues. . . . We see this in the way that the deaths of black women often go unreported, but also in the invisibility of the women doing the behind-the-scenes organizing in a movement that the media so often describes as leaderless. (para 9)

More paradoxically, is the fact that the hashtag of the movement was actually coined by three Black women Alicia Garza, Patrisse Cullors, and Opal Tometi. Yet, there is a potential as a powerful force for Black women to fight back sexism and give a voice to the voiceless (Chittal 2015).

In a February 2015 Huffington Post Live discussion regarding how Black women have used social media to reclaim global beauty standards, Martinez (2015) contends that diversity in news media, particularly social media, is advantageous in comparison to traditional media in which Black women are now creating the images that they want to see on social media. Davis (2015) furthers this belief in the following statement:

A lot of the images that we have been consuming over the years have been created through a male fantasy, whether it's oversexualized or desexualized. We're defining it [our beauty] for the first time. We've been living out some-one else's narrative, someone else's fantasy for such a long time, that this is the age of us saying who we are. And, blogs and Instagram and Pinterest are now this place where women, and anybody, can say this is what I think this is beautiful, what do you think? No one ever asked us what we think; about who was in the videos, or who was on the cover of every single magazine.

This is significant as Walker (2007) argues that African-American images, beauty culture and its promotion have unremittingly reflected tensions since the early twentieth-century for African-American women. Walker contends that this time period invoked questions of black independence and economic power, and provided a base for ambitious Black women to create personal wealth and social and political influence in the black communities, yet also highlighted deep problems with racially limited standards of feminine beauty. She further explains that respectability would have particular urgency, as African-American women sought, and continue to seek, to combat prevailing hypersexualized and promiscuous stereotypes:

Increased urbanization of black women and their extensive public participation as wage workers, churchgoers, club members, and leisure seekers ensured that they, like white women, would have to decide what sort of public image they wanted to convey. (pg. 30–31)

Tyree (as cited in Holland 2014, para 8) advocates that it matters who the owners are, it matters who the producers are, it matters who the editors are, because that's often the agenda or the slant of the media and coverage. She further argues that stereotyping of African Americans in the media, and a distrust of systems in the United States rife with racism contributes to the distrust of media to portray their communities accurately (para 6). Thus, African American beauty standards, and commodification of beauty standards in media (traditional media), largely shaped within black society are more so formed in reaction to, and imposed by the majority culture.

HASHTAGS AS A FUNCTION OF FEMINISM, RECIPROCITY AND BENEFIT ANALYSIS

Instagram can provide African-American women an outlet for creative story-telling and engagement with tight communities of people who share a pas-sion for the same values (Peterson 2014). One particular feature employed that builds a community of values is the use of a hashtag. Hashtags are essential on Instagram, and other social media channels, in building a fan base and community by delivering images to users who are most interested.

Hashtags enable people to easily search and track related tweets and spread ideas digitally to amplify your message (Flemings 2011). It's a community of people that engage by creating and sharing content around a specific topic, conference, event, crisis or news story (para 1). Use of Lawler's (2001) affect theory of social exchange best explains this concept and the use of hashtags to build communities as it suggests that emotions can be an explicit and central feature of social exchange, as exchanges are dyadic and connected:

> Individual actors make decisions about whether to exchange, with whom to exchange, and under what terms. They do this repeatedly over time with the same others, because the network structure creates recurring opportunities or constraints on who can exchange with whom. (pg. 326)

As avid users who understand the value in and relevancy of their posts and encouragement to like their photos, Black women are able to use it as a tool to get other women, more than likely other women of color, to repost or join their community by clicking on a hashtag. That value and relevant content subsequently drives engagement. Thus, a commitment to exchange relations and the effects of repeated exchange occurs among the same users. Knowing how to use such tools can be influential for African-American women in raising awareness of and add value and relevancy to their individual brand, as well as the collective message and/or narrative.

Despite being disproportionately at risk for abuse and harassment online, women, in general, proved the real power of social media in 2014, utilizing it for thoughtful conversations about inequality and social change (Plank, 2014). Plank (as shown in Table 7.1) cites online feminist publishing site

Table 7.1.   *The 12 Most Powerful Feminist Hashtags of 2014*

1. #RenishaMcBride and #RememberRenisha*
2. #YouOKSis*
3. #YesAllWomen
4. #AllMenCan
5. #BringBackOurGirls*
6. #SurvivorPrivilege
7. #RapeCultureIsWhen
8. #HobbyLobby
9. #WhyIStayed
10. #NMOS14*
11. #DudesGreetingDudes
12. #MediaWritesWOC *

Note: * = a topic specific to African American women or women of color.
Adapted from Plank (2014). Retrieved from http://mic.com/articles/104970/the-12-most-important-feminist-hashtags-of-2014.

Hashtag Feminism and online news organization *Mic*'s ranking of the biggest feminist hashtags. Hashtags were selected based on national and global trending power; national online and/or independent news media attention; sustainability; impact on social, political and cultural issues offline; and influence with notable Twitter users and thought leaders in social media and feminist spaces. Five of the twelve hashtags specifically addressed African-American women's or women of color issues including the way the lives of Black women and girls are often downplayed, exploited or altogether ignored in mainstream media and other public discourses (#RememberingRenisha); the way women of color experience street harassment at the intersection of gender, sexuality, disability, culture and race (#YouOKSis); the Boko Haram terrorists kidnapping of school girls in Nigeria (#BringBackOurGirls); silent vigils to honor victims of police brutality around the country (NMOS14); and discussion around how media reports and frames violence against girls and women of color (#MediaWritesWOC). Thus, the use of the hashtag on social media is shaping the way information is transmitted to the public, impacting how those events are remembered, and in some cases become a huge part of the stories themselves (Mason 2012).

Social media democratizes feminist activism, opening up participation to anyone with an account and a desire to fight the patriarchy (Chittal 2015).

"PRESENTATION" OF SELF AND IDENTITY: SELFIES AS SELF-LOVE FOR BLACK WOMEN

For African-American women, social media can put an interesting lens on the creation of the self. The ideal self is the self we aspire to be and our self-image is the person we actually are based on the actions, behaviors, and habits currently possessed (Sunstrum 2014). "In curating the 'perfect' social media self, Instagram enables us [African American women] to put an aspirational front on our lives, to create our own brand, and in a sense, like a personal magazine, meticulously curate based on things we like, or more often than not, things we know other people will like" (Fleming 2014, para 15). It appeals to the notion of maximized perception, presenting the best possible version of ourselves (Lynch 2014), in that users are able to not only share a photo, or upload a video up to fifteen seconds, but apply filters and edit posts for best-self presentation. "It is axiomatic that if we do not define ourselves for ourselves, we will be defined by others—for their use and to our detriment" (Lorde 1978, 31). Lorde contends that the development of self-defined Black women, ready to explore and pursue our power and interests within our communities, is a vital component in the war for black liberation.

With this notion, Black women's images shared on Instagram appeal to the lifestyle and values of followers as posting an image is not only about you but who's viewing your image. Understandably, photographs are more likely to drive self-esteem effects than likes and comments (Winter 2013). Moritz (2014) proposes that visual content leverages images in which they must first directly appeal to a target audience, then solve a problem, inspire its community to take action or give instantly actionable advice that is highly sharable (para 9).

Using Collins's (1990) Black Feminist Thought it can be asserted that all African-American women share the common experience of being Black women in a society that denigrates women of African descent; an experience in spite of differences created by historical era, age, social class, sexual orientation, or ethnicity that binds threads of struggle against racism and sexism and stimulates Black women's independence and self-reliance. Consequently, in this context, Instagram connects African-American women with other users, highly likely other minority women, with shared interests, values and visual sensibilities. Black Feminist Thought insists that both the changed consciousness of individuals and the social transformation of political and economic institutions constitute essential ingredients for social change. Moreover, creation of visual content is about connecting visual shared identities; building community.

Instagram's popularity is its voyeuristic nature, transparency, and ability to communicate authentic stories; thus appealing to people's need for belongingness and acceptance (Jung 2014). For anyone who believes in self-promotion, the selfie should be celebrated as a marketing tool, stringing together the changing of our times and the fascination we have with our own image and how we want others to view us (Hodges 2013). McFadden (2015) describes selfies as "pixelated bits of confection to remind us that we are all interconnected, no matter how we try to tear each other apart" (para 1). A photographer, she questions how societies celebrate a singular definition of beauty to the exclusion of others as she sees stray posts of young black girls, dark skin girls sharing carefree moments, perfect and imperfect (para 2). Gervais (2013) supports this notion in suggesting that Instagram actually has allowed the public to reclaim photography as a source of empowerment in a way that has never been possible before. In applying Gervais's declaration, Instagram offers a quiet resistance to the barrage of perfect [white] or negative [black] images that African-American women face each day:

> We can look through Instagram feed and see images of real people—with beautiful diversity. Imperfect images that make their way onto my Instagram feed are much more interesting and no less beautiful. Instagram also allows us the opportunity to see below the surface. We capture a glimpse into the makings of people's daily lives. We get a sense of those things that make the

everyday extraordinary—the things that inspire us, pique our curiosity, deeply touch us, and make us smile. (Gervais 2013, para 5)

Selfies allow Black women to say "we are here, and we are beautiful" (McFadden 2015).

Due to Instagram's unadulterated voyeurism, it's not unusual to scroll through an Instagram feed and feel suffocated by fabulousness (Williams 2013). Yet, Lee (2013) contends the "selfie" habit isn't unique, and instead reflects a universal human proclivity to preserve, document, record and share ourselves. Moreover, the use of the term "selfie," which is believed to have been coined by an Australian student in 2003, in itself has helped to reduce the narcissistic quality of self-portraits and turned them into something rather more endearing (Pearlman 2013). Tatum (2014) refutes this notion of the selfie as passive narcissism and self-indulgence facilitated by social media (para 4) in the following:

> The great thing about selfies is that they can be just what the name implies: all about you. Selfies challenge the idea that you need a justification to be seen. You're announcing that you exist in the world and are going about your day. Strategic selfies can also change the way you perceive yourself, both literally and metaphorically. Various effects like lighting, angles, and filters can turn your selfie into a work of art. (para 9, 12–13)

Women have for years been surrounded by images of other women who are mostly underweight, mostly white, and often hyper-sexualized, at younger and younger ages Schreker (2014). Schreker expounds that adding social media ups the social comparison gauge:

> Women are put in the position to compare themselves on a daily basis, not only to celebrities and models, but to their peers, everyday comparing themselves to friends and celebrities (who may even be photoshopping their photos). It's a constant cycle of comparison and "improvement" fueled by the multi-billion dollar diet, plastic surgery and cosmetics industries. (Scherker 2014, para 16)

Hodges suggests use of the selfie is an experience in self-awareness in that we should "think not of the selfie as a sign of moral decay, but the preservation of our existence" (para 6). Wilson (2015) argues that while selfies can be seen as narcissistic, they are an expression of self-love, looking at uniqueness, a celebration of our beauty and our differences, instead of being influenced by dominant images.

INSTAGRAM AS AN EMPOWERMENT TOOL FOR AFRICAN-AMERICAN WOMEN

While most of us represent many things, Instagram indicatively asks for the matching of the visual imagery of photos with the narrowed text posted: finding keywords and phrases that express your personality but are also able to attract followers in limitation. Using Instagram specifically for personal and professional branding and curating is becoming more ubiquitous, and lucrative, for African American women who have mastered the social media branding concept. With that understanding, Instagram is continuously looking into ways to strengthen its authenticity and consumption experience as the archetypal mobile application (Constine 2014). More so, its engagement simplicity and strategic call to action are its best features for marginalized and excluded communities. This engagement through likes, shares and "regrams," help identify what efforts resonate with a target audience; in this case, an African American female audience that is engaging at a rate far higher than other social media channels (Delzio 2015). The call to action is simple: attract fans and build a loyal fan base by liking and/or commenting (Pere 2014; Kerpen 2014).

Understanding this relationship, social media can empower and amplify the voices of Black women against all systems of oppression, centering their narratives (Savali 2014) and allowing for the presentation of the self in the best light. Social media platforms, like beauty/barbershops, are a place where people come to voice their opinions, share funny stories, and connect with others. "There are a lot of amazing conversations happening within those comment threads section about people and the things that they thought were not beautiful—but actually are—and people are telling them that 'I love that about you'" (Wilson 2015). Hence, the year 2014 found black women positioning self-preservation as an act of political warfare on both individual and institutional levels (Savali 2014). Savali asserts that Black women can be the change agents at the forefront and heart of digital protests and more by engaging in social media movements and hashtag activism. She believes that this activism was authentic and effective through their social media influence. Instagram thus becomes an essential vehicle, taking full advantage of hashtags to help deliver images to people who are most interested in seeing them (Altos 2014).

Black women are using their Instagram accounts and social media platforms to do just that, celebrate "self" in communities of difference. "Black Women Do. . . ." niche online communities are emerging and on the rise. Apparently Black women workout (@BlackWomenDoWorkout), travel (@BlackGirlsTravelToo), run (@BlackGirlsRun), and rock (@BlackGirlsRock)! "We fiddle with Instagram filters, use other photo apps to adjust light curves values that render us magical, mysterious—the center in our own stories—with beauty, drama, and complexity, teaching us to see ourselves anew and across multiple situations (McFadden, 2015, para 3). In the article, "'We Out Here': Inside the New Black Travel Movement," Ferguson (2015) describes how young, hip, urban millennials are using tools like Instagram to become one of the fastest growing travel markets. Travel communities Nomadness Travel Tribe and Travel Noire, created by black millennial women, Evita Robinson and Zim Ugochukwu, respectively, are not only shifting perceptions on black travel but changing lives, untapped by the trillion-dollar travel industry (Ferguson 2015). The tagline on the Nomadness Travel Tribe website reads, "(started with) one woman. (grew to) one tribe. (taking over) one country at a time." Black women are seeing these online communities as movements, using Instagram as their photographic diary, changing the visual landscape.

Subsequently, Instagram can be an effective social media tool to create, curate, and build congruent and integral layers of "best self" identity for African-American women. As we continue to grow in numbers on Instagram, and other social media channels, African-American women will need to understand the significance of selection strategy, hashtag keyword choice in drawing attention and building community, as well as the corresponding working relationship of complementary appealing visuals. Without them the content just will not circulate. Having a photo without any hashtags is like having a text message in your drafts folder; you have something to say, but nobody is getting it (Altos 2014). Mastering these tools on Instagram are fundamental to conveying the narrative imagery of our sometimes silenced, or ignored, voices and promotion of an act of understanding through presentation of "maximized perception" of our "selves."

REFERENCES

Adler, E. (2014, September 26). *Social Media Engagement: The Surprising Facts About How Much Time People Spend On The Major Social Networks*. Retrieved January 10, 2015, from Business Insider: http://www.businessinsider.com/social-media-engagement-statistics-2013-12#ixzz3OXzja61A.

Altos (2014, July 25). *Hashtag Research in 30 Minutes and 3 Seconds on Instagram*. Retrieved from Altos: https://altosmarketing.com/blog/13-social-media/155-hashtag-research-in-30-minutes-and-3-seconds-on-instagram.

Collins, P. H. (1990) *Black Feminist Thought: Knowledge, Consciousness, and the Politics of Empowerment*. New York: Routledge.

Chittal, N. (2015, March 26). *How Social Media Is Changing the Feminist Movement*. Retrieved April 2, 2015, from MSNBC.com: http://www.msnbc.com/msnbc/how-social-media-changing-the-feminist-movement.

Constine, J. (2014, December 10). *Instagram Hits 300 Million Monthly Users To Surpass Twitter, Keeps It Real With Verified Badges*. Retrieved from TechCrunch: http://techcrunch.com/2014/12/10/not-a-fad/.

Davis, M. A. (2015, February 5). *How Black Women Are Using Social Media To Reclaim Global Beauty Standards*. Retrieved February 25, 2015, from Huffington Post Live: http://

on.aol.com/video/how-black-women-are-using-social-media-to-reclaim-global-beauty-standards-518637243.

Delzio, S. (2015, March 9). *New Research Reveals Instagram Users Like to Shop.* Retrieved March 9, 2015, from socialmediaexaminer.com: http://www.socialmediaexaminer.com/instagram-users-like-to-shop/.

Duggan, M., and J. Brenner (2015, January 9). *Social Media Update 2014.* Retrieved from Pew Research Center Internet & America Life Project: http://www.pewinternet.org/2013/12/30/social-media-update-2013/.

Ferguson, C. (2015, January 4). "'We Out Here': Inside the New Black Travel Movement." Retrieved April 12, 2015, from The Daily Beast: http://www.thedailybeast.com/articles/2015/01/04/we-out-here-inside-the-new-black-travel-movement.html.

Fleming, O. (2014, November 18). "'Why Don't I Look Like Her?': How Instagram Is Ruining Our Self Esteem." Retrieved from Elle: http://www.elle.com/beauty/tips/a2531/how-instagram-is-ruining-our-self-esteem/.

Gervais, S. (2013, January 22). *Does Instagram Promote Positive Body Image?* Retrieved January 11, 2015, from Psychology Today: http://www.psychologytoday.com/blog/power-and-prejudice/201301/does-instagram-promote-positive-body-image.

Harvey, K. (2014). *Encyclopedia of Social Media and Politics.* Thousand Oaks, CA: SAGE Publications, Inc.

Holland, J. J. (2014, September 16). *African Americans, Latinos Really Don't Trust The Media To Tell Their Stories Well.* Retrieved March 5, 2015, from Huffington Post: http://www.huffingtonpost.com/2014/09/16/blacks-hispanic-media-trust-united-states_n_5831228.html.

Jung, W. (2014, August 5). *10 Ways To Use Instagram For Community Engagement.* Retrieved from Brightkit: http://brightkit.com/10-ways-instagram-community-engagement/.

Kerpen, C. (2014, May 12). *The Trouble With Instagram—and Why You Should Be on It.* Retrieved January 10, 2014, from Inc.: http://www.inc.com/carrie-kerpen/the-trouble-with-instagram.html.

Lee, A. (2013, November 6). *Me, My Selfie and I.* Retrieved January 12, 2015, from Read-Write: http://readwrite.com/2013/11/06/selfies-are-not-narcissism.

Lorde, A. (1978, April). "Scratching the Surface: Some notes of Barriers to Women and Loving." In L. Taylor and Francis (eds.), *The Black Scholar*, 31–35.

Mason, L. (2012, July 11). *Impact of Social Media on Society: 5 Times Social Changed the World.* Retrieved March 20, 2015, from Social Media Sun: http://socialmediasun.com/impact-of-social-media-on-society/.

Martinez, J. (2015, February 5). *How Black Women Are Using Social Media To Reclaim Global Beauty Standards.* Retrieved February 25, 2015, from Huffington Post Live: http://on.aol.com/video/how-black-women-are-using-social-media-to-reclaim-global-beauty-standards-518637243.

McFadden, S. (2015, February 24). *Selfies allow black women to say we are here, and we are beautiful.* Retrieved April 12, 2015, from The Guardian: http://www.theguardian.com/commentisfree/2015/feb/24/selfies-black-women-we-are-here-we-are-beautiful.

Moritz, D. (2014, February 26). *5 Ways to Make Shareable Images That Drive Traffic.* Retrieved January 10, 2014, from Social Media Examiner: http://www.socialmediaexaminer.com/shareable-images/.

Nicholson, A. (2014). "The Classification of Black Celebrity Women in Cyberspace." In A. Y. Goldman, V. S. Ford, A. A. Harris, and N. R. Howard (eds.), *Black Women and Popular Culture: The Conversation Continues* (p. 326). Lanham, MD: Lexington Books.

Nielsen and The National Newspaper Publishers Association (2013). *Resilient, Receptive and Relevant: The African-American Consumer.* The Nielsen Company.

Perez, S. (n.d.). *5 Best Types of Instagram Photos to Drive Engagement.* Retrieved January 10, 2014, from Wishpond: http://blog.wishpond.com/post/56884222190/5-best-types-of-instagram-photos-to-drive.

Pierre-Louis, K. (2015, January 22). *The Women Behind Black Lives Matter.* Retrieved April 2, 2015, from In These Times: http://inthesetimes.com/article/17551/the_women_behind_blacklivesmatter.

Plank, E. (2014, December 10). *The 12 Most Powerful Feminist Hashtags of 2014*. Retrieved March 25, 2015, from Mic.com: http://mic.com/articles/104970/the-12-most-important-feminist-hashtags-of-2014.

Savali, K. W. (2014, December 29). *Change Agents of 2014: Black Women on Social Media*. Retrieved from The Root: http://www.theroot.com/articles/culture/2014/12/black_women_on_social_media_in_2014_as_agents_of_change.html.

Scherker, A. (2014, October 20). *Why It's Harder Than Ever For Women Not To Obsess Over Their Appearances*. Retrieved February 28, 2015, from Huffington Post: http://www.huffingtonpost.com/2014/10/20/women-beauty-culture-obsess-over-appearance_n_5754382.html.

Social Media Plays Greater Role in Cause Engagement For African Americans and Hispanics. (2011, May 11). Retrieved March 25, 2015, from Ogilvy Public Relations: http://www.ogilvypr.com/en/press/social-media-plays-greater-role-cause-engagement-african-americans-and-hispanics.

Sunstrum, K. (2014, March 14). *How Social Media Affects Our Self-Perception*. Retrieved January 11, 2015, from Psych Central: http://psychcentral.com/blog/archives/2014/03/14/how-social-media-affects-our-self-perception/.

Tatum, E. (2014, April 24). *Selfies and Misogny: The Importance of Selfies as Self-Love*. Retrieved January 12, 2015, from everyday feminism: http://everydayfeminism.com/2014/04/selfies-as-self-love/.

Walker, S. (2007). *Style and Status: Selling Beauty to African American Women, 1920–1975*. Lexington, KY: The University Press of Kentucky.

Weedston, L. (2014, December 19). *12 Hashtags That Changed the World in 2014*. Retrieved March 25, 2015, from YES Magazine: http://www.yesmagazine.org/people-power/12-hashtags-that-changed-the-world-in-2014.

Williams, A. (2013, December 13). *The Agony of Instagram*. Retrieved January 11, 2015, from New York Times: http://www.nytimes.com/2013/12/15/fashion/instagram.html.

Wilson, J. (2015, February 5). *How Black Women Are Using Social Media To Reclaim Global Beauty Standards*. Retrieved February 25, 2015, from Huffington Post Live: http://on.aol.com/video/how-black-women-are-using-social-media-to-reclaim-global-beauty-standards-518637243.

Winter, J. (2013, July 23). *Selfie-Loathing*. Retrieved from Slate: http://www.slate.com/articles/technology/technology/2013/07/instagram_and_self_esteem_why_the_photo_sharing_network_is_even_more_depressing.html.

Chapter Eight

A Blog, a Bittersweet Mess, and Black and White Identity Development

Makini L. King

We are now well-immersed in an era where social media have become one of the primary ways that people create and maintain relationships. While some may consider connecting with others via Facebook, Twitter and blogs as impersonal, these media offer an innovative method of self-expression and learning. More importantly and with regard to racial justice, social media may play a unique and important role in the racial identity development of American citizens.

The aim of this chapter is twofold; to compare the differences in intent between bloggers of color and those of the dominant group and to explore the impact of my personal blog, written as a woman of color, on my black identity and the identity of my white audience members.

More specifically, in the exploration of these differences in blogging intent, I examine how bloggers of oppressed minority groups utilize the blogosphere as both a form of resistance of dominant culture and solidarity of minority culture. Secondly, I discuss my blog's content and impact within the context of racial identity development for myself, as an African American female blogger, and the racial identity development of my white audience members. I discuss how my blog encourages and supports my personal transitions through particular stages of William Cross's Black Identity Development model and Downing and Roush's Feminist Identity Development Model. Similarly, I examine how the blog's content may influence the transition of white readers through the stages of Janet Helm's White Identity Development Model.

A BLOG'S PURPOSE: BLACK AND WHITE

Since the first recorded blog in 1997 (Nardi, Schiano, Gumbredt, & Schwartz 2004), the number of blogs has grown exponentially over the years in addition to the reasons that people choose to blog. Generally, blogs have been an avenue of self-expression on topics ranging from politics and sports to simply tracking the events of bloggers' daily lives. In the United States bloggers tend to be younger in age, city-dwellers, highly educated and white (Lenhart & Fox 2006). Like most people, in the beginning I believed that most blogs were run as businesses for either marketing purposes or political commentary. In theory I knew that anyone could purchase a domain and write things on the internet for other people to read. Embarrassingly, I learned this piece of information from the movie *Julie & Julia*, but I never considered the reality that regular people like myself blogged. Of the hundreds of millions of bloggers that exist today, most of them have small audiences composed of people they already know (Nardi et al. 2004). Generally, the content of majority of the blogs are as unique as the people who manage them, yet the common denominator resides in the content, which is often autobiographical in its representation of the bloggers' interests, opinions, travel or record of daily life. An added benefit of blogging involves the ability to express one's opinion without being intrusive as no one is forced to read it. Similarly, readers only have to respond if they want to, it's not required. So, blogs allow people to discuss what's important to them; the anonymity supplied by not having to communicate face-to-face makes it easier to express sensitive and personal content; and the readers are making a conscious choice to participate. These factors provide a foundation that is supportive of a community in which people can voluntarily participate in the exchange of experiences and information.

More and more, researchers have been examining differences in blogging between those members of the dominant racial group and those of the non-dominant group. However, bloggers who represent oppressed groups may utilize their blogs for very specific reasons. For example, minority bloggers may see blogging as a safe space in which to freely challenge the dominant cultural structure and seek affirmation of a shared racialized experience from other people of color (Steele 2011). Additionally, a blog may provide a space for a black woman to participate in the re-telling of her personal narrative and the restructuring of her individual story (Steele 2001). As a black woman I am in a unique position between two forms of oppression; my racial group and gender.

I view the blog as an opportunity for a black woman to share her opinion on a multitude of topics. So often we only ever get exposed to the white perspective. It is after all the status quo. I'm fairly confident that I know far more about white culture than whites know about my culture. Most of our media represents majority opinion. When I read reviews of books or movies, they are more than likely the reviews of a white person. I know the kinds of hair and beauty products white women enjoy, the foods white people like, the news that's important to them, their healthcare concerns. For minorities, our knowledge of white culture is a requirement of our survival, our ability to navigate the system in order to achieve some modicum of success.

On the other hand, white people have very little reason to learn about a non-majority culture. Their ability to live fruitfully is not dependent upon their knowledge of someone else's opinion or whether they take the time to understand someone else's experience in the world. This does not mean that some whites are incapable of this or do not take the time to do these things because some whites take very deliberate interest in the experiences of the "Other."

In his book *White*, Richard Dyer argues that it is necessary to impose the racialization of whiteness, that it must be separated from its pedestal of normalcy, dislodged "from its centrality and authority" (Dyer 1997, 10). He further states that as long as being white is equal to being human, they secure a position of power.

> White people have power and believe that they think, feel and act like and for all people; white people, unable to see their particularity, cannot take account of other people's; white people create the dominant images of the world and don't quite see that they thus construct the world in their own image; white people set standards of humanity by which they are bound to succeed and others bound to fail. Most of this is not done deliberately and maliciously. . . . White power none the less reproduces itself regardless of intention, power differences and goodwill. . . . White people need to learn to see themselves as white, to see their particularity. In other words, whiteness needs to be made strange. (Dyer 1997, 9)

What this means for many bloggers of color is that the blog becomes a way to challenge the dominant discourse through their content. As a non-white I inevitably engage in a world that consistently reminds me of my racial identity and thus my contributions in interactions invariably reflect my experiences as a black woman. According to Dyer, whites struggle to talk about their whiteness because it tends to lead to feelings of guilt; a reminder of their awful history, what whites have done and what whites continue to do to maintain their status and privilege. Like many American minorities, I am often required to engage with whites in a way that does not threaten their place of privilege. When non-whites are brave enough to express a racialized viewpoint, they risk bringing attention to and challenging the white person's whiteness, which will likely lead to negative consequences; intentional or not. The blog, therefore, becomes a safe medium through which unfiltered opinions, ideas and viewpoints can be shared in an ocean of otherwise whitewashed perspectives that are propagated in our culture. I would much rather be able to execute my perspective face-to-face with no reservations about the consequences that may ensue, but white fragility limits this possibility.

A BITTERSWEET MESS AND IDENTITY DEVELOPMENT MODELS

Originally racial identity models were developed as a means to define one's racial group as a sociopolitical and economic construct that determines how members of that group adapt in racially oppressive environments (Cross 1991; Helms 1990a). In psychotherapy such identity development models are used to help therapists understand patients' relationship in the contextual world. Black Identity Models help explain how a black individual might develop a healthy racial identity in a racially oppressive environment. Subsequent models for the majority population were important in understanding how whites also developed a healthy racial identity and non-racist attitude in the same racially oppressive environment (Helms 1990b).

The first stages of both the black and white identity models usually represent a less well-adjusted racial identity; where blacks will reject or deny their African perspectives as a result of past and present European imposition on non-European groups and whites will adopt a "color-blind" attitude so as not to have to confront the benefits they obtain from past and present white domination of other groups. Ironically, a deflated sense of black identity parallels an inflated sense of white identity in these early stages and are both supported by a racially oppressive environment which favors Eurocentricity. The early stages are necessarily intertwined and dependent on one another where in order for whites to feel superior, blacks must be inferior and both groups must acknowledge these roles. The latter stages are characterized by the person's awareness of one's cultural history, desire to work towards social justice, and the ability for healthy and meaningful relationships between minority and white majority people to be created and maintained.

A BITTERSWEET MESS: A TOOL FOR RACIAL IDENTITY DEVELOPMENT

An important factor that leaves both blacks and whites stagnant in the earlier stages of their racial identity development is their lack of awareness of their own history as it relates to oppression in a white society. The assumption is that when a black person begins to understand and respect his racial history and can understand whites as both separate from and integral to past and present oppression, his cultural identity shifts so that he can then work towards racial justice and have meaningful engagement with whites. Similarly, a white person's racial identity shifts when he is given the opportunity to

learn and understand the minority perspective in America. Through his transformation he not only acknowledges the role of the white race in black
oppression, but accepts this as basis for his own white privilege and then
makes deliberate efforts towards racial and social justice.

As a woman of color, I view blogging as a method to reach a larger
audience through which I can safely share my thoughts on my own experiences in white culture beyond the safety of other people of color. The blog
allows one to deliberate, to process, to explore the complexities of events—
specifically regarding race and gender—in front of an audience. Ideally blogs
allow others to participate; to offer their opinion, to foment a conversation
that addresses the experiences of a black woman in this majority culture.

For example, in June 2015, Dylann Roof walked into the Emanuel
American Methodist Episcopal Church murdering nine black church-goers in
prayer study. When the shootings in Charleston, South Carolina, happened I
was restless, angry, frustrated, and my hands literally shook in emotional
turmoil. I wondered how people were able to walk around in apparent normalcy when I was so agitated by what happened and what it represented that
my stomach churned.

Posts about the events in Charleston offer an opportunity to engage my
audience with difficult and provocative content about race. These conversations need to be had, even if they are controversial, off-putting and uncomfortable; but the goal, hopefully, is growth of understanding the "Other"
perspective, racial cohesiveness, and genuine community.

The variations in understanding the events in Charleston between black
and white people represent the complexity in fully grappling with racial
oppression in America. On the surface blacks and whites generally agree that
the murder of those nine people was grotesque and unthinkable, but the
details in both groups that lead to these judgements embodies the persistent
racial tensions that continue to exist.

Like Dyer explains, our culture makes it extremely difficult for whites to
consider a perspective different from their own. White people can choose not
to be a part of their complete world; the one that includes black and brown
experiences and suffering. After Charleston I observed how difficult it was to
verbally engage with whites and express my inner turmoil on race relations
in this country. In an ideal world I would have been able to grieve over
Charleston by conversing with others, both black and white, validated by the
shared sense of sadness in our history and inspired by the shared pursuit of
racial equality and justice. In reality, I was only able to commiserate with
other blacks and very few whites. Again, for many whites their assumed
position of dominance and normalcy is directly aligned with the early stages
of their racial identity development where they assume a color-blind attitude
and possess an erroneous understanding of race relations. Thus, their open-
ness to difficult conversations that bring light to the history of racial oppres-

sion is often met with defensiveness. This is unfortunate for the racial identity development of both parties involved. Healthy relationships between black and white individuals are critical to the later stages of racial identity development and these are predicated upon the knowledge and acceptance of racial history. So, if these honest conversations about race cannot be had, growth may remain stagnant for one or both parties.

BLACK IDENTITY DEVELOPMENT

There are several models of black identity development and the purpose of many of these models is to define the progress of a black person's way of thinking and self-assessment in relation to her reference groups. In these models an individual will move from the least healthy, white-identified stage to the healthiest, self-defined stage of racial transcendence (Helms 1990a). One of the more popular models was created by William Cross. According to Cross's Black Identity Development Model (BIDM), the transition to a positive black identity occurs in five stages. In the first Pre-encounter stage, the individual devalues his/her blackness and favors a white, Eurocentric perspective. Since the Eurocentrism is the dominant culture, the black individual finds a way to separate himself from blackness (the inferior culture) in order to adopt the superior one.

Typically a significant event or experience will occur that pushes the individual into the Encounter stage. In this stage the individual finally recognizes her inability to effectively conform to white standards, begins to reject white culture and seek contact with black culture. This is followed by the Immersion/Emersion stage where she completely immerses herself into black culture and denigrates white culture. Here the amount of anger felt towards whites for their hand in oppression, past and present, may be tantamount to the black person's idolatry of blackness and African heritage. Whereas the Immersion/Emersion stage is an exaggerated expression of black identity which is defined by others in her reference group, the Internalization stage marks the synthesis of the individual's personal identity with her cultural or black identity, thus setting the stage to reevaluate her position in white society and a healthier and more effective relationship with white people. Ultimately, the black person develops a positive black identity in the fifth stage of Internalization-Commitment where she maintains an appreciation of black culture, its history and the impact on his/her life. Not only is she comfortable with her blackness, but she is able to interact in the world according to her black perspective. That is, even when others are unable to relate or understand her black perspective, she does not deny the value of her blackness. In this stage the individual is also able to identify with other oppressed minorities and is able to establish meaningful relationships with whites (Helms 1990a).

If I consider my own transformation over the years and the blog to be a medium through which I am able to healthfully and safely explore and manage my identity as a black person in a white majority culture, the BIDM is a useful map by which to explore my transformations. I might assume that my early years in middle and high school represented my Encounter stage. I have always been aware of my blackness, but certainly attending a predominantly white elite boarding school made my blackness ever apparent. In many developmental models, people rarely transition smoothly from stage to stage, achieving complete bliss having permanently arrived at the ultimate developmental milestone. One's progression through stages of identity are fluid, sometimes messy and complex—much like life—and thus overlap and regression through the stages are par for the course. College may have been the time where I began to deliberately seek out opportunities to learn about black American culture and since then I have consistently slipped in and out of the last three stages of the BIDM. I remember that in college I had a visceral anger towards whites and their inability to understand their history of oppression and consequential privilege. While I still maintained genuine, healthy interpersonal relationships with whites, in retrospect those relationships may have been rather superficial. I can't recall any conversations with whites about race and its significance in my life, which may have contributed to this interpersonal superficiality.

Blogs are often considered a form of journaling. The most apparent difference is that the traditional format of journaling defined as the more personal written expression of one's emotional experiences generally discourages feedback unless the writer intentionally shares the content, or is less fortunate and the content is read by an unintended audience. The written expression of one's emotional experiences is beneficial because it permits the exploration and evaluation of one's thoughts, emotions and behaviors surrounding one's experiences (Smyth 1998; Ullrich & Lutgendorf 2002). When a person reflects on the complexity of an experience, he gains more information that he might have missed before. Having gained more insight he may make better decisions and be more effective at problem solving. Blogging, on the other hand, assumes that feedback is permissible. An added benefit in addition to the introspection that occurs in traditional journaling is that others are now able to participate in the reflection of your experiences. This type of interaction can inspire community-building, a sense of belonging, validation, and support (Gumbrecht 2004).

These benefits might be especially important in the identity development of black minority bloggers. If blogs supply the medium by which black bloggers can freely express how race impacts their daily experiences and both blacks and whites are permitted to reflect and provide feedback, the blogger may not only reduce her distress around these experiences, but elicit emotional support from both readers of color and whites. These types of interactions may be instrumental for the blogger's positive black identity in addition to an improved ability to find merit in relationships with whites.

This phenomenon can be seen in several of my posts. After Charleston a political debate ensued over the benefit of removing the Confederate flag from the statehouse grounds in South Carolina. I had a personal experience involving the rebel flag during this national debate, which led me to post about it. In this particular experience I went to a fourth of July celebration where a Confederate flag was displayed in a parade and in the yard of the adjacent property where the event was held. The post was extremely personal, heavy with emotion and the experience caused me significant distress. The following is an excerpt.

> I think it's incredibly disturbing that everyone around me carried on as though everything was normal. Perhaps that's because it was only abnormal to me. While everyone else carried on, I couldn't think of anything else, but that stupid flag? Whose flag is it? Does everyone know each other here? How many people here are in support of that flag and what it represents? How many of these people say the word nigger regularly? How many of these people hate niggers? How many of these people are pissed that a nigger showed up to their party ruining their fun?

> That flag was a big deal. That flag said "Heritage Not Hate," which means putting that flag up was a very deliberate act likely in response to Charleston. That flag had a very specific message for and to me. That flag couldn't exist without me, without black people. There would be no need. That flag might as well say "Niggers died and niggers will die." There is nothing else that flag could mean.

> What does it mean that I had this experience? That I tolerated 3.5 hours in the presence of that flag and no one came to my rescue? That no one thought to ask that someone take the flag down, or take me away from that place, or even speak directly to me about that issue?

> I live in an America where we still struggle to acknowledge racial oppression, where even when that oppression is literally hoisted over our heads and can be directly linked to the murder of black people, we choose to turn a blind eye. I live in an America where I, an educated black woman, still feel I must shuck and jive to appease white fragility rather than advocate for myself and my dignity.

> Just another day in our America. (King, July 6, 2015)

While the act of writing about my experience provided relief, the feedback from black and white readers was crucial in validating my emotional experience as a black woman and helped me maintain a positive perception of whites and their ability to sympathize with my experiences with race in a white society.

Presently, I have deeper interpersonal relationships with whites and I believe the critical piece which has allowed me to develop these relationships is that within these relationships I am able to have meaningful conversations about how race has impacted my life. More importantly, in my closest relationships I have been able to talk openly without any negative consequences. I have found that I am only able to develop these deeper relationships when I feel safe enough to talk openly on these topics, and freely share my black perspective. There are moments when I struggle to disentangle my hate of the oppressive system from white individuals, but over the years, along with my growth and knowledge about my own culture, this feat has become easier. The blog has been quite helpful in navigating relationships with whites and possibly in creating new relationships with whites where only superficial relationships existed in the past.

FEMINIST IDENTITY DEVELOPMENT

Downing and Roush (1985) adapted the five stage Feminist Identity Development Model from Cross's BIDM in which a woman transitions from a passive feminist identity to a more active feminist identity. In the first stage termed Passive Acceptance, a woman conforms to the idea that men are superior to women and accepts the traditional gender roles associated with white, North American ideals. In the second stage, Revelation, a woman may have a significant encounter that challenges these traditional gender roles. She may consequently develop anger toward men and toward herself for contributing to her and other women's oppression through her past conformity. The third stage of Embeddedness-Emanation marks the woman's desire for meaningful relationships with other women and cautiousness in her interactions with men. This is followed by Synthesis, where the woman develops a positive feminist identity, transcends rigid gender roles and identities, becomes flexible in her understanding of these structures and develops her own sense of these roles as they apply to herself and other individuals. Finally the woman develops a strong commitment to social change for gender equality in the last stage of Active Commitment.

One of my first posts on the blog tackled gender disparity issues. Over the years as I have more thoroughly entrenched myself into adulthood as a mother, stepmother, divorcée, second wife, homeowner, and psychologist, I have become more sensitive to gender differences that I encounter quite regularly. I am of the mindset that most people believe, at least publicly, in equalizing the pay gap, women's access to opportunities and even ability to choose their healthcare. I like to highlight and support those issues as well, but I also use my blog to highlight gender issues that many people have never considered.

> It's 2014 (*at time of this post*) and we still have a ways to go in terms of understanding and then actively resisting behaving in ways that propagate the ideology of women as second class citizens. By nature of my profession as a psychologist, I am probably better primed at observation and analysis of human behavior than most. I also understand that much of what we do, willingly or not, is likely a result of conditioning that began the minute we were born and began receiving information in the world. We take our conditioning for granted and want so desperately to believe we control a lot more than we do (more blogging on this later). I don't have time to address every act of sexism in our society, but I'll give you a few of my favorites to consider. What is the underlying message when the husband and child direct statements such as "what's for dinner?," "where are the batteries?," and "we are out of toilet paper" only towards the mother. Why is it still expected that women take on their husband's last name in marriage? I don't have a maiden name, but I do have a name. Why is it still okay for men to "hit on women" who were otherwise minding their own business in the grocery store? I am pretty sure that there are female sport's commentators that are way more competent than a retired football player who has a history of concussions (no offense to them). Why are we still more likely to see women's giblets all over the television and giant billboards instead of men's? Why do people have such a strong reaction to hairy legs and armpits ONLY on women? No, it's not because "it just feels better," or "looks better." My goodness, we are just now beginning to have a proper conversation about rape culture which is rampant in our society. It's not that women send mixed messages to men, it's our society that sends us these messages. . . . (King, September 24, 2014)

In this blog post I speak to how frequently we miss the underlying sexism in our society. As I often imply in my posts, "People typically think of "isms" as these broad stroke behaviors that are easily identifiable and therefore easily extinguished, but they are more accurately a deeper mindset, a skillful and secret infiltrator that is rendered more effective at its destruction given its camouflage" (King, September 24, 2014). I think the post is fairly representative of my heightened sensitivity to everyday sexism. In it I list several apparently small indecencies that women experience that tend to, overtime, become significant annoyances and threats to gender equality.

I have expanded on some of these topics in separate posts on rape culture and the disapproval of body hair on women. I also make a point to promote other media and celebrities that uphold the ideals of feminism and gender equality such as my posts highlighting Chimamanda Ngozi Adichie's speech We Should All be Feminists and Emma Watson's He For She speech at the United Nations.

WHITE IDENTITY DEVELOPMENT MODEL

One of the topics that I explore on my blog is white racial identity develop-ment. The irony in that statement is that many whites don't consider that they have an ethnic identity. When you ask the average white American what they are, they inevitably say "American." When you ask an ethnic minority what they are, they typically describe their color, or their family background: black, Korean, Native, or Latino. The implication is that their color and ancestry informs how they behave in the world and how they interact with other people, specifically whites. When you are the norm and all things are measured by the standard set by you, there really is no need to consider your racial identity and what that may entail. It's normal to be white and so what might it mean if a white person deliberately recognizes his whiteness in the context of other Americans. It immediately renders him different from some-one else who is non-white. This type of awareness can completely change how a white person sees himself in the world. No longer is that person the norm, but now he is asked to see himself within the context of not being "regular," but different. He might then see what makes up those differences and more importantly, all the potentially disquieting evidence of how those differences came to be. I imagine that is not an easy thing to do.

Janet Helms (1990c) created the White Racial Identity Development Model specifically to address how whites are affected by their own racist identity and how they then can transition to a healthy, non-racist white iden-tity in a persistently racist society. The assumption here is that white Americans are racist, whether conscious of it or not, and that in order to be non-racist, whites must transition through certain developmental identity stages. Like Dyer, Helms suggests that white Americans rarely identify their racial group membership and instead have assimilated into what is consid-ered "mainstream culture," or as Dyer states, "just human."

In Helms's model, the first stage of white identity development occurs in the Contact stage where the individual maintains an identity of racelessness by denying a racial identity, denying the existence of racism as well as their role in it. This is followed by Disintegration where the person feels caught between white and black culture, is becoming more aware of the social implications of race, and is hesitant to acknowledge his or her whiteness and therefore discrimination. In Reintegration, the third stage, the individual may feel anger towards people of color and blame them for their own hardships. This stage is characterized by the idealization of all things "white" and deni-gration of all things considered "black."

The transformation from denial and a "color-blind" attitude finally begins to change in Pseudo-Independence, the fourth stage. The individual begins to internalize his whiteness; accepting personal responsibility for his part in racism and the structure of white privilege in the United States. Feelings of guilt and shame are common, but the ability to sit with these feelings of discomfort makes it possible for the individual to become more comfortable in his whiteness and move towards an action stage. This occurs in the fifth stage of Immersion/Emersion. Whereas in Reintegration, the person may have looked for answers from black people, in this stage he looks to other whites to help find solutions to racism. In the last and sixth stage of this model, Autonomy, the white individual finally exemplifies a self-actualized, white racial identity when he becomes more informed about white privilege and deliberately engages in antiracist and social justice-oriented behaviors with both whites and people of color.

I often think about how the white readers of my blog receive some of the more direct racial content that I post. It is worth reiterating that I have made certain assumptions about my white readers. Most of them know me, if not directly, then indirectly by only a degree or two of separation. Most of my white readers are friends and via selection bias are likely to be more conscious of race and gender issues, white privilege and race relations in the country. They also lean left politically. Given these assumptions it may be a fair assessment that many of them are likely in the fifth and sixth stages of the WIDM; Pseudo-Independence and Autonomy.

Still, I often wonder how reading some of the more euro-critical posts impact them personally. One of my most popular posts is called "Whiteness Demands Not-the-Truth." I posted this around the time that I was reading Edward Baptist's *The Half Has Never Been Told*, in which he examines how slavery made the American economy. I had been in correspondence with Baptist specifically about how whiteness influences the reception of information that highlights the detrimental impact of white supremacy, past and present. In his response he said that "Whiteness demands not-the-truth, which is why telling the truth creates such controversy" (E. Baptist, personal communication, January 30, 2015). I appreciated that a white man was able to express this seemingly with ease. I wondered how white people progress to these later stages of WID, comfortable in their whiteness and very aware of the privilege it provides them. This type of progress means that a white person can receive the truth about their whiteness and manage the chasm of guilt and shame that creates the defensive barrier that halts actual racial progress. It's not easy recognizing one's role in racism, but some white people are able to do so beautifully and then push back against it.

In that particular post I make a point to expand on Peggy McIntosh's Invisible Knapsack by sharing my own experiences under the thumb of white privilege. The post was a call to correct non-believers of white privilege.

1. When people say "our forefathers" or "the good ole days," I cringe because I know that those allusions to a happier history placed my ancestors in chains. I vow that whenever I hear someone make refer-

ence to our country's "glorious" history, it will be my duty to remind them of our country's "inglorious" history and how it has impacted my life still. We all should do this and stop using those played out phrases.

2. No one will ever mistake me for a doctor (which I am), even at my own place of employment, and people are more likely to assume my husband (a white man) is a professional (which he is) even when he is not acting in that capacity. I cannot count the times that I have been mistaken for someone's administrative assistant and then had to explain their error and pretend not to be offended.

3. If I choose to voice my concern at my place of business about the lack of minority representation, or attention to minority concerns, it is almost inevitable that there will be some type of (in)direct backlash and blame directed toward myself. In other words, I have been reprimanded for pointing out areas of growth for my employer when those areas of growth have to do with the topic of race. If only they knew how hard it is for me to work up the courage to address those issues in the first place AND that addressing the issues will benefit everyone.

4. I also get reprimanded for not calling the police when I hear gunshots. Growing up my family rarely called the police. My parents (who grew up during Civil Rights) have a very specific and unfortunate history with the police, which certainly colors their present view. Sure, I shouldn't stereotype. All police aren't bad, but given the history of our country, and the very real injustices experienced presently by black and brown minorities by lawmakers and law enforcers, one certainly shouldn't be faulted for being a bit skeptical.

5. I also know that my presence in any neighborhood, no matter my credentials, decreases the property value for the homes in that neighborhood. The only way to get the property value of a neighborhood to increase is to increase the number of white people in that neighborhood. How's that for evidence of one's worth?

6. There are a lot of great books in the world. A small number of these great books are written by black authors. There should be far more great black books except that the publishing industry is pretty racist. They simply don't support black writers even though black females happen to read more books than any other group in this country. I have been forced to read books written by white authors my whole life. I have been taught that great writers are white and that there are also a few great black writers. People typically don't have to read books by authors of color unless they take an elective class in school. Most white readers probably have to work really hard to recall the last non-white author they read. When whites do read non-white books, they find it extremely hard to empathize with the characters, not because

it's impossible, but because they haven't practiced enough. Then, it might be years, if ever, that they read another black author. I read a lot of white books and if my appreciation of a book was dependent upon my ability to empathize with a character solely on race, well, I wouldn't read as much as I do.

7. My last name is not my own. It's a relic of a time not so long ago where my ancestors and others who looked like me were stolen from their land and forced to live in captivity, separate from their families, humiliated, debased and tortured for the sole purpose of a white man's profit. My family and other black Americans with last names not-their-own will never see the massive wealth owed to us/them from centuries of enslavement. Yet, we still shamelessly carry around the last names trying to ignore the gaping wealth gap between ourselves and the progeny of the name's actual owner (King, March 17, 2015).

In this post I explain how being white directly benefits a person in ways that hurt another group. When I publish posts like these, I am often conflicted because I am only slightly less afraid of hurting white readers' feelings as I am angry at the injustice. The blog then becomes an important tool in protecting me from this fear and forcing me to expose my experiences and emotions as a black woman onto the consciousness of majority society. This is a very deliberate act. In her book *Sister Outsider*, Audre Lorde, a black feminist, explains that the path towards growth is promoted via the expression of black anger and that white sentiments of guilt and shame should not prevent the expression of this anger. She states

> I cannot hide my anger to spare you guilt, nor hurt feelings, nor answering anger; for to do so insults and trivializes all our efforts. Guilt is not a response to anger; it is a response to one's own actions or lack of action. If it leads to change then it can be useful, since it is then no longer guilt but the beginning of knowledge. Yet all too often, guilt is just another name for impotence, for defensiveness destructive of communication: it becomes a device to protect ignorance and the continuation of things the way they are, the ultimate protection for changelessness. (Lorde 1984/2007)

Lorde contends that without this expression of black anger; or relatedly, action within the BID stage of Internalization-Commitment where one can freely express her black perspective, there can be no growth. The status-quo of white normalcy is a function of the repression of one's black perspective and emotional turmoil in order to maintain white comfort. The guilt and shame felt by whites when confronted with the black perspective are required in order to stimulate action towards change and racially-just community.

While some of the more direct posts on race may be offensive, it is also a necessary step for any progress to be made. Perhaps the blog format makes it easier for white readers to receive. Rather than being directly confronted by a person who is accusing you of unearned racial privilege, which incites fear, anger, sadness, confusion and defensiveness, the blog gives white readers a chance to grapple with their emotions in isolation, in safety. This perhaps makes it less likely that the message will fall flat. When one has time to reflect quietly rather than debate aggressively, she is more likely to alter her opinion on things even if it's counter to her core beliefs. This phenomenon may be even more likely on topics of race.

It may seem ironic that in order for white people to acknowledge their own privilege it has to be delicately handed to them, but this careful handling of difficult topics may be necessary in order for whites in the Pseudo-Independent stage to fully digest this information that might easily induce feelings of guilt and defensiveness. The isolation and anonymity provided by the blog format permits whites to sit with those difficult emotions; working towards acceptance of their privilege, moving them forward into the final stage Autonomy. As in the case of BIDM, these stages, too, are fluid. As I share new perspectives and experiences on race as a woman of color, white readers will likely encounter new information that challenges their identity in new ways. Thus, they may move back and forth between the last two stages of the WIDM. But given the safety of receiving the information in blog form, they are free to reflect safely and hopefully reestablish their place in Autonomy.

SUMMARY

At some point in our society the ability to discuss race and gender issues between groups may not require such strategic maneuvering. In a future society whites and their culture may no longer be considered the norm against which all else is measured. The standing question, though, is how we get there. I have asked this question to some of my white readers. I wanted to understand how they envision a more racially-just future. Given their own transition through white identity development, what have they gleaned from their transformation? Some white readers cited ethnic or race courses they took in high school and college, or intimate friendships they had with racial and ethnic minorities that led to their Autonomous identity development. Others said it was a result of having been raised in a multi-ethnic neighborhood, or having experienced first-hand some significant racial injustice perpetrated by whites.

The common factor in all of these experiences is one of education. It becomes extremely difficult to become Autonomous if you have little to no

experience with non-white culture. This type of education is not easily ac-
quired either, for it requires a deliberate effort on the part of the white person
to reach beyond mere contact with a minority. It requires an immersion in the
non-white perspective, forcefully rejecting the normalcy of whiteness and the
comfort that it bestows and embracing the discomfort that emerges from
recognizing the delusion of white supremacy and one's persistent role in it.
But it is the education piece which seems critical to the emergence of a
positive white anti-racist identity. Without it there is no possibility of challenging the white, dominant discourse. How could whites know that they
exist in a world that caters strictly to them unless they are exposed to a non-
white perspective that argues against that injustice?

My blog is an attempt, albeit small, to remedy this ignorance by building
a community in which this type of education is fostered. The goal is to get
the introspection percolating; the conversation started. The anonymity of the
reader presents a non-threatening platform on which this type of introspection can occur. Ordinarily when one's ties to white supremacy are challenged, the individual's discomfort with having to confront his unearned
privilege renders him unready to transition to the anti-racist stages of white
identity. The blog remedies the white instinct for defensiveness, creating a
safe space for reflection rather than protection.

The blog supports my own black identity development as a black female.
In the real world (as opposed to the virtual one), I am often limited in my
expression of topics related to gender and racial oppression. Like many minorities, I am forced to hold secret my experiences as a black woman because
any expression of my racial and gender-based sentiment might lead to retri-
bution. Part of a positive black identity entails not denying the truth of my
blackness and black perspective, which is very difficult in majority society.
The blog platform represents a community that permits my truth to be shared
in a safe space. Through the blog I can relieve the distress from my daily
experiences as a woman of color and receive validation from both black and
white readers.

Given the current resistance to address race and gender oppression head-
on, minority blogs play a very unique and important role in our progression
towards a just world. In the meantime we can consider this type of blogging
as practice for a time when we are able to have these difficult and necessary
conversations about white oppression in person.

REFERENCES

Cross, W. E. (1991). *Shades of Black: Diversity in African American Identity.* Philadelphia:
    Temple University Press.
Downing, N. E., and K. L. Roush (1985). "From Passive Acceptance to Active Commitment: A
    Model of Feminist Identity Development for Women." *The Counseling Psychologist* 13:
    695–709.

Gumbrecht, M. (2004, May). "Blogs as 'Protected Space.'" In *WWW 2004 Workshop on the Weblogging Ecosystem: Aggregation, Analysis and Dynamics* (Vol. 2004).

Helms, J. E. (1990a). "An Overview of Black Racial Identity Theory." In J. E. Helms (ed.), *Black and White Racial Identity: Theory, Research, and Practice* (pp. 932). Westport, CT: Greenwood.

Helms, J. E. (1990b). "The Beginnings of a Diagnostic Model of Racial Identity." In J. E. Helms (ed.), *Black and White Racial Identity: Theory, Research, and Practice* (pp. 83–104). Westport, CT: Greenwood.

Helms, J. E. (1990c). "Toward a Model of White Racial Identity Development." In J. E. Helms (ed.), *Black and White Racial Identity: Theory, Research, and Practice* (pp. 49–66). Westport, CT: Greenwood.

King, M. L. (2015, July 6). "Shuckin' and Jivin' on the Fourth of July." Retrieved from http://abittersweetmess.com/?p=402.

King, M. L. (2014, September 24). "Feminism in 2014 May Not Be Beyonce." Retrieved from http://abittersweetmess.com/?p=53.

King, M. L. (2014, March 17). "Whiteness Demands Not-The-Truth." Retrieved from http://abittersweetmess.com/?p=320.

Lenhart, A., and S. Fox (2006). "Bloggers: A Portrait of the Internet's New Storytellers." Retrieved from http://www.pewinternet.org/files/old-media/Files/Reports/2006/PIP%20Bloggers%20Report%20July%2019%202006.pdf.pdf.

Lorde, A. (1984/2007). "The Uses of Anger: Women Responding to Racism." In A. Lorde (ed.), *Essays & Speeches by Audre Lorde* (pp. 124–133). New York: Crossing Press.

Nardi, B. A., D. J. Schiano, and M. Gumbrecht (2004). "Blogging as Social Activity, or, Would You Let 900 Million People Read your Diary?" *Communications of the ACM* 47(2): 41–46.

Smyth, J. M. (1998). "Written Emotional Expression: Effect Sizes, Outcome Types, and Moderating Variables." *Journal of Consulting and Clinical Psychology* 66: 174–184.

Steele, C. K. (2011). *Blogging White Black: A Critical Analysis of Resistance Discourse by Black Female Bloggers.* Association of Internet Researchers: Performance and Participation. Seattle, WA. October 2011.

Ullrich, P. M., and S. K. Latgendorf (2002). "Journaling about Stressful Events: Effects of Cognitive Processing and Emotional Expression." *Annals of Behavioral Medicine* 24(3): 244–250.

Conclusion

Sonja M. Brown Givens

Since January 1, 2012, at least sixty-one women of color have been killed by a member of law enforcement, according to the website http://www.killedbypolice.net. In the rare occurrence that these cases are shared with the public, they are typically shared as short news broadcasts which focus on the victims' lifestyles, conviction records, toxicology reports or employment histories. These women's *life* stories, whose ages at the time of their death range from sixteen to ninety-three, are seldom told by conventional media. In fact, some would argue that the circumstances leading to their unfortunate deaths were (and in some cases continue to be) intentionally withheld from the public. These mothers, daughters, sisters, and aunts of "The Village" all have stories. Stories that provide insight into the challenges they were forced to navigate as "double minorities." Stories we would likely never know if not for hashtag activism through social media. For example, hashtag campaigns like #SayHerName, #YesAllWomen, #NoMakeup, #BringBackOurGirls, #WhyIStayed, #SolidarityisforWhiteWomen, #WeAreSlient, #womenshould, and #BlackLivesMatter give visibility to social injustices by creating spaces to share case-specific information to mass audiences and to engage in deep cultural critique about the current state of our communities and future livelihood. Likewise, virtual petition, GoFundMe, and meme campaigns enable women-of-color-users to feel empowered to advocate for change. They provide spaces for nurturance and healing.

Collectively, these spaces "clear room" for us to vent, cry, grieve and mobilize in the face of what could be considered overt attacks on people of color in America. They provide sister circle communities that we've come to rely on to check our own perceptions and remain engaged with the issues we are most concerned about. It is in these spaces where our roles in the struggle for justice are debated and challenged. It is in these spaces where we feel

163

most free to express our views. It is in these spaces where we share the soul-shattering pain we feel without suggestion that we should "be strong." It is in these spaces where we tell our truths.

This book explores how Women of Color utilize social media networks in order to navigate the demands and experiences of their lives. In the process of completing this project we've found that (1) social media networks provide opportunities for immediate escape from environmental conditions that may be harmful to our socio-emotional/socio-psychological well-being; (2) social media networks provide opportunities to re-frame the stories we're told by conventional media for close interrogation and critique; (3) social media networks "stand in the gap" for us when we need to feel affirmed, valued and beautiful—in light of the tumultuous social climate we find ourselves in every day; (4) social media networks provide a means for us to compare our experiences with other women of color in order to make sense of them; and (5) social media networks provide a means for us to fully immerse ourselves in the topics/issues that matter to us most, in judgement-free environments. In summary, these networks are sustainable communities built on the values of common ground discourse and function to empower community members in ways that are seldom experienced during encounters as the "Other."

Social media have evolved in order to accommodate users' increasingly complex preferences, expectations and imaginations. Networking groups have emerged for users with varied interests and perspectives to connect with other users who share those interests and perspectives. This evolution doesn't distinguish users at-large in any particular way; rather, it allows users to channel their social media activity to create rich user-environments that appeal to their sense of place in the world. Women of color have utilized the tools of social media to create safe spaces for themselves to do, think, and simply . . . be. This book offers the reader an opportunity to understand some of the conditions which inspire that activity, and why it is important.

Without social media networks, stories about the women whose names, ages, and death dates that appear below would likely be little-known. Through them we give these women voice, and their legacies mass-reading, so they are not forgotten:

> Shereese Francis, 30—March 15, 2012; Rekia Boyd, 22—March 21, 2012; Sharmel Edwards, 49—April 21, 2012; Shantel Davis, 23—June 14, 2012; Alesia Thomas, 35—July 22, 2012; Malissa Williams, 30,—November 29, 2012; Darnisha Harris, 16—Dec. 2, 2012; Shelly Frey, 27—Dec. 6, 2012; Kendra Diggs, 37—May 8, 2013; Jacqueline Reynolds, 54—May 8, 2013; Kourtney Hahn, 21—May 15, 2013; Andrea Rebello, 21—May 18, 2013; Mhai Scott, 38—May 29, 2013; Keoshia L. Hill, 28—June 3, 2013; Lana Morris, 46—June 6, 2013; Jessica Gonzalez, 35—June 23, 2013; Kyam Livingston, 37—July 24, 2013; Maria Rita Zarate, 31—October 1, 2013; Miriam

Carey, 34—October 3, 2013; Amy Reyna, 35—October 28, 2013; Rosa Flores Lopez, 50—November 1, 2013; Jeanette Anaya, 39—November 7, 2013; Andrea Naharro-Gionet, 61—November 16, 2013; Elizabeth Arellano Renteria, 21—December 1, 2013; Hilda Medrano, 21—December 1, 2013; Yvette Smith, 47—February 16, 2014; Gabriella Monique Nevarez, 22—March 2, 2014; Chieu-di Thi Vo, 47—March 27, 2014; Natividad Nuñez, 44—April 17, 2014; Karina Sandoval-Jiminez, 18—April 19, 2014; Veronica Rizzo-Acevedo, 50—April 20, 2014; Pearlie Golden, 93—May 7, 2014; Tiffany Morton, 27—May 21, 2014;Yanira Serrano-Garcia, 18—June 4, 2014; Jacqueline Nichols, 64—July 4, 2014; Maria Rodriguez, 42—August 3, 2014; Donyale Rowe, 37—August 5, 2014; Michelle Cusseaux, 50—August 14, 2014; Maria Fernada Godinez, 22—August 19, 2014; Vernicia Woodward, 26—August 28, 2014; Latandra Ellington, 36—October 1, 2014; Tracy A. Wade, 39—October 2, 2014; Iretha Lilly, 37—October 7, 2014; Elisha Glass, 20—October 11, 2014; Aura Rosser, 40—November 10, 2014; Tanisha Anderson, 37—November 13, 2014; Keara Crowder, 29—November 19, 2014; Guadalupe Manzo-Ochoa, 27—December 9, 2014; Mayra Cornejo, 34—December 31, 2014; Jessica Hernandez, 17—January 26, 2015; Yuvette Henderson, 38—February 3, 2015; Natasha McKenna, 37—February 8, 2015; Janisha Fonville, 20—February 19, 2015; Jessica Uribe, 28—March 1, 2015; Monique Jenee Deckard, 43—March 8, 2015; Meagan Hockaday, 26—March 27, 2015; Alexia Christian, 25—April 30, 2015; Sarah Lee Circle Bear, 24—July 12, 2015; Sandra Bland, 28—July 13, 2015; Tamala Anne Satre, 44—July 23, 2015; Ralkina Jones, 37—July 26, 2015. . . .

Index

About the Editors and Contributors

Fatima Zahrae Chrifi Alaoui is a scholar of culture and communication. She is currently a post-doctoral fellow at the Center of Contemporary Arab Studies at Georgetown University, where she is working on a book manuscript titled "The Vernacular Discourse of the Arab Spring: An Analysis of the Visual, the Embodied, and the Textual Rhetorics of the Karama Revolution." She holds a PhD in communication studies from the University of Denver. Dr. Chrifi Alaoui received a Fulbright scholarship to pursue her MA in intercultural and international communication at the Department of Media, Film & Journalism Studies and the Josef Korbel School of International Studies at the University of Denver. Her research and teaching engage international and intercultural communication, cultural studies, critical rhetoric, political communication, gender studies, and social change in a variety of contexts, including social movements, political discourse, and pop culture. More particularly, Dr. Chrifi Alaoui's scholarship considers how the often non-normative, un-institutionalized voices of resistance work to change their communities, and how normative or institutionalized discourses reinforce their ability to maintain power, with a specific focus on the MENA region. She also investigates issues of Arab and Muslim representation, performance, and identity in the United States and around the world.

Minu Basnet is a PhD candidate in rhetoric at Wayne State University. Her research interests include transnational feminist movements, border rhetoric, and culture with a focus on critically exploring the formation of transnational public spheres. She is currently working on her dissertation titled "Traversing Borders through Nomadism: Resistance and Activism of Migrant Care Workers." This research interest has grown out of her engagement with feminist inquiry into the transnationalization of gendered labor.

Sonja M. Brown Givens is associate vice president for academic affairs at Medaille College. Since earning her PhD in interpersonal communication and media studies from the University of Georgia in 2001, she has held various faculty and administrative appointments. Her scholarly interests include representations of women of color in media, marginalization and feminist praxis among women of color, and multicultural approaches to organizational leadership in higher education. Her ongoing research agenda explores how women of color make sense of their "place" in organizational environments, and how they sometimes articulate resistance to place-making.

Bernice Huiying Chan is a Toisanese writer, activist, and scholar. She will receive her BA in ethnic studies and education studies from Wellesley College in spring 2016. At Wellesley, she helped organize a student movement demanding the college create ethnic studies programs and allocate more resources to students of marginalized identities. She has worked at the Wellesley Centers for Women for three years researching how women of color use and are impacted by social media and televised media. She is also a Mellon Mays Fellow whose research intersects race, gender, homeland, and the power of ethnic studies. Huiying Chan constantly strives to make her research accessible to those outside of the academy, and to always ground her work in her family and community. As a means of survival, she explores writing and the creative arts as tools for social change.

Linda Charmaraman, PhD, is a research scientist at the Wellesley Centers for Women and a former National Institute of Health Child Health and Human Development (NICHD) postdoctoral scholar. She received her PhD in human development and education from the University of California, Berkeley's Graduate School of Education. Currently a New Connections grantee with the Robert Wood Johnson Foundation, and collaborating with the Boston Children's Hospital, Center on Media and Child Health, Dr. Charmaraman is focused on how the use of media and social networking communities influence adolescent risk or resiliency, given potentially negative media stereotypes or stigma about one or more of their social identities, such as race/ethnicity or sexual orientation. Besides RWJF, Dr. Charmaraman has been a principal investigator, co-investigator, or consultant on projects funded by National Institute of Child Health and Human Development, the Centers for Disease Control and Prevention, the Department of Education, Kellogg Foundation, William T. Grant Foundation, Schott Foundation for Public Education, Planned Parenthood League of Massachusetts, Borghesani Community Foundation, and Aids Action Committee of Massachusetts. She has published on adolescent media use, teen sexuality, peer sexual harassment, racial/ethnic identity, youth development, and drop-out prevention in

Journal of Adolescent Health, Sexuality Research & Social Policy, Journal of School Health, Cultural Diversity & Ethnic Minority Psychology, New Directions for Youth Development, Sociological Studies of Children, Journal of Youth Development, Journal of Youth & Adolescence, Journal of Early Adolescence, Journal of Family Issues, and *Learning, Media, & Technology.*

Robin R. Means Coleman is a professor in the Department of Communication Studies and the Department of Afroamerican and African Studies at the University of Michigan.

Caitlin Gunn is a PhD student in feminist studies at the University of Minnesota, Twin Cities. Her research interests include womanist and black feminist theory, Afrofuturism, race and gender in speculative fiction, and digital performances of race and gender. At the University of Minnesota, she was a 2014 recipient of the Diversity of Views and Experiences (DOVE) fellowship and currently serves the Department of Women, Gender, and Sexuality Studies as a digital humanities fellow. She graduated cum laude from Beloit College in 2014, where she was a McNair Scholar in the Ronald E. McNair Post-Baccalaureate Achievement Program.

Alexa A. Harris, PhD, is a communications consultant in Atlanta, Georgia. Her background is filled with a myriad of experiences in the media, ranging from television, film, and print journalism to marketing, event planning, and public relations. Dr. Harris earned her doctorate in communication from Howard University, holds a master's degree in "Documentary Film and History" from Syracuse University, and a bachelor's of arts from Spelman College. Her research focuses on black millennial women in popular culture and alternative media. In her spare time, she enjoys travelling and working with organizations to encourage young women to follow their dreams.

Kandace L. Harris is associate professor and chair of the Department of Mass Media Arts at Clark Atlanta University. Dr. Harris's baccalaureate teaching and administrative honors include being department chair at both Johnson C. Smith University and Shaw University, the 2012 recipient of the Shaw University *Excellence in Academic Teaching* Award, and co-director of the UNCF/Mellon Teaching and Learning Institute at Shaw University, "*Using Social Networks to Enhance Writing across the Curriculum.*" She was also honored as a 2014 Who's Who in Black Atlanta "Leader in Academia." She recently co-authored "Cloud Computing and Citizen Privacy" in the *Encyclopedia of Social Media and Politics*, "Black History Dot Com: The Role of Social Media Technology in Linking the Black Atlantic in the Barack Obama Campaign" in *Global Migration, Technology & Transculturation*, and published "Using Social Networking Sites as a Student Engagement Tool" in *Diverse Issues in Higher Education*. She is also currently the board chair of the 411 Brand Foundation, a non-profit organization in Atlanta that creates, develops, and produces educational, athletic, and entertainment programs for kids and young adults. Dr. Harris holds a BA in print journalism and two advanced degrees from Howard University: a MA in human communication studies and a PhD in mass communications and media studies.

Makini L. King, PhD, is a licensed psychologist in Kansas and Missouri. She works in a community health clinic in Kansas City, Missouri, where she does therapy, behavioral health consultation, program development, and evaluation. She teaches adjunct for the counseling psychology department at University of Missouri–Kansas City and has published empirical articles and book chapters about primary and secondary education. In addition to her work as a psychologist, she created and runs the blog Abittersweetmess.com, where she posts about race, culture, gender, current events, and life in general.

Latoya Lee is a PhD candidate in the sociology department at SUNY Binghamton. Her research interests include Africana studies, black feminisms and women of color feminisms, critical race theory, and cyber/social media studies. Her current research focuses on the engagement with, and contemporary uses of, social media by black women and men in the United States. Lee teaches at Adelphi University where she offers classes on the intersections between gender, sexual constructions and identities, race and class, and social media. Both her teaching and research are strongly influenced by her commitment to building community(ies) and diversifying academia.

Temple Price is a graduate student in the Department of Education and Counseling at Xavier University of Louisiana. She has worked closely with underserved populations in rural Louisiana and Washington, DC. Price has spoken at the national convention of the American Psychological Association and at the Ruhlman Conference at Wellesley College. She is the co-author of a paper published in *Journal of Addictive Behaviors, Therapy & Rehabilitation*. Her research interests include culturally competent counseling and community-based mental health care. Price holds a bachelor's degree in psychology from Wellesley College, with a minor in Africana studies.

Amanda Richer, MA, is a research associate for the National Institute on Out-of-School Time (NIOST) and assistant methodologist for the Wellesley Centers for Women, Wellesley College. She has been involved in psychometric testing of after school assessment tools and has experience analyzing diverse datasets, including nationally representative secondary datasets. She has supported research in youth development, youth program quality, adolescent media use, teen sexuality, and social psychology. Prior to coming to NIOST, Richer completed her MA in general/experimental psychology from UMASS Dartmouth, where she conducted research on nonverbal communication, personality traits, and cooperation in young adults.

Keisha Edwards Tassie is associate professor of communication at Morehouse College. She earned degrees in speech communication with emphases in interracial communication and media studies from the University of Georgia. For almost two decades, Dr. Tassie has explored the intersectionality of communication, race, gender, and mass media—presenting her scholarship through dissertation studies on intraracial skin tone bias within the black race, mediated images, and perceptions of communicator competence; through numerous professional presentations in the fields of communication and sociology; and through publications focusing on mediated images of black culture, and black women in leadership. In recent years, an organic transition into focused-exploration and scholarship of the experiences of women of color living within multiple tensions of race, class, gender, and sexuality has positively transformed her evolving research agenda.

www.ingramcontent.com/pod-product-compliance
Lightning Source LLC
Chambersburg PA
CBHW071153050326
40689CB00011B/2093